Sponsorship Strategy

Evidentiary Tactics for Winning Jury Trials

Robert H. Klonoff
and
Paul L. Colby

THE MICHIE COMPANY
Law Publishers
CHARLOTTESVILLE, VIRGINIA

Library of Congress Catalog Card No. 90-60874
ISBN No. 0-87473-577-7

Robert H. Klonoff

J.D., Yale University. Member, District of Columbia Bar. Formerly Assistant to the Solicitor General of the United States; Assistant United States Attorney (District of Columbia); and Visiting Professor of Law, University of San Diego.

Paul L. Colby

J.D., Columbia University. Member, District of Columbia and Virginia Bars. Formerly White House Attorney-Adviser (Iran/Contra Investigation); and Assistant United States Attorney (District of Columbia).

Table of Contents

Part Two
Selection of Evidence

Foreword

It is very rare that a book appears that substantially reorients thinking in any area of human endeavor. It is rarer still that we come upon inspired thinking capable of rerouting pathways deeply worn by the foot traffic of long experience. Review of *Sponsorship Strategy* convinces me that it is such a book and that it will have that sort of effect. It is a major advance in understanding the activity of trying lawsuits and offers an analytical framework — obvious once stated, but unstated for hundreds of years — that will greatly assist lawyers in thinking more clearly about what they are doing in the courtroom.

As anyone who has taken a trial advocacy course or been a beginning trial lawyer lucky enough to receive the advice of more experienced hands knows, trial practice has long been a discipline lacking any substantial conceptual or theoretical dimension. The teaching provided in that area has been almost entirely mechanical or anecdotal. We can tell someone where to sit or stand, how close to get to the jury, and when to approach the witness. We can also offer up a blueprint for putting in real evidence of various types or getting the best out of our own experts on different subjects. We can even give some pointers on that most imponderable act of courtroom legerdemain, cross-examination. But most of all, we pass along our own war stories (and those we have heard from others), and thereby convey the messages — of strikingly limited utility — that certain techniques work sometimes and that (our own) inspiration and personal genius ultimately tell the tale.

What has hitherto been lacking is any serious effort to understand what the jury perceives to be going on in a courtroom. In our system, jurors do not simply decide what resolution of the legal dispute is appropriate, based on the law and their understanding of the facts. They are rather adjudicators of a contest in which victory for either side is governed by the application of sometimes obtuse rules. The central insight of *Sponsorship Strategy* is that the evidence and events occurring at trial are viewed by the jury as parts of a contest in which the participants on both sides are seeking, above all else, to prevail.

Given this concept of the lawyer's role, which is inherent in the adversary system, jurors expect and believe that an advocate will strive to put his client's case in the best possible light. The truth, the jury will assume, can be no better for a party than his advocate represents it to be, and it is a fair inference that the advocate will try to give a rosier impression than an impartial observer would draw from a full understanding of the facts. Not only can the lawyer be expected to overstate the affirmative aspects of his own case, but in fulfilling his obligation to seek victory zealously he will be expected to challenge every material aspect of the opposing case that is open to question. Thus any material assertion by the opposition that the advocate does not attack can be taken as correct.

The image of the trial as a quest for victory therefore shapes the effect that arguments and evidence will have on the jury. A lawyer's decision to present certain evidence is a statement that that evidence is important to the resolution of the dispute and, more specifically, to the acceptance of his client's own position. Thus, weak evidence offered by the prosecutor in support of criminal guilt is not simply another small plus on the prosecution side of the ledger — it is more significantly a statement of his concern about his standing in the contest. Why would a lawyer present such uncertain evidence, other than out of a belief that the outcome of the contest may ultimately turn on it? Jurors assume that everything done at trial is aimed at convincing them to return a favorable verdict. A lawyer who puts in shaky or inconsequential evidence, for reasons of candor or completeness, or simply without thinking, will likely suffer what the authors describe as the cost of overtrying.

The failure to introduce evidence may likewise take on a special significance. Sometimes omitting evidence in the course of presenting other evidence (e.g., the testimony of a particular witness) may seem strained and unnatural. In that circumstance the lawyer may pay a penalty in the jury's eyes for his unusual efforts in omitting the evidence. Taking notice of that omission, and ever-conscious that the lawyer is seeking to prevail, the jurors may assume the worst about both the lawyer and the evidence.

From these and other examples the authors demonstrate that the significance and weight attached by the jurors to what they see and hear in the courtroom may vary greatly based on who presents or omits particular arguments or pieces of evidence. *Sponsorship Strategy* is above all else a careful and precise playing out of the implications of this thought throughout the length and breadth of the jury process. The authors work through the consequences of sponsorship on most of the types of decisions that can confront a lawyer at trial. They are never doctrinaire and do not offer the sort of cut and dried recipes that mark much existing trial practice literature. They rather consider with care and insight the components to be identified and evaluated in each case. Not surprisingly, they often find themselves convincingly at odds with the conventional wisdom.

Sponsorship Strategy thus can be expected to have a major impact on the way lawsuits are tried in this country. Its effect should be a salutary one, rendering advocacy both more streamlined and more persuasive. But the book has implications that transcend the instructional purpose for which it was written. The authors have offered a compelling and comprehensive new conceptual framework where none previously existed. Like Darwin's *Origin of the Species,* they have opened whole new areas for thought and reflection.

There is, for example, a great deal to be learned here about the role of lawyers in our society, and about the concept of truth in the adversary system of justice. Our legal system is one that defines the lawyer's role as one of zealous advocacy, presenting the position of his client in the best possible light while doing his best to diminish that of the opposition. Truth in this context is not any independently knowable reality. It is rather whatever emerges from the struggle of advocates before the jury. This notion of lawyers as ones who create rather than pursue the truth is one more evidence of our society's distrust of orthodoxy and its celebration of individual autonomy. It may also, however, have something to do with the low esteem in which lawyers are held. Moreover, the penalties that await those who depart from the role of zealous advocate, that is, those who respond to concerns for candor with a full presentation of the facts to the jury, may raise even more sweeping questions in some minds.

Donald B. Ayer
Deputy Attorney General
of the United States

Preface

We wish to acknowledge the assistance of several friends and colleagues. We are grateful to Donald B. Ayer, Paul H. Desan, Timothy Dickinson, T. Mark Flanagan, John P. Giraudo, Joseph M. Jones, Gregory Tosi, Alexine von Keszycki and Christopher T. Wonnell for their comments. In addition we extend our thanks to Judy-Lynn Lawson and RoAnne Shamsky for their excellent word processing services. We also wish to note our appreciation for the cooperation of the University of San Diego School of Law and the District of Columbia litigation firm of Schwalb, Donnenfeld, Bray & Silbert. Finally, we dedicate this book to our parents.

For convenience, we use the male pronoun when referring to attorneys. An alternative, such as "he/she," would have been more accurate, but also would have been far too cumbersome.

Part One
Fundamental Concepts

1

Introduction

The Sponsorship Dilemma

The young prosecutor sat in the back of the courtroom waiting for his case to be called for trial. It was a tough case for the government. A robber had snatched a purse from an elderly and very frightened woman and was making his escape. A good samaritan, who had not seen the snatch itself, gave chase for several blocks until, in a dimly lit alleyway, the robber pulled out a knife, warded him off, and completed his escape.

The victim made clear at the outset of the police investigation that she could not identify her assailant. Thus, the entire case depended on the pursuer. Nearly a month after the robbery, at the local precinct house, an investigating detective asked the good samaritan to view a large mugbook containing randomly arranged photographs of local rogues. The witness selected the defendant as the person whom he had chased, but the significance of that selection was dubious because the defendant's photograph was the first one in the book.

The defendant was later placed in a lineup. As expected, the elderly victim was unable to identify anyone.

The good samaritan again identified the defendant, but the selection — which was captured on videotape — was anything but ideal. When called forth to make his identification, the witness paused, crossed his arms, and rested his chin in his hand with apparent bewilderment as he viewed the seven men in the line. After 30 seconds, he asked, "Could I see them from the right?" After at least another minute and a half, spent getting a closer view, he stated slowly and with some hesitation: "Number ... Five [the defendant]." The lineup identification of the defendant was uncorroborated by any other evidence: no purse had been recovered and no confession had been made. A tough case indeed.

Nonetheless, the prosecutor was convinced that he had the right man. The good samaritan had stated at a witness conference that he had had an excellent opportunity to view the fleeing assailant and that he was "100 percent positive" of his identification. He had explained that his delay at the lineup was simply an effort to be cautious — to make sure that he selected the right man or none at all. Moreover, the witness was highly credible and had no motive to fabricate. Under the circumstances, the prosecutor believed that the witness had correctly identified the assailant and that the interests of justice demanded a trial rather than a dismissal of the case.

The young prosecutor was soon joined in the back of the courtroom by one of the senior and most experienced trial hands in the office. In hushed tones, they discussed the case. The younger one noted for his mentor that he did not intend to display the lineup videotape for the jury. The seasoned one sternly warned him that failing to present such problematic evidence to the jury would constitute a major tactical error, since the defense was certain to present it if he did not do so. Only by introducing the tape himself could the prosecutor "take the sting out of it." If the government let the *defense* introduce the tape, the learned prosecutor explained, an acquittal was a virtual certainty, since the defense could then argue that the government deliberately withheld the most important piece of evidence demonstrating reasonable doubt. The veteran prosecutor therefore recommended that the tape be introduced during the good samaritan's direct examination, and that the witness be asked to explain to the jury, as the tape was being shown, precisely what he was thinking at each moment during the selection process. While the experienced prosecutor may not have realized it, his advice was consistent with that of virtually all of the leading trial manuals and treatises: an advocate should bring out the weaknesses in his own case instead of letting his opponent do so.[1]

Contrary to his mentor's advice, the young prosecutor never introduced the videotape in his trial of the case. He simply elicited from the pursuing witness the fact that he had identified the defendant at the lineup. The prosecutor was somewhat surprised that defense counsel, who had been present at the lineup and had reviewed the videotape during discovery, never used it in the defense case. Upon reflection, however, defense counsel's decision not to use the tape was tactically justified.

To be sure, the defendant's introduction of the tape may have cast some doubt on the identification. This is true even though the witness's explanation of his conduct at the lineup — that he was certain of his identification at the lineup and was merely being cautious — might have diluted the impact of the tape as a means of discrediting the witness. Defense counsel therefore would not have been acting unreasonably in using the tape as part of his case or during the cross-examination of the witness. By introducing the tape, the defense could have argued that the good samaritan's hesitancy at the lineup confirmed that there was a reasonable doubt with respect to the defendant's guilt.

---

[1] *See* page 96 & n. 42, *infra.*

Such a strategy, however, would have carried serious disadvantages as well. In particular, the prosecutor could have commented during summation that defense counsel had gone to all the trouble to roll in a television set and darken the room, only to have his client ultimately chosen as the robber. The prosecutor could have argued:

> You must have expected, after all this effort, that the tape would show the witness selecting someone else as the perpetrator. You must have been surprised, to say the least, when the witness in fact identified the defendant.

Even without such an argument, the jury might well have viewed the videotape as a rather odd piece of "defense" evidence.

The critical point, however, is that the prosecutor was better off not introducing the tape himself regardless of what the defense decided to do with that evidence. By introducing evidence damaging to his case, the prosecutor would have implicitly conceded the central significance of the tape to the verdict. Defense counsel would then have been able to argue along the following lines in his summation:

> You must have asked yourself: Why was the prosecutor so concerned that you see a tape showing a very hesitant and unconvincing witness? One thing is clear, at the very least. The prosecutor cannot deny that the tape is the most important item of evidence for you to consider in this case. Isn't that why he went out of his way to set up the video equipment and darken the room, only to present evidence so devastating to his case? He obviously recognizes that his duty as a prosecutor is not necessarily to get a conviction but to see that justice is done.

Such an argument would have left the prosecutor without an effective reply, since he could not credibly claim that the tape was unimportant, given his introduction of it.

To summarize, the government's strategy of not introducing the tape left the defense in a difficult dilemma. Only the *prosecutor's* introduction of the tape would have resolved that dilemma. Put another way, what the seasoned prosecutor failed to realize was that, while the introduction of the tape by the defense may have been damaging to the government's case, the prosecutor's introduction of that evidence would have been even more damaging.

The foregoing case — based on an actual trial conducted by one of the authors — illustrates a central thesis of this book: that the impact of an item of evidence on the jury's verdict will often be decisively influenced by the identity of the party who introduces that item into evidence. Thus, in the foregoing trial, the weight that the jury would attach to the videotape could not be determined in a vacuum. An informed prediction regarding the impact of the tape could be made only by taking into account which side would introduce it. As we have noted, the tape would have been more damaging to the government's case if it had been introduced by the prosecutor rather than by the defense. In this book, we use the term "sponsorship" to describe a party's introduction of evidence, since that term emphasizes that an attorney, by offering any item into evidence, in effect endorses the significance of that item to the resolution of the case.

The jury's association of evidence with the party introducing it follows from the requirement of our judicial system that evidence be marshaled by the parties to the controversy. Under this system, each side is represented by a professionally trained advocate who is responsible for presenting his client's case in its most favorable light. So long as the attorney appears competent, the jury will assume that the case can be no better than he states it.[2]

[2] *See, e.g.,* W. LaFave and J. Israel, *Criminal Procedure* § 1.6, at 23 (West 1985) (noting jury's expectation that each party will present evidence in light "most favorable to its side"); L. Fuller, "The Adversary System," 31, *reprinted in* H.

At the same time, the advocate's favorable evidence will be viewed with skepticism, since the jury will assume that such evidence is being packaged in its best light.[3] In this manner, the weight given by a jury to a piece of evidence will depend heavily on which side introduces that evidence.

This phenomenon of "sponsorship" can be highlighted by assuming, for comparative purposes, a hypothetical system in which all evidence is presented to the jury by a disinterested source, such as the judge himself. Such a system is analogous to the "inquisitorial" system, a mechanism that preceded the adversary system as a way of resolving disputed issues of fact. Under that system, the judge not only decided the case but also investigated the facts and questioned the witnesses.[4] Furthermore, the decision-maker did not view the witnesses as being associated with the parties.[5] By contrast, under the adversary system, the decision-maker typically regards a witness as identified with the party who calls him.[6]

Berman, ed., *Talks on American Law* (Vintage Books 1961) ("[The advocate's] task is not to decide but to persuade. He is not expected to present the case in a colorless and detached manner, but in such a way that it will appear in that aspect most favorable to his client.").

[3] *See, e.g.*, S. Hamlin, *What Makes Juries Listen* 186 (Law & Business, Inc. 1985) ("[Juries] expect you to slant questions and get answers that will only favor your witness and your case. Therefore, they're always a little suspicious of a direct examination."); *cf.* R. Carlson & E. Imwinkelried, *Dynamics of Trial Practice: Problems and Materials* § 3.3(D), at 32 (West 1989) (noting that because attorneys are "hired guns," the jury "tend[s] to discount what the attorneys say during trial").

[4] *See generally* S. Landsman, *The Adversary System: A Description and Defense* 49 (American Enterprise Institute 1984); Sward, *Values, Ideology, and the Evolution of the Adversary System,* 64 Ind. L.J. 301, 313-315 (1989).

[5] *See, e.g.*, Ladd, *Impeachment of One's Own Witness — New Developments,* 4 U. Chi. L. Rev. 69, 79 (1936); *cf.* Fed. R. Evid. 614, Advisory Comm. Note Subdiv. (a) (noting that when the court calls a witness, "[t]he tendency of juries to associate [the] witness with the party calling him ... is avoided.").

[6] *See, e.g.*, Ladd, *supra* note 5, at 79; H. Spellman, *Direct Examination of Witnesses* § 4:3, at 66 (Prentice-Hall 1968) (noting that under the adversary system, "there is a subconscious tendency on the part of those hearing the case to identify the witness with a party").

In the foregoing armed robbery case, if the judge had presented the jury with all of the evidence, including the videotape, the impact of that tape would not have been complicated by its association with one of the parties. Under the adversary system, however, the weight assigned to the tape would depend on which side introduced it.

To demonstrate this point, assume that the strength of a piece of evidence on a disputed matter can be measured on a scale from plus ten to minus ten, with plus ten being the strongest, minus ten being the most harmful, and zero being neutral. Under the adversary system, the association of evidence with a particular party will influence the jury's determination of the weight of such evidence. As later chapters explain, if an item of evidence would be evaluated as a plus five when introduced by the judge, its value would typically be diminished, perhaps to a plus three, if introduced by the side that stands to benefit from it. On the other hand, introduction of the evidence by the party who is harmed by it will typically *enhance* its impact on the jury, perhaps to a plus seven or more.

To summarize, there is a cost associated with sponsorship that influences the weight that the jury will assign to a given item of evidence. Specifically, a party will generally be worse off if *his* attorney, rather than his opponent's attorney, introduces the evidence. This phenomenon, which we call the "cost of sponsorship," is examined in detail in Chapter Two.

Purposes of this Book

This book demonstrates the importance of sponsorship as a guide in conducting all aspects of a trial. As the following chapters will reveal, virtually no tactical decision can be fully analyzed without considering the sponsorship costs involved.

As we explain below, this book's conclusions, borne of simple logic, confirmed by longstanding evidentiary principles, and tempered by the authors' experience in conducting approximately one hundred trials (primarily jury trials), contradict many of the basic teachings of the trial tactics literature. The reason for the contradiction is clear: no other book has identified sponsorship as a pervasive principle of trial strategy. Accordingly, as this book demonstrates, much of the advice given in the literature is unsound and even counterproductive. Throughout this book, we identify advice that we find to be misguided.

By the same token, however, portions of the literature are consistent with sponsorship principles. The problem is that the manuals provide no general theory to explain *why* certain advice is given. Thus, while we identify advice from other manuals with which we agree, we provide the theoretical underpinnings to demonstrate *why* such advice is sound.

Since our experience is primarily in the criminal area, most of our examples involve criminal cases, including many cases in which we were involved as trial lawyers. Nonetheless, the book's basic concepts — and its strategies for effective trial advocacy — operate at a level of generality that transcends the differences between criminal and civil cases. Of course, certain distinctions — involving, for example, the scope of discovery — must be taken into account when applying some of this book's recommendations. These differences are addressed where appropriate.

A major purpose of this book is to provide basic concepts and strategies that an advocate can apply almost automatically during trial, when he does not have time to consult a manual. An attorney obviously cannot request a recess every time he needs to determine, for example, whether to cross-examine a witness or object to a question. The advocate who understands sponsorship can resolve such questions quickly and confidently. Contrary to a number of commentators, who assert that there is "no right way" to try a case,[7] we believe that there are a few basic rules — derived from sponsorship theory — that can be applied to resolve virtually every tactical issue at trial.[8]

Since its purpose is to provide basic concepts and strategies, this book does not catalogue every available trial technique for achieving a particular end. The literature is replete with advice of this sort.[9] Nonetheless, the principles of this book can be readily applied in evaluating the wisdom of such techniques.

Prior to recognizing and applying sponsorship theory, both authors lost several strong cases after faithfully applying conventional trial techniques. These losses occurred notwithstanding the authors' thorough familiarity with trial procedure and techniques, developed through training seminars and "hands on" experience. By contrast, both authors repeatedly won even their most difficult cases — many in verdicts of less than twenty minutes — once they identified and perfected the principles outlined in this book. Furthermore, as prosecutors, both authors secured convictions in retrials of cases in which other prosecutors, applying conventional techniques, had ended up with hung juries stacked heavily in favor of acquittal. These experiences convince us that the chances for success at trial can be improved considerably by understanding and applying sponsorship principles.

---

[7] *See, e.g.,* T. Mauet, *Fundamentals of Trial Techniques* at xix (Little, Brown 2d ed. 1988) ("In trial work, ... there is no 'right way' to try cases .... [E]ffective [methods] are as varied as lawyers are numerous.").

[8] *Cf.* II R. Jebb, *The Attic Orators from Antiphon to Isaeus* 370-371 (Russell and Russell, Inc. 1962) ("It was the essence of Greek oratory ... that its practice should be connected with a theory ... [and] from the first there was a fixed tendency to regard oratorical composition as susceptible of regular analysis....").

[9] *See, e.g.,* J. Tanford, *The Trial Process: Law, Tactics and Ethics* 302 (The Michie Co. 1983) (explaining how repeated valid objections can serve to fluster an advocate's opponent); *see generally* E. Imwinkelried, *Evidentiary Foundations* (The Michie Co. 2d ed. 1989).

The Existing Trial Practice Literature — Inadequate and Misleading

Given the availability of numerous trial manuals on the market, the question will no doubt arise concerning the need for yet another. In our view, there is a critical need. As beginning trial lawyers, the authors searched in vain for a manual containing meaningful *tactical* guidance. More recently, in writing this book, we concluded that the existing trial manuals generally suffer from a number of major flaws.

Most fundamentally, we found — as we had years earlier as young trial lawyers — that there is no trial book on the market containing any overarching principles. Existing manuals generally treat each phase of the trial as *sui generis,* and thus provide rules, observations, and anecdotes that apply only to the phase of the trial that is being discussed. For instance, there is no relationship between the suggested techniques for opening statement and those for cross-examination. Although some techniques set forth in the literature may be useful, the reader is still left in a state of confusion. He has derived no theme that he can put to use in resolving the difficult — and often unique — issues that are certain to arise in his own trials. And when an issue arises that happens to be addressed in a manual, the reader is expected to accept the advice wholly on faith.

In addition, many manuals, by not recognizing the importance of sponsorship, offer advice that can harm the advocate's case. For instance, virtually all of the leading trial manuals advise attorneys to bring out the weaknesses in their own cases rather than letting their opponents do so.[10] As we will demonstrate, this approach is generally counterproductive.

Furthermore, many manuals focus heavily on elementary techniques, such as impeachment with prior state-

---

[10]*See* page 96 & note 42, *infra.*

ments and the introduction of various types of exhibits.[11] While these procedures are important and must be mastered, such procedural proficiency does little to guarantee effective trial strategy. At bottom, knowledge of how to execute such techniques does not tell the advocate how to *win* trials.

Finally, many manuals devote more attention to matters of etiquette and personal style than to tactical issues. The view, apparently, is that such matters are important in persuading a jury. In our view, such advice elevates form over substance and achieves little in the way of concrete benefits. Accordingly, unlike other manuals, this book does not provide guidance on such subjects as what clothing or jewelry to sport in the courtroom,[12] how to breathe in a relaxed manner,[13] how often to smile,[14] when to be humorous before the jury,[15] and where to sit and stand in the courtroom.[16] This book, in short, is a *tactics* manual, not a book on style or how to execute basic techniques. It

---

[11] *See, e.g.,* Mauet, *supra* note 7, § 5.3(14), at 193-194 (laying foundation for use of past-recollection-recorded exhibits); *id.,* § 5.3(3), at 169-170 (introduction of photographs and motion pictures); *id.,* § 5.3(13), at 192-193 (introduction of computer records).

[12] *See, e.g.,* 1 S. Gazan, *Encyclopedia of Trial Strategy and Tactics* 1-2 (Prentice-Hall, Inc. 1962); L. Smith & L. Malandro, *Courtroom Communication Strategies* §§ 1.17-1.22 (Kluwer Law Book Publishers, Inc. 1985).

[13] *See, e.g.,* 1 *Goldstein Trial Techniques* § 1A.07-1A.09, at 1-4 to 1-6 (Callaghan & Co. 3d ed. 1984) (describing relaxation techniques and techniques for abdominal breathing).

[14] *See, e.g.,* B. Palmer, *Courtroom Strategies* 172 (Prentice-Hall, Inc. 4th ed. 1966) (recounting the success of the "laughing defense," namely, defense counsel's use of "frequent smiles").

[15] *See, e.g.,* L. Decof, *Art of Advocacy: Opening Statement* § 1.13, at 1-33 to 1-34 (Matthew Bender 1987).

[16] *See, e.g.,* Mauet, *supra* note 7, § 3.3, at 52 (discussion and diagrams concerning where to stand for delivery of opening statement); *id.,* § 7.2, at 279 (similar diagram and discussion pertaining to where to stand in delivering a summation); R. Carlson & E. Imwinkelried, *supra* note 3, § 10.2(J), at 170-173 (five separate courtroom diagrams relating to an attorney's positioning for the conduct of cross-examination). *See generally* S. Goldberg, *The First Trial: Where Do I Sit? What Do I Say?* at xxi (West 1982) (stating in the preface that the advice contained in the book is "so introductory that it will not be of any value after your first trial — certainly not after your third").

begins where most other manuals leave off by providing guidance on how to *win* trials, not simply how to conduct them competently.

Structure of the Book

The following chapters elucidate and apply the theory of sponsorship. Chapter Two identifies the basic concepts. In particular, it discusses various characteristics of the jury system and identifies three separate sponsorship costs: the cost of introduction, the cost of unusual efforts, and the cost of overtrying. Chapter Three provides guidance on identifying the issues in the case. In addition, it sets forth the method for evaluating the strength of evidence bearing on those issues.

Chapters Four, Five, and Six describe the process for selecting evidence to use at trial. Specifically, Chapter Four develops and explains the fundamental rule of evidence selection for disputed issues: use only strong evidence. This simple rule, if followed, will ensure that the attorney does not "overtry" his case.

Chapter Five discusses two categories of evidence selection decisions to which different rules must be applied. The first category involves evidence that an advocate must introduce if he is to meet a legally imposed burden of proof. This burden applies to plaintiffs, prosecutors, and defendants putting on affirmative defenses. As we will explain, the advocate's failure to meet a legal burden of proof, even on an issue that is not disputed by his opponent, will prevent his case from even reaching a jury. The second category involves selection decisions relating to evidence that is uniquely associated with one party. The prime examples are the plaintiff (or complainant) and the defendant. Chapter Six focuses on the decisions to defend and rebut. The rules governing such decisions are based on those set forth in Chapters Four and Five.

Chapters Seven through Twelve apply the principles discussed in earlier chapters to all phases of the trial. Specifically, Chapter Seven addresses jury selection and opening statements. Chapter Eight focuses on direct examination and redirect examination. Chapter Nine discusses real evidence, demonstrative evidence, and stipulations. Chapter Ten considers issues relating to the opponent's case. In particular, Chapter Ten describes techniques for monitoring the opponent's opening statement, closing argument, and questions to witnesses. In addition, Chapter Ten discusses whether to voice objections. Chapter Eleven discusses cross-examination. Finally, Chapter Twelve provides guidance on crafting a persuasive closing argument.

2

Sponsorship Theory

In the moments before opening statements begin, every trial lawyer is tempted to glance at the jurors to see what he can glean from their demeanor. Invariably, the jurors return stone-faced, impassive looks that provide little clue of what is on their minds. The lawyer will no doubt be wondering what will persuade them and how they will arrive at their verdict. In short, he will want to know what makes them "tick." This chapter answers that question. As will be seen, because juries are composed of ordinary citizens, they will act much like ordinary individuals act any time someone is trying to persuade them of a point. For that reason, this chapter develops the theory of sponsorship not only from trial examples but also from everyday situations arising outside of the courtroom. The chapter concludes by providing a formal statement of the three costs of sponsorship.

The Jury and the Advocate

The Jury's Assumption of Best Case with Minimum Effort

When the jurors are empaneled in a case, they face the awesome duty of deciding which party should prevail. They are told, usually at the outset of the trial, that it is their responsibility alone "to resolve any conflicts in the testimony ... and to determine where the truth lies."[1] In discharging this duty, the jury generally cannot draw on prior courtroom experience, since the members typically consist of lay persons who are unfamiliar with how to evaluate trial evidence.[2] Moreover, the jury receives precious little assistance from the judge. Indeed, where the judge has intimated even the slightest personal opinion regarding the merits of the case, he will typically instruct the jury to disregard it.[3]

To be sure, the instructions of the court give general guidance on a number of topics, including the evaluation of evidence. Most of these instructions, however, ultimately leave discretion in the jury's hands.[4] Although

[1] *Criminal Jury Instructions, District of Columbia* § 1.02, at 5-6 (3d ed. 1978); *see also* 1 E. Devitt & C. Blackmar, *Federal Jury Practice and Instructions* § 10.01, at 258; § 10.10, at 268 (West 3d ed. 1977); 3 E. Devitt, C. Blackmar & M. Wolff, *Federal Jury Practice and Instructions (Civil)* § 70.06, at 10 (West 4th ed. 1987).

[2] *See, e.g.,* B. Kaplan, "Trial by Jury," at 49-50, *reprinted in* H. Berman, ed., *Talks on American Law* (Vintage Books 1961) (noting that juries consist of "untrained citizens ignorant of law, often of limited education, brought together to serve for a short time and unable to acquire experience in the art of judging").

[3] *See, e.g., Criminal Jury Instructions, District of Columbia, supra* note 1, at 6 (containing model jury instructions providing that "[i]f you come to believe during the course of the trial that I have expressed or even hinted at any opinion as to the facts, you should disregard it"); 1 Devitt & Blackmar, *supra* note 1, § 10.01, at 260; *id.,* § 10.11, at 271.

[4] *See, e.g.,* 3 Devitt, Blackmar & Wolff, *supra* note 1, § 72.01, at 31 (sample jury instructions on burden of proof in civil cases); *id.,* § 73.01 (sample jury instructions providing that jurors are sole judges of credibility); 1 Devitt & Blackmar, *supra* note 1, § 17.09, at 544 (sample jury instruction providing that "[i]t is the province of the jury to determine the weight to be given to any prior conviction

judges in some jurisdictions are empowered to comment on the evidence,[5] this privilege is rarely utilized. Since the jury is unable to rely on the judge or draw on its own legal experience, it has no choice but to turn to the advocates for guidance in evaluating the weight of the evidence.[6] When it does, however, it faces a difficult dilemma.

It is basic that the jury views the advocate as the client's champion and spokesman and thus as fundamentally biased. Put another way, the jury views each attorney in the case not as a neutral arbiter, but as a "hired gun" with one task to perform: to win the case for his client.[7] Therefore, as a number of commentators have recognized, the jury assumes that everything an advocate says and does is calculated to reflect his client's case in its best possible light.[8]

---

as impeachment"). Of course, the jury is occasionally given mandatory guidance on the evaluation of certain evidence or the absence of evidence. *See, e.g., id.,* § 17.14, at 556 (sample jury instruction providing that no inference may be drawn from the failure of a criminal defendant to testify).

[5] *See, e.g.,* 1 Devitt & Blackmar, *supra* note 1, § 8.04, at 248 (noting that "[a] federal judge ... may summarize and comment on the evidence and also express his opinion on the facts" but also noting that this practice is "no longer permitted in the courts of most of the states").

[6] *Cf.* Brown, *A Juryman's View,* 2 Ga. B.J. 225, 227, 229 (1965) ("The most important persons in the courtroom to the juryman are the attorneys who participate in the trial .... [W]hat the attorneys did, said, or what they did not do or say overpowers other factors and influences the jurors' decision.").

[7] *See, e.g.,* R. Carlson & E. Imwinkelried, *Dynamics of Trial Practice,* § 3.3(D), at 32 (West Pub. Co. 1989) ("The jurors know that the attorneys are ... 'hired guns.'").

[8] *See, e.g.,* W. LaFave and J. Israel, *Criminal Procedure* § 1.6, at 23 (West 1985) (noting that under the adversary system, "[e]ach party is expected to present the facts and interpret the law in the light most favorable to its side, and through a searching counter-argument and cross-examination, to challenge the soundness of the presentations made by the other side"); S. Landsman, *The Adversary System: A Description and Defense* 4 (American Enterprise Institute 1984) (noting that under the adversary system, the attorneys are expected "to find and present their most persuasive evidence" and that "[a]dherence to this principle affords the decision maker the advantage of seeing what each litigant believes to be his most consequential proof"); S. Hamlin, *What Makes Juries Listen* 186 (Law & Business, Inc. 1985) (noting that the jury "expect[s] each lawyer to put the best face on his or her story" and "to slant questions and get answers that will only favor [his] witness and [his] case"); *cf.* E. Morgan, *Some Problems of Proof Under the Anglo-American System of Litigation* 3 (Columbia Univ. Press 1956) ("The

As Professor Lon Fuller observed, an advocate "is not expected to present his case in a colorless and detached manner." Unlike "a jeweler who slowly turns a diamond in the light so that each of its facets may in turn be revealed," the attorney "holds the jewel steady, as it were, so as to throw into bold relief a single aspect of it."[9] Stated more formally, the jury assumes that each advocate will make every contention and introduce all available evidence that he believes will materially favor his case. At the same time, it makes the corresponding assumption that each advocate will make no contention and introduce no evidence unless he believes that it will materially favor his case. This follows from the jury's adoption of the fundamental principle of human behavior that individuals seek to accomplish their tasks with minimum effort.[10]

At bottom, the jury's dilemma is how to evaluate an advocate's biased presentations and contentions and use them to arrive at a correct verdict. As the following section explains, its basic rule is to take from each advocate the bad regarding his own case and view with great skepticism his favorable evidence. How it does this is not difficult to understand.

In essence, the jury utilizes its assumption of best case in a negative manner. Specifically, it is apt to infer that each side's case can be *no better* than that stated by the attorney. For this reason, the jury will not be inclined to identify contentions that are more favorable than those made by the advocate. Similarly, it will not be apt to speculate on

---

theory of our adversary system of litigation is that each litigant is most interested and will be most effective in seeking, discovering, and presenting the materials which will reveal the strength of his own case and the weakness of his adversary's case...."); *cf.* G. Kennedy, *The Art of Persuasion in Greece* 23 (Princeton Univ. Press 1963) (terming the "right to present [one's] case in the best light possible" as "an inheritance from Greek justice imposed by the debates of the sophists").

[9] L. Fuller, "The Adversary System," at 31-32, *reprinted in* H. Berman, ed., *Talks on American Law* (Vintage Books 1961).

[10] *See, e.g.,* G.K. Zipf, *Human Behavior and the Principle of Minimum Effort* 6 (Addison-Wesley Press, Inc. 1949) ("[A]n individual's entire behavior is subject to the minimizing of effort.").

the existence of favorable evidence that was not presented.

In using its assumption of best case, the jury will have little or no difficulty holding the actions of the lawyer against his client, assuming that it views the attorney as competent. This is because the advocate is perceived to be his client's agent or, indeed, his *alter ego.* Everything the advocate says or does is treated as if the party he represents had said or done it.[11] The assumption is generally a reasonable one, since the client usually sits in the courtroom during the trial, listens to his lawyer's contentions, and thereby implicitly ratifies such contentions.[12]

If the lawyer's actions, in hindsight, prove to be unwise, the jury will not assume that such actions were taken without the client's authorization. For instance, if the lawyer contends in opening statement that his client entered into a contract under duress, and if that contention is later undermined by the evidence at trial, the jury will not be likely to conclude that the duress theory was advanced against the wishes of the client and that the client had other viable defenses, such as a claim that there never was a contract.

The Jury's Negative Use of the Assumption of Best Case in Reaching a Verdict

General Principles

The recognition that the jury assumes each advocate to be presenting his best case is, by itself, of little practical

[11] *Cf. McLhinney v. Lansdell Corp. of Maryland,* 254 A.2d 177 (Md. App. 1969) (holding that a client is legally bound by admissions of an attorney in opening statement).

[12] *Cf.* 1 B. Elliott & W. Elliott, *The Law of Evidence* § 256, at 380-381 (Bobbs-Merrill Co. 1904) ("[S]tatements as to facts in controversy made by the attorney in the presence of his client may be shown as admissions, where it is also shown that the client heard them and made no objections.").

use to the trial lawyer. What is of value is understanding *how* the jury utilizes this assumption in a negative manner.

In brief, because of its assumptions, the jury will accept nothing at face value that either advocate says, with one critical exception: any concession made by the advocate will be fully credited and held strictly against him. The reason for this is clear. If a competent advocate is presenting his case in its best light, then it can be no better than he states it. No juror, after all, can be expected to espouse to his fellow jurors a position more favorable to a party than that embraced by the party's own advocate.

The jury's reasoning is quite logical. If what it sees and hears is the *best* the advocate has to offer, then it can conclude that there is nothing better. Moreover, because it assumes that the advocate will minimize his effort in seeking to present his best case,[13] it will view him as *conceding* that every contention that he makes and every item of evidence that he introduces is necessary and was therefore worth the effort to marshal. These implicit concessions are highly useful to the jury; they enable it to translate the advocate's mere words and deeds into concrete information that it can use to decide the case.

Juries have an insatiable appetite for concessions from the advocates. Concessions make a jury's task easier. They narrow the issues that it must resolve, and they remove what would otherwise be obstacles to reaching the ultimate issue, namely, which side should prevail. Accordingly, the only parts of the advocate's presentation that will be strictly relied upon in the jury room, even in the absence of any proof, are those that are *unfavorable* to his case, such as weaknesses acknowledged in opening statement, elicited in direct examination, and conceded during summation.[14] These concessions allow the jury to draw lines constituting the outer boundaries of its decision.

---

[13] *See* page 20 and note 10, *supra*.

[14] *Cf.* Fed. R. Evid. 801(d)(2), Advisory Comm. Note (noting the "freedom which admissions have enjoyed from technical demands [of hearsay rules] of

The jury will generally choose either one counsel's position or that of his opponent (or a compromise between the two). Rarely will it venture beyond those bounds. To be sure, on infrequent occasions, a jury will issue a note during its deliberations suggesting that it is considering a theory that neither advocate has advanced. But these rare instances do not undermine the point that the jury will seldom stray from the boundaries set by the advocates.

The jury's assumption of best case operates in evaluating what the attorney *says* and what he *does* by way of introducing evidence. The following sections explain how and why this occurs.

The Advocate's Statements

It is a common observation regarding human behavior that if a person speaks falsely he is apt to do it when it benefits him but not when it harms him.[15] The jury views the statements of lawyers no differently: it tends to credit lawyers' negative statements about their cases but to view lawyers' favorable statements with suspicion. To illustrate the jury's perspective, assume a child being confronted by his mother who tells him that she waited until midnight for him to come home, at which point she went to sleep. If the child admits that he did not return until 1:00 a.m., the mother will assume that he was out until *at least* that time, and perhaps considerably later. She will not consider the possibility that he returned sooner, at 12:30 a.m.

---

searching for an assurance of trustworthiness in some against-interest circumstance"); *Bruton v. United States,* 391 U.S. 123, 139-140 (1967) (White, J., dissenting) (noting the "profound impact [of out-of-court admissions] on the jury," and stating that "an admission of guilt by the defendant ... constitutes direct evidence of the facts to which it relates. Even the testimony of an eyewitness may be less reliable than the defendant's own confession.").

[15] *Cf.* Jefferson, *Declarations Against Interest: An Exception to the Hearsay Rule,* 58 Harv. L. Rev. 1, 8 (1944) ("People are apt to speak freely and falsely in their own favor but are reluctant to speak falsely to their pecuniary or proprietary detriment.").

It follows that if the advocate states something favorable about his client's case, the jury will be apt to view it as a concession that the matter is no better — and perhaps a lot worse — than he has stated it. By the same token, if the advocate says something unfavorable about the case, the jury will be apt to view it as a concession that the matter is *at least* as bad as he has stated and is perhaps even worse.

The jury views an attorney's statements no differently than a prospective customer views those of a salesman. Consider, for example, a vacuum cleaner salesman who is trying to convince a prospective customer to purchase his product. The consumer assumes that the salesman is making the best presentation for his product. The salesman's praise for his product — "finest on the market," "will last a lifetime," "cleans perfectly" — will thus be heavily discounted.

On the other hand, if the salesman concedes that there is an equally good product by another company for the same price, that concession will be fully credited. The only open question is how much *better* the competitor's product may be, and the result is that the salesman will almost certainly lose the sale unless the competing product is unavailable. No potential customer will conclude from such a presentation that the salesman's product is *better* than his competitor's. Indeed, in the absence of independent verification, such a customer will be unlikely to conclude that the product is *as good* as the competition. Stated more broadly, the consumer will be skeptical of any claim by the salesman that is either favorable regarding his own product or unfavorable regarding that of his competitor. At the same time, he will tend to give considerable weight to anything said by the salesman that is either unfavorable concerning his own product or favorable concerning the competing product.

Similarly, when a restaurant posts a newspaper review of its food, the consumer will be apt to conclude that this is the *best* review and that other reviews not reproduced and posted — if any — are no better and, perhaps, are much worse. Here again, the customer's reaction to the posted review is no different than a juror's reaction to an advocate's statement about his case.

The foregoing phenomenon is mirrored in how statements are evaluated in the political arena. For instance, prior to federal election reform legislation, it was a time-worn campaign practice to disassociate a political communication from the candidate benefiting from the communication. Thus, in the late President Lyndon Johnson's first campaign for a Congressional seat, his staff composed newspaper releases that were later printed as articles rather than as paid advertisements. The communications were believed to "carry more weight [that] way."[16] Significantly, current federal election law requires all paid political advertisements to identify the individual financing the communication, including his association, or lack thereof, with any candidate.[17]

In the same vein, political commentators have traced the Senate's rejection of former Senator John Tower, President George Bush's first nominee for Secretary of Defense, to the early revelations by presidential aides that the President himself "had his doubts" about the merits of the nomination. These revelations were termed "the first drops of poison."[18]

To illustrate the foregoing points in a setting closer to the jury trial, assume an arbitration proceeding in which the party seeking relief estimates his claim at $5,000 and the defending party acknowledges liability of only $1,000. It is highly unlikely that the arbitrator's award will fall

[16] R. Caro, *The Years of Lyndon Johnson: The Path to Power* 406-407 (Alfred A. Knopf 1983).

[17] *See* 2 U.S.C. § 441d(a). This statute by its terms applies regardless of whether the communication is true or false. *Cf. United States v. Insco,* 365 F. Supp. 1308, 1311 (D.Fla. 1973).

[18] R. Evans and R. Novak, "The Tower Scorecard," reprinted in Wash. Post, Mar. 15, 1989, at A23.

outside of these boundaries. Like a jury, the arbitrator assumes that the case is no better than each advocate has stated. The $5,000 figure of the plaintiff is viewed as a concession that the case is worth no more. And the $1,000 figure of the defendant is viewed as a concession that the claim has validity *at least* in the amount of $1,000.

It should be clear from the above examples that jurors, like consumers, voters, and arbitrators, screen statements of interested spokesmen for their negative content. For this reason, an advocate can harm his case by explicit concessions in opening statement and closing argument. By telling the jury that his case is somehow weak or unpersuasive, he has ensured that the jury will view the case in that light.

In sum, apart from the party himself, there is no better witness against a party than his own hired gun. To paraphrase a familiar admonition, the advocate should be on notice that anything he says to the jury "can and will be used against [him] in court."[19]

The Advocate's Evidence

The above discussion has illustrated how the jury evaluates statements or assertions by reference to which attorney is making them. The jury's assumption of best case also colors its view of the advocate's evidence. This occurs in several ways.

First, an item of evidence introduced by an advocate will likely be viewed as his best evidence on the point. A non-courtroom example illustrates the point. Assume that, in interviewing to hire a lawyer, an executive visits a partner at his office in a leading Wall Street law firm. During that visit, the executive notices, prominently displayed among pictures of the lawyer's family, a commendation from the City Bar Association for the lawyer's contribution to a particular Bar subcommittee. The executive

[19] *Miranda v. Arizona,* 384 U.S. 436, 469 (1966).

will probably conclude that this commendation reflects the lawyer's most notable professional accomplishment to date.

Second, the jury's assumption of best case will lead it to suspect that an advocate undertook to "package" the item of evidence so that, when viewed by the jury, it would appear in the light most favorable to his case. This suspicion will cause the jury to seek to "unpackage" the item. Again, a non-courtroom example illustrates the point.

Assume a television commercial in which the Brand A Cola Company is reporting the results of a taste test it conducted involving its own brand and that of its competitor, Brand B Cola. The viewer is apt to be highly skeptical of the results showing that Brand A Cola won. He may suspect, for example, that several such tests had to be conducted before Brand A Cola prevailed in one, or that the sample of Brand A Cola used for the test was from a special stock. In short, he will have many misgivings about the validity of the test. And assertions by Brand A about the objectivity of the test will not completely eliminate the viewer's skepticism.

On the other hand, if the same television viewer opens a copy of a leading consumer magazine and reads an article about a taste test conducted under the magazine's supervision that yielded similar results, he will be apt to place far greater weight on the conclusion that Brand A was found preferable to Brand B. Finally, assume that the same television viewer goes to his accounting job and is told by a fellow accountant working on the Brand B account that everyone in Brand B's management is concerned about how to handle the results of a secret taste test conducted by Brand B in which Brand A won. In this circumstance, the viewer is apt to give the taste test the greatest weight of all. In fact, he is likely to consider it settled beyond all doubt that Brand A has a better taste.

The jury is no different. It will evaluate a piece of evidence by reference to the advocate introducing it. For example, it will assume that witnesses are extensively coached and prepared so that their testimony favoring the attorney's case emerges at trial in the best light. For that reason, it will assume that the only parts of a witness's testimony that it can strictly rely upon without hesitation, even in the absence of any other proof, are those that *disfavor* the case of the advocate calling the witness. And even with respect to those unfavorable portions of the testimony, the jury will assume that the witness has presented those matters in the best light.

It follows from the foregoing that when an advocate presents evidence that is *inconclusive,* the jury will almost certainly construe such evidence in the light *least* favorable to the sponsoring advocate. To illustrate the point, assume an automobile accident case in which the issue is whether the defendant was speeding. Assume further that an expert is available to testify concerning his analysis of skid marks. If, based on the expert's analysis, the skid marks show that the defendant was traveling 60 mph in a 30 mph zone, then the evidence should be introduced by the plaintiff. If the expert can give only a range of between 25 mph and 50 mph, then such evidence is consistent with the defendant's case, and plaintiff should *not* introduce it. The jury is apt to deem it significant that the best expert that the plaintiff could find allows for a finding that the defendant was driving within the speed limit. The common ground for decision is a finding that the defendant was driving 5 mph under the speed limit, and the jury is very likely to so decide.

On the other hand, if the *defense* introduces that evidence, then the plaintiff can point out that the best expert testimony the defendant could produce is consistent with the plaintiff's contention that the defendant was speeding. This analysis reveals that *neither side* should introduce this inconclusive skid mark evidence.

The jury's assumption of best case with minimum effort colors the view of evidence in yet a third way. When the advocate introduces an item of evidence or calls a witness, he is making an implicit statement that the evidence is material and important to the case. In the worst case scenario, his introduction of favorable evidence will be viewed as a concession that, without such evidence, he loses. The jury thus will not pause to consider whether the advocate would win without the item of evidence. The only disputed issue is whether the additional evidence is sufficiently favorable to require a verdict contrary to what it would have been without the item. In deciding that issue, the jury will preoccupy itself with considering all the reasons why the evidence is *not* sufficiently favorable. It will not dwell on the positive features of the evidence.

To use another non-courtroom example, assume that a consumer who is unfamiliar with electronics is deciding between two brands of stereo receivers carried at two competing stores. Assume further that the salesman at one store stresses above all else that his brand delivers more watts per channel for the dollar than the competitor's brand. Finally, assume that a consumer magazine study test conducted after the sales presentation found that the *competitor's* brand delivered more watts per channel for the price. The salesman who made the erroneous statement would thereafter have great difficulty claiming that a receiver's watts per channel is irrelevant and that his product beats the competition on sound alone. The significance of a receiver's watts per channel will have been implicitly conceded.

The harm from conceding the materiality of a point is not limited to situations where the advocate cannot prove that point.[20] As the next section demonstrates, even if he can prove the point, his case still might suffer if he endeavors to prove more than he needs to in order to win.

[20] *Cf.* Letter from Abraham Lincoln to Usher F. Linder (Feb. 20, 1848), *reprinted in* 1 *The Collected Works of Abraham Lincoln* 453 (R. Basler ed. 1953) ("In law it is good policy to never plead what you need not, lest you oblige yourself to prove what you can not.") (emphasis omitted).

The Advocate's Use of Inferior Evidence

As noted above, the jury assumes that an attorney will *not* introduce an item of evidence unless he believes that it will materially favor his case.[21] To illustrate using a non-courtroom example, if a civil engineer's plans for boring a tunnel through a mountain call for anything other than a straight path, a person reviewing the plan is apt to assume that the engineer believed that a straight path would not have accomplished the goal.[22] Similarly, the jury will view an advocate who calls a witness as believing that the testimony was important enough to justify the effort.

Thus, where the advocate goes to the effort of introducing evidence that is inferior to other evidence that he has introduced, the jury is apt to assume that he views the inferior evidence as materially favoring his case. When the jury makes this assumption, the advocate's case is almost certain to suffer.

In the worst case situation, the jury will assume that the advocate felt that he needed the inferior evidence to win. Put another way, the jury may conclude that he has implicitly acknowledged that his other evidence is inadequate. This concession assists the jury in resolving the most fundamental decision that it faces, and the one that it is least equipped to resolve: how much evidence is enough, under the applicable burden of proof,[23] to sustain a given verdict.

---

[21] Juries tend to agree with Professor Wigmore's observation that "possible witnesses whose testimony would be for any reason comparatively *unimportant*, or *cumulative*, or *inferior* to what is already utilized, might well be dispensed with by a party on general grounds of expense and inconvenience." II J. Wigmore, *Evidence* § 287, at 202-203 (Little, Brown & Co. Chadbourn rev. 1979) (emphasis in original). *Cf. Patton v. Rambo*, 20 Ala. 485 (1852) (where only one of two examining physicians called, no adverse inference may be suggested to the jury as to uncalled physician without a showing that his testimony would have been *more* valuable).

[22] *See, e.g.*, Zipf, *supra* note 10, at 2 (giving factually analogous example).

[23] *See, e.g.*, 1 Devitt & Blackmar, *supra* note 1, § 11.14, at 310 (instruction on proof beyond a reasonable doubt standard); 3 Devitt, Blackmar & Wolff, *supra*

As we will show, this concession from the use of inferior evidence is one that the advocate will have trouble overcoming. He will have difficulty convincing the jury, for example, that he presented evidence that was unnecessary or irrelevant. The jury will therefore be inclined to focus not on his superior evidence but on whether the inferior evidence is enough to put an otherwise inadequate case "over the top." The attorney is unlikely to benefit from this microscopic critique of his inferior evidence.

Accordingly, the weight given to an advocate's superior evidence will be influenced by any inferior evidence that he introduces. In general, the introduction of inferior evidence reduces the probative impact of the advocate's other, superior evidence. The reason is that the introduction of the inferior item is viewed as a statement by the advocate that he needs that item in light of the inadequacy of his superior evidence. For example, when an attorney puts on a strong witness and a weak witness on the same point, the jury is likely to conclude that the attorney himself was not sufficiently convinced by the strong witness and felt compelled to produce additional evidence to make his case. In short, the advocate who uses inferior evidence risks that the consideration of his superior evidence will be significantly prejudiced.

The Advocate's Unusual Efforts

Because of the principle of minimum effort,[24] jurors are influenced by any unusual efforts they perceive to have been required of the attorney to marshal an item of evidence. In general, the greater the perceived effort, the less favorably the jury will view evidence. This phenomenon is reflected in common experience.

For example, when a man is complimented on his sports jacket, his statement, "Oh, I was in a rush. It was

---

note 1, § 72.01, at 31-32 (instruction on preponderance of the evidence standard).

[24] *See* page 20, *supra*.

the first thing I grabbed," is an attempt to enhance the viewer's impression. A contrary response — "This is my best and most expensive jacket. It took me weeks of shopping in Europe to find it." — would leave the viewer thinking, "It's not that great."

Similarly, a student's classmates will be more impressed by his high grade if he achieved that grade without studying. The student will substantially reduce the impact of his grade if he states, "I did nothing else but study for the test for two months." His fellow students will then view him as an over-achiever and will conclude, "Anyone could have gotten that high a grade with *that* much studying."

The same phenomenon applies in the courtroom setting. Thus, in the trial involving the lineup tape discussed in Chapter One, the exhibit was made less desirable as a potential defense exhibit because of the unusual efforts that would have been required to display it to the jury. Similarly, a lawyer's meager results on cross-examination will be magnified if the questioning is lengthy and labored. For example, in Robert Traver's novel, *Anatomy of a Murder,* defense counsel in summation effectively ridiculed the prosecutor for having "hammered and clawed" throughout his fruitless "terrier cross-examination."[25]

The foregoing examples illustrate the concept of the concession of no better evidence for a given level of effort. Specifically, the jury will assume that, for any given level of effort necessary to marshal an item of evidence favorable to his case, the advocate could not have produced evidence of that probative value by using less effort. The result is that the greater the effort necessary to produce an item of evidence, the less inclined the jury will be to

[25] R. Traver, *Anatomy of a Murder* 464 (Dell 1958). *See also* S. Turow, *Presumed Innocent* 168-169 (Farrar Straus Giroux 1987) (fictional criminal defense lawyer, explaining to his client that he did not want to conduct an investigation into the accuracy of certain government records, noted that "'I would not want to see [the government] introduce the fact that we made efforts to challenge the accuracy of these records and failed'").

assume that the advocate could have produced even stronger evidence had he undertaken greater effort. Furthermore, whether evidence is favorable or unfavorable, attorney effort translates into a concession of materiality and thereby triggers jury skepticism.

The Advocate's Use of the Attack — The Importance of the Attack

Some trial manuals caution against spending much time attacking or responding to the opposition. They reason that the advocate, by so doing, is communicating that he has nothing of his own to offer and that he is forced out of desperation to attack his opponent.[26] Such advice is inconsistent with what the jury expects of an interested advocate.[27]

The jury's assumption of best case includes a mirror-image expectation as well: the jury looks to each advocate to highlight the shortcomings of his opponent's case. Thus, while the advocate must strive to demonstrate the merit in his own position, he must likewise strive to demonstrate the lack of merit in his opponent's position. As the following section explains, if the advocate succeeds in convincing the jury of the latter, then it will be largely constrained to rule in his favor. For this reason, it may be as much to the advocate's benefit to show the flaws in his opponent's side as it is to show the strengths in his own side.

---

[26] *See, e.g.*, J. Sonsteng, R. Haydock & J. Boyd, *The Trial Book — A Total System for the Preparation and Presentation of a Case* § 10.6 at 337 (West 1984) ("It is not wise to spend significant portions of the closing argument responding to the opponent's issues, positions, and arguments. The jury may perceive an attorney [who] does this as an advocate without any substantial positions."); 1 S. Schweitzer, *Cyclopedia of Trial Practice* § 185, at 503 (Lawyers Co-op. Pub. Co. 2d ed. 1970) ("Under no circumstances should the defendant in his opening make a direct criticism of any claim of the plaintiff.").

[27] It is also inconsistent with the practice of the ancient Greek orators. *See, e.g.*, G. Kennedy, *The Art of Persuasion in Greece* 131 n.13 (Princeton Univ. Press 1963) (noting view of 19th Century scholar that the "attack on the opponent" was a "characteristic fifth-century [Greek] feature of the proof").

To illustrate the point in a common setting, assume that a prospective home buyer has conclusively narrowed his choice to two houses in different neighborhoods and is trying to decide between them. The real estate agent for one of the houses will, of course, attempt to influence the buyer by stressing the desirability of the house that he is selling, such as the high quality of schools and easy access to public transportation. If the buyer states that he is considering another house being handled by a competing agency, the thorough agent will also stress the undesirability of the other house, such as its location in a high crime area.

This principle was illustrated by events during the course of the 1988 presidential election. Then Republican candidate George Bush demonstrated that he could reap as great a benefit from attacking his Democratic opponent, Michael Dukakis, as he could from simply stressing the merits of his own candidacy. Once he applied that strategy, he climbed dramatically in the polls and ultimately won the election.[28]

Theoretical Underpinnings for the Attack

Most experienced defense lawyers need no instruction on the value of attacking the government's or plaintiff's presentation. For them, the two methods for persuading the jury could not be more obvious: they can win both by putting on their own case and by contending that the prosecutor or plaintiff has not met his burden.

Nonetheless, we have found that among many plaintiffs' lawyers and prosecutors the requirement of a burden of proof has been an obstacle to their full appreciation of the value of attacking the defense. They reason

---

[28] *See, e.g.,* P.J. Buchanan, "Keep up the Pressure, George," reprinted in the San Diego Union, Aug. 30, 1988 at B7 (noting that George Bush went from an 18-point disadvantage to a 6-point lead during the month of August by going on the offensive and attacking Michael Dukakis's views).

that because *they* have the burden, their success in demonstrating the lack of merit in their opponent's defense will not make the jury more likely to find in their favor. In our view, this analysis is flawed.

To be sure, a jury is not constrained to select between the two positions urged by the parties. The jury could conceivably find for one party on a theory that was not even urged by that party. For example, if a suit filed by a plaintiff can be defended in three possible ways, the lack of merit in one of the defenses does not necessarily imply the validity of the plaintiff's claim. In logical terms, given the alternative defenses, the plaintiff's claim and the invalid defense are at best "contrary" (*i.e.,* both could be false but only one can be true) and not "contradictory" (*i.e.,* if either one is false, the other must be true).[29] If that is so, then it would seem to follow that showing that the opponent's defense is without merit does not substantially help establish the merit in the advocate's position. The jury could still rule for the opponent on a theory that the advocate has not advanced.

Nonetheless, where defense counsel has urged only the one meritless defense, the jury will not likely seek to identify and evaluate defenses that have not been advanced. Rather, it will be apt to assume that defense counsel has selected the *best* defense and that, if that one is not enough, then the others are *a fortiori* inadequate.[30] As a result, the plaintiff's claim and the defense urged by defense counsel assume, as a practical matter, a contradictory relationship in which showing the falsity of one implies the truth of the other. Thus, the plaintiff's attorney

---

[29] *See* Webster's New World Dictionary 308, 309 (Simon & Schuster Second College Ed. 1980) (definitions of "contrary" and "contradictory" as used in logic).

[30] *Cf.* T. Twiss, *Life of Lord Eldon* (1844) (quoting comment of English jurist Edward Thurlow: "'I was with you, Mr. Scott — until I heard your argument.'"), *reprinted in* D. Shrager and E. Frost, *The Quotable Lawyer* 14 (Facts on File Pub. 1986).

or prosecutor who succeeds in meeting his legal burden of proof will derive as much benefit from exposing the weaknesses of his opponent's case as he will from advancing the strengths of his own case.[31]

The Costs of Sponsorship

It is useful at this point to formalize the foregoing analysis by recognizing the existence of three fundamental costs of sponsorship incurred by the advocate in making contentions and introducing evidence. Each of these costs ultimately rests on the fundamental assumption of best case with minimum efforts.

These costs bear on virtually every tactic and strategy recommended by this book. Furthermore, familiarity with them will enable an advocate to make his own tactical decisions in the heat of trial, when time does not permit him to consult a manual for guidance.

The First Cost: Introduction of Evidence

When an interested advocate introduces an item of favorable evidence, the jury will conclude that the item was the best evidence on the point that he could marshal using that degree of effort. This constitutes a harmful conces-

[31] Some commentators have suggested that a prosecutor should not adopt an aggressive trial strategy. *See, e.g.,* Alschuler, *Courtroom Misconduct by Prosecutors and Trial Judges,* 50 Tex. L. Rev. 629, 636 (1972) (arguing that a prosecutor "should avoid the 'glow and flow of the heat of forensics' and should, in fact, strive for more 'Chesterfieldian politeness'"); *cf.* Model Code of Professional Responsibility, EC 7-13 (instructing prosecutors "to seek justice, not merely to convict"). Other commentators point out, however, that while a prosecutor's goal is not simply to convict but to see that justice is done, this in no way relieves him from his duties as an advocate once he decides that there is a valid basis for bringing criminal charges. *See, e.g.,* W. Seymour, *Why Prosecutors Act Like Prosecutors,* 11 Record of NYCBA 302, 312-313 (1956) ("When we decide to prosecute, it is because we decide that this is how justice will be done .... [At trial, the prosecutor is] a full-fledged fighting advocate; and he should be.... To do otherwise would be to violate his duty in the most real sense.") We generally favor the latter view.

sion of no better evidence. Furthermore, the attorney's effort in introducing the item of evidence is received by the jury as a "statement" — whether intended or not — that the attorney deems the item of evidence probative and material to the resolution of the case. Thus, when an advocate introduces an item of evidence favorable to his case, he will, in the worst case, be viewed as making a statement that the item of evidence is *needed* to prove his case. The jury will be apt to credit that concession of need but view the evidence with skepticism and discount the attorney's assessment of its favorable probative value.

Correspondingly, when an advocate introduces an item of evidence that is *unfavorable* to his case, his implicit "statement" or concession that the evidence is important will result in the unfavorable evidence being given enhanced weight. Put another way, the jury will view that statement as an admission that it is *his* job to show that the damaging item does not compel a verdict against him. This is far worse than the alternative of having his opponent burdened with showing that the item is important to the verdict.

Introduction of an item of evidence — whether favorable or unfavorable — triggers a further prejudicing of the jury's evaluation of that item. This impact stems from the jury's assumption that the advocate has packaged the item to appear in its best light. For example, when an advocate introduces a witness, the jury assumes that the advocate had one or more pretrial conferences with the witness. The jury will normally assume that such conferences afford the advocate the opportunity to probe all dimensions of the witness's recollection and to select only those aspects that favor his client's case. It may further suspect that, if a witness at a pretrial conference initially recalls something inconsistent with the advocate's case, the advocate will confront him with the statements of other witnesses in the hope that the witness will reconsider his own recollection.[32]

Similarly, with respect to items of physical evidence, the jury will be apt to assume that such evidence was packaged in its best light. For example, when it sees a photograph, the jury will assume that the picture contains the best possible angle, lighting, and distance to make the advocate's point.

Given these two consequences of introduction — the attorney's statement of materiality[33] and the jury's assumption that he packaged the evidence in its best light — it should be apparent that an advocate introducing evidence is generally worse off than he would have been had the evidence been introduced by his opponent. This is true regardless of whether the evidence is favorable or unfavorable. This influence can be graphically illustrated as a uniform shift to the left along a continuum, as represented in the figure below, where the numeric value represents the weight assigned to the evidence by the jury.

Figure 2-1: Axis of Materiality

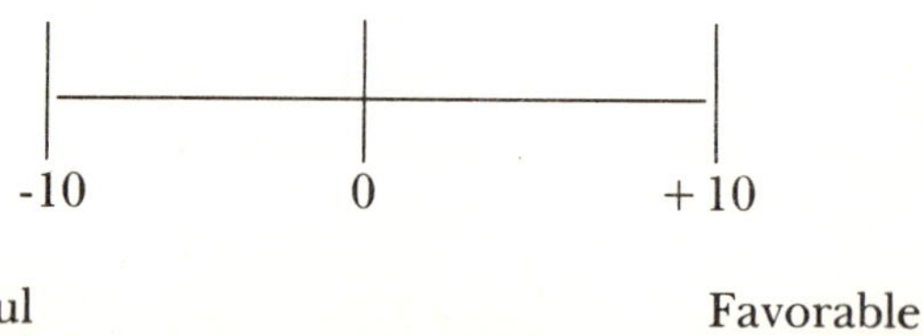

We term this uniform shift "the cost of introduction." This shift reflects the cost associated with the introduction

[32] *Cf.* Markus, *A Theory of Trial Advocacy,* 56 Tul. L. Rev. 95, 102-103 (1981) (noting the advocate's desire in a pretrial witness conference to "develop characteristics of the event favorable to [his] client's position," and also noting how "the witness will be encouraged to reconsider the accuracy of [his] recollection(s)" by the advocate's confronting him with the contrary recollections of other witnesses).

[33] For convenience, the terms "statement of materiality" and "concession of materiality" are used throughout this book as encompassing the concession of no better evidence as well.

of any item of evidence, whether favorable, neutral, or unfavorable. Put another way, other things being equal, *the act of introducing an item of evidence will influence the weight that the jury gives to that item in a manner that disfavors the sponsoring advocate's case.*

In general, the more an item of evidence favors the advocate's case, the lower will be the cost of introduction. This is because the concession of no better evidence is less significant when the quality of the evidence approaches perfection. It is also because the jury expects the advocate to present all evidence that materially favors his case.

As we show in Chapter Four,[34] recognition of this cost of sponsorship leads to the rejection, as a general tactical rule, of a fundamental principle of the current trial tactics literature: that an advocate invariably gains by bringing out a weakness in his case rather than leaving it to his opponent to introduce. The reason why this principle is unsound is that when the advocate brings out the harmful evidence, *he* incurs the cost of introduction, and the item of harmful evidence is therefore given heightened weight by the jury. In addition, the opponent benefits from the cost that he saves in not having to bring out the weakness himself.

By the same token, when the opponent brings out a weakness in the advocate's case, such as eliciting during cross-examination the prior conviction of one of the advocate's witnesses, the benefit to the opponent's case is reduced because of the opponent's introduction of it. Put another way, the impact of the weakness on the advocate's case is not as great as it would have been had the advocate himself elicited it. For these reasons, while the strategy of volunteering weaknesses has applicability in exceptional circumstances (discussed in Chapter Four), it is untenable — and must be rejected — as a general principle of advocacy.

[34]*See* pages 86-105, *infra.*

The Second Cost: Unusual Efforts

The second cost of sponsorship is based on the phenomenon discussed earlier in this chapter regarding the efforts of attorneys as perceived by the jury. Specifically, any unusual efforts perceived to have been expended by an advocate to marshal an item of evidence will influence the weight given to that item in a manner that disfavors that advocate's case. Like the cost of introduction, the impact of the cost of unusual efforts can be graphically illustrated as a uniform shift to the left along the continuum depicted in figure 2-1 above.

The cost resulting from perceived efforts represents an impact on the probative value of evidence that is distinct from that resulting from the cost of introduction. To be sure, there is an overlap between the cost of unusual efforts and the cost attributable to the advocate's implicit concession of materiality when he introduces any evidence. The act of calling a witness represents a fixed quantity of effort on the attorney's part. The attorney must go out of his way to contact the witness, interview him, give him directions to the courthouse, and occasionally issue a subpoena to secure his attendance at trial. It is largely the expenditure of effort in calling the witness that causes the jury to conclude that the attorney deems the witness material to the case. For analytical convenience, however, this book treats the two costs separately.[35]

To illustrate the distinction between the two, assume that a witness has testimony about four facts and gives testimony concerning all four. The advocate introducing such testimony will suffer a loss in evidentiary weight as to each of these four facts by operation of the cost of introduction. If, in order to prove one of the four facts, he

[35] For the most part, this book refers to the cost of unusual efforts as simply the "cost of efforts." This shorthand term is for convenience only. Thus, the "cost of efforts" refers solely to additional efforts beyond introducing a witness or piece of evidence or questioning a witness.

must conduct an elaborate and lengthy examination involving multiple documents and diagrams, the jury will be apt to discount even further the weight given to that one fact.[36]

It is important to note that, on rare occasions, consideration of the cost of efforts may make it tactically advisable for an advocate to introduce harmful evidence himself. This will arise when the apparent effort required of the advocate to *omit* evidence from his presentation causes the jury to give that evidence *greater* weight when his opponent later introduces it than it would have received had the advocate introduced it himself. A detailed discussion of this point is contained in Chapter Four.

The Third Cost: Overtrying

Special considerations apply when an advocate has more favorable evidence than is required to establish a *prima facie* case or disprove his opponent's case, and is therefore faced with the question of whether to use that additional evidence. As we will show, the introduction of such additional evidence can result in a negative impact on the weight that the jury assigns to the advocate's *other* evidence. This impact is distinct from that predicted by the costs of introduction and efforts.

The jury's tendency to discount the weight it attaches to an advocate's other evidence when he introduces an item of additional evidence stems from the implicit concession that the advocate believes the evidence to be important enough to warrant introducing it. As previously noted,[37] the jury assumes that an advocate will be apt to dispense

[36] The analytical relationship between the costs of introduction (excluding packaging) and unusual efforts can be understood by considering the two sponsorship costs in combination as a function of the strength of the item of evidence and the effort required to marshal it, where costs decrease with strength and increase with effort.

[37] *See* page 37, *supra.*

with an item of evidence if it does not *materially* advance his case. Thus, when an advocate calls a witness who appears cumulative or inferior to another witness whom he has previously called, he is apt to be viewed as taking a dim view of that other witness. If the advocate himself appears to feel this way about the other witness, the jury will tend to discount that witness's testimony.

When the advocate introduces evidence favorable to his case, the jury may assume that he is concerned that he *needs* such evidence. As noted above,[38] the ultimate hazard is that the jury may conclude that the advocate is of the view that his other evidence, standing alone, is insufficient to win.

If this negative effect is substantial enough, a net harm can result from introducing more rather than fewer favorable witnesses or items of evidence. This phenomenon reflects the cost associated with what is commonly termed "overtrying" one's case. The critical step in understanding the cost of overtrying is to recognize the counter-intuitive point that there exists *favorable* evidence that, when introduced along with other of the advocate's favorable evidence, reduces the overall persuasiveness of his presentation. Evidence causing such an effect should be omitted from the advocate's presentation.[39]

For example, assume an assault case where the defendant is claiming misidentification and the complainant has testified unequivocally that the defendant is the one who committed the assault. Assume further that a second witness is available to testify that he is sixty percent certain

[38] *See* page 37, *supra*.

[39] For those versed in mathematics, several of sponsorship theory's relationships between strength and effort (and how, for example, overtrying costs are incurred) can be described using constrained optimization techniques advanced by the 18th Century French mathematician Joseph Lagrange. The problem can be formulated by positing an effort-minimizing advocate constrained to put on at least what he considers to be sufficient evidence to win. An analogous problem is set forth in A. K. Dixit, *Optimization in Economic Theory* 9 (Oxford Univ. Press 1976) (production of target output at minimum cost).

that the defendant was the assailant. In these circumstances, the advocate's calling of the second witness to corroborate the complainant is apt to diminish significantly the probative value that the jury assigns to the complainant's testimony. In our experience, the decrease in weight that the jury would give to the complainant's testimony would easily outweigh the incremental probative value of the second witness (as adjusted by any costs of introduction and efforts). For this reason, the second witness should *not* be called.

In sum, an item of *favorable* evidence, when added to the other evidence in the advocate's case, can sometimes cause a net *reduction* in the overall persuasiveness of his case. Employing the graph in figure 2-1, the effect is to *reduce* the weight placed on the other evidence, standing alone, by an amount that is *greater* than the positive increment gained from the probative value of the additional evidence.

The advocate should also recognize that it is possible for his use of an item of favorable evidence to reduce his chances of securing a favorable verdict even where he introduces no other evidence. As explained more fully in Chapter Six, this can be true for defense attorneys, who must assess the impact of introducing *any* defense evidence on the weight given to the *opponent's* foregoing presentation. By putting on any defense, defense counsel is communicating a concern that he *needs* to do so because of the persuasiveness of his opponent's case.

The jury may view the defendant's decision to put on a defense as a concession that his opponent has made out a case which, if not rebutted, would be sufficient for a verdict in the opponent's favor. In those circumstances, the impact would be to enhance the weight that the jury will give to the opponent's evidence. Employing the graph in figure 2-1, the effect is represented by a positive or rightward shift in the weight that would otherwise be accorded to the sum of the *opponent's* evidence. The attorney considering whether to put on a rebuttal or surrebuttal case faces similar issues.

By itself, the simple principle that overtrying a case can be harmful is not a new one. Many commentators have recognized it.[40] Nonetheless, the rationale typically given — that the jury will become bored or confused[41] — does not begin to explain the real reason for the danger from overtrying a case.

It is important to note that the cost of overtrying incurred by the use of additional evidence will normally be influenced by the strength of that additional evidence. Other things being equal, the stronger the additional evidence is (relative to the other evidence), the lower the cost of overtrying is apt to be. This is because the jury expects the advocate to present all evidence that *materially* favors his case. To whatever extent the introduction of the additional evidence comports with this expectation, the advocate will reduce his cost of overtrying.

Moreover, the weaker the advocate's evidence is (relative to the additional evidence), the lower will be the cost of overtrying incurred by the use of the additional evidence. In this circumstance, the advocate's acknowledgement of the weakness of his other evidence by introducing the additional evidence will be less significant because the jury will to a great extent already see that weakness.[42]

The advocate, of course, should not lose sight of the inherent probative value of the additional item of evidence. Net costs of overtrying from the use of evidence are incurred only where the benefit from the additional item is exceeded by the harm to the probative value of the

---

[40] *See, e.g.*, J. Appleman, *Preparation and Trial* 211 (Coiner Pub., Ltd. 1967) ("[D]on't forget one primary rule. Never overtry a case.").

[41] *See, e.g.*, *id.*, at 211 ("A jury will become bored by a constant stream of witnesses upon trivial matters.").

[42] Two further factors influence the cost of overtrying: the efforts expended in marshaling the additional evidence (which result in increased costs) and the efforts expended in marshaling the other evidence already presented (which result in decreased costs).

other evidence. Where there is a net benefit, then it is obvious that the evidence should be used.

****

This chapter has demonstrated how an attorney's words and deeds can influence the jury's perception of the strength of his case and that of his opponent. Most fundamentally, it has shown that the same item of evidence may be given significantly different weight depending on which side introduces it.

Some may believe that the adversarial system's requirement that the parties marshal the evidence (rather than the court or another neutral source) results in an undesirable distortion of the weight given to such evidence.[43] Nonetheless, whether an advocate approves or disapproves of this feature of the adversary system, he must consider the costs of sponsorship in virtually every tactical decision he makes if he wishes to maximize his success at trial.

---

[43] *See, e.g.*, Sward, *Values, Ideology, and the Evolution of the Adversary System,* 64 Ind. L.J. 301, 316 (1989) ("adversarial adjudication may overemphasize party control to the point of distortion"); *but cf.* 2 U.S.C. § 441d(a) (disclosure of candidate affiliation utilized as an *aid* to the voter in interpreting political communications). The inquisitorial system is not without its own distortions. *See* Chapter Eight, *infra,* note 50.

3

Issue Identification and Evidence Evaluation

You have just returned from court. The judge has set a trial date in a case that you were certain would settle. You now sit in a conference room amid a morass of witness interview summaries, documents, exhibits, deposition transcripts, charts, and graphs. You ask yourself: How do I make sense out of all of this? What is my theory of the case? What is the other side going to argue? This chapter will equip the advocate with the tools he needs to make order out of the chaos.

Any advocate facing trial must perform two critical threshold tasks before deciding upon a trial strategy. First, he must identify the issues in the case and determine which ones are going to be disputed. Second, he must evaluate the strengths and weaknesses of the available evidence in light of the disputed issues. This chapter addresses those two tasks.

Identifying Issues Capable of Being Disputed

Identifying disputed issues — or, in the case of the defense, choosing which issues to dispute — is a critical task of an advocate preparing for trial. The first step in accomplishing this task is for the advocate to identify his interpretation of the available evidence — commonly known as his "theory of the case." For the plaintiff or prosecutor, this interpretation of the evidence must satisfy the requirements of the legal burden of proof applicable to the claim or offense in the case.[1] Similarly, a defendant who is disputing one or more elements of the claim or offense or who is asserting an affirmative defense must have in mind an interpretation of the evidence that defeats his opponent's claim.

The key to identifying the disputed issues in the case is for the advocate to determine, based on his knowledge of all of the evidence available to both parties, those elements of the claim or affirmative defense for which both sides have a non-frivolous position. To illustrate, assume that a defendant has been sued for breach of contract. His attorney, in planning his defense, should consider a variety of issues, such as whether there is evidence that his client even entered into a contract. The attorney may conclude that the discussions between the parties were simply preliminary negotiations that did not culminate in an offer and an acceptance.

Moreover, if a statute of frauds applies, the attorney should determine whether a sufficient writing exists to satisfy that statute. In addition, he may consider whether, if a contract was formed, any affirmative defenses are available, such as undue influence or duress. After he has considered these and other available means of defeating the claim, defense counsel will presumably have identified those elements of his opponent's claim that he is capable of disputing.

[1] *See* Chapter Five, *infra,* pages 114-117 (describing the method for ascertaining the legal elements of a claim).

Predicting the Issues That Will Be Disputed

Where there is more than one issue for which both sides have a non-frivolous position, each advocate has an important additional determination to make. For the plaintiff's attorney or prosecutor, an educated guess should be made as to which elements of his claim his opponent will deny or which affirmative defense, if any, his opponent will advance. If he anticipates an affirmative defense, he must determine which element of that defense he is capable of disputing.

For defense counsel, a decision must be made as to which elements of the claim to deny or which affirmative defense, if any, to advance. If the defense decides to advance an affirmative defense, it must make an educated guess regarding which element its opponent is capable of disputing. The following two sections give guidance in accomplishing these tasks.

Ascertaining What the Defense Will Be

As noted, the plaintiff's lawyer or prosecutor must assess which elements or aspects of his case, if any, the defendant will deny and what affirmative defenses, if any, will be presented. In a civil suit, the rules of civil procedure facilitate this determination, and civil discovery procedures permit an in-depth exploration of a defendant's contentions.[2] By contrast, in a criminal case, the defense must normally be inferred, if possible, from defense counsel's opening statement or from such evidence as recorded statements of the defendant at the time of his arrest. Even here, however, the prosecutor may, in limited circumstances, be legally entitled to learn the nature of the defense prior to trial.[3]

---

[2] *See, e.g.*, Fed. R. Civ. P. 26-37 (various discovery rules, including procedures for depositions, interrogatories, and requests for documents and admissions).

[3] *See, e.g.*, Fed. R. Crim. P. 12.1 (government may request notice of defendant's intention to offer an alibi defense; such notice shall specify the defen-

Deciding Whether to Advance More Than One Defense

This section addresses the considerations pertinent to whether a defense attorney should advance more than one defense. For instance, in the foregoing contract suit example, the defendant may find that more than one defense is available under the facts of the case. The question here is whether he should assert more than one defense.

If the available defenses are inconsistent — for example, no contract negotiations ever took place, but if they did, the resulting contract was entered into under duress — the cost of overtrying instructs that only *one* defense, the stronger one, should be selected. By offering an inconsistent theory and suggesting that it could be credited, the defense would be conceding that a reasonable interpretation of the evidence exists that precludes its primary theory. Advancing both defenses would substantially reduce the weight that the jury would place on the evidence supporting the stronger defense. For this reason, we unequivocally counsel against advancing inconsistent theories in any circumstance. This conclusion comports with the position taken by most experienced trial lawyers.[4]

The more difficult issue is whether an advocate should advance alternative theories that are not inconsistent — for example, defending a contract suit by claiming duress and also arguing that the defendant's performance did not constitute a breach of the contract. Because of the cost of overtrying, advancing the second defense may be viewed by the jury as revealing the attorney's lack of confi-

dant's whereabouts at the relevant time and list "the names and addresses of the witnesses upon whom the defendant intends to rely to establish such alibi"); Fed. R. Crim. P. 16(b)(1)(A) (requiring, upon a similar defense demand on the government, that the defendant disclose documents and tangible objects that he intends to produce at trial); Fed. R. Crim. P. 16(b)(1)(B) (requiring, after he makes a similar request to the government, that the defendant disclose the results of tests or experiments that he intends to use at trial).

[4] *See, e.g.*, R. Carlson & E. Imwinkelried, *Dynamics of Trial Practice* § 3.3(D), at 30 (West Pub. Co. 1989) ("The threshold question is whether the attorney should urge all [factually inconsistent] theories at trial. Most experienced attorneys answer that question in the negative.").

dence in his first defense. Here again, most experienced attorneys advise against advancing multiple theories to the jury even if such theories are not inconsistent.[5]

Sponsorship analysis agrees, for the most part, with the approach of not advancing alternative but consistent defenses. The agreement stems largely from the fact that in the typical case, the alternative defense is not compelling. In such a case, the jury will be apt to attribute the espousal of the weaker defense as an act necessitated by defense counsel's view that his other defense is insufficient. In this respect, the jury's reasoning is similar to the reasoning it applies when inconsistent defenses are advanced.

The jury will be less likely to reach this conclusion, however, where the alternative defense is supported by equally compelling evidence. This is because, as we have stated,[6] the jury is inclined to view any advocate as committed to presenting any available evidence or argument that will *materially* advance his case. In this situation, advancing more than one defense may be appropriate.[7]

For example, assume an undercover narcotics distribution case in which the defendant has credible alibi evidence showing that he was not the seller. Assume further that he can also call into serious question the accuracy of the government's tests showing that the substance purchased by the agent was heroin (as opposed to a harmless substance used to defraud buyers, such as baking soda). Here, the advocate may well be advised to advance both

---

[5] *See, e.g.,* Carlson & Imwinkelried, *supra* note 4, § 3.3(D), at 30-31 (citing practices of experienced lawyers); *cf.* R. Keeton, *Trial Tactics and Methods* § 10.6, at 370 (Little, Brown & Co. 2d ed. 1973) (noting dangers in asserting multiple or inconsistent defenses before the jury, but pointing out that such an approach is appropriate in drafting pleadings).

[6] *See* page 20, *supra.*

[7] As will be shown, the advocate faces a similar dilemma when he has more than one item of evidence available to prove the same point. *See* Chapter Eight, pages 190 to 194, *infra.*

theories, assuming that he is careful in how he crafts his argument.[8]

Evaluating Evidence on the Disputed Issues

Once the disputed issues are discerned, the advocate can evaluate the probative value of the evidence in light of those issues.[9] It is basic that a given item of evidence, when considered in its totality, can either help, harm, or have no influence on the strength of the advocate's case. The terms used in this book to describe these categories of evidence are "favorable," "neutral," and "harmful."

Favorable evidence is evidence that, on balance, makes the position urged by the advocate more probable in the jury's eyes than it would have been without such evidence. Harmful evidence is evidence that makes the advocate's position less probable in the jury's eyes than it would have been without such evidence.[10] Neutral evidence is evidence that, on balance, makes the advocate's position neither more nor less probable than it would have been without such evidence. In classifying evidence, the advocate must compare the persuasive impact on the jury of using the item of evidence along with his other evidence and the impact of using the other evidence alone.[11] The advocate must also recognize that, as used in this book, the terms for classifying evidence refer to the strength of evidence

---

[8]Chapter Twelve provides guidance in making such an argument. *See* pages 260-261, *infra.*

[9]The special considerations pertinent to evaluating the strength of evidence on undisputed issues are addressed in Chapter Five. *See* page 119, note 18, *infra.*

[10]*Cf.* Fed. R. Evid. 401 (defining "relevant evidence" as "evidence having any tendency to make the existence of any fact that is of consequence to the determination of the action more probable or less probable than it would be without the evidence").

[11]*Cf.* 11 C. Wright & A. Miller, *Federal Practice and Procedure* § 2883, at 278 (West 1973) (in discussing, *inter alia,* whether the erroneous admission or exclusion of evidence is harmless, the probative effect of the item of evidence in question is to be determined "in light of all the evidence").

as introduced by a neutral source, not to the strength of evidence as adjusted for sponsorship costs.

Evidence cannot be considered favorable, as defined in this book, merely because it seems in some respect to advance the advocate's position on a disputed issue. Before an advocate can conclude that an item of evidence is, on balance, favorable, he must assess the item in its totality.

For example, in an assault case involving a claim of self-defense, the testimony of an attentive and observant passer-by witness who can give an unequivocal account of the assault which, if credited, precludes the possibility of self-defense would unquestionably constitute favorable evidence. Since the passer-by is not acquainted with either of the parties, he has no motive to fabricate, and his credibility is virtually impossible to impeach. The same testimony, however, from a relative of the victim who had previously told the police that the defendant had acted in self-defense may, on balance, constitute favorable, neutral, or harmful evidence when the testimony as a whole, including impeaching materials, is considered. In making this determination, the advocate would need to consider, among other things, the strength of the other evidence available, the closeness of the relationship between the defendant and the victim, and the persuasiveness of the witness's explanation for the prior inconsistent statement.

The three categories — favorable, neutral, and harmful — coincide with the positive, negative, and zero portions of the materiality graph depicted in Chapter Two (figure 2-1). In addition to these three categories, this book identifies a fourth category of evidence — designated as "marginal" evidence — clustering closely around zero on the graph.[12]

---

[12] Courts have used the term "marginal" to describe evidence that, although erroneously admitted, was not likely to have swayed the verdict. *See, e.g., Lokos v. State,* 434 So.2d 831, 835 (Ala. 1983) (noting that "the inflammatory aspect of [the] evidence would have been only marginal at most and certainly insufficient

The test for whether evidence is marginal is likewise a relative one. An item of evidence is marginal if, when considered in conjunction with any other evidence supporting the advocate's case, it has no *realistic* chance of causing an otherwise unconvinced trier of fact to render a verdict in the advocate's favor.

Given the foregoing test, an item of evidence can be marginal even if, as a theoretical matter, it makes the proposition that the advocate is asserting more probable than it would have been without the item. For example, where an eyewitness to a rape can state only that the rapist was white (the defendant's race), such evidence, although technically favorable to the prosecutor, is unlikely to persuade the jury to rule in his favor.

It is important for the advocate to be familiar with the categories described above. They are employed throughout this book as a framework for evaluating the costs of sponsorship incurred by the use of evidence.

Evaluation of Evidence Bearing on More than One Disputed Issue

Although the basic categories of favorable, neutral, and harmful evidence carry simple titles, the determination of the appropriate category for a given piece of evidence can be a difficult one. In a case where there is more than one issue, evidence may fall into one category for purposes of one issue and another category for purposes of a second issue.

For instance, an eyewitness to an automobile accident might have favorable testimony on behalf of the victim that the defendant was driving recklessly. That same witness, however, might testify that he observed the victim walking with a noticeable limp immediately before being struck, thereby undercutting the victim's claim for dam-

to establish any likelihood that the jury would have reached a different result without it").

ages. Thus, while the witness may be favorable on liability, his testimony might be categorized as harmful on the issue of damages. The advocate considering the use of such a witness must balance these two features of the testimony. Similarly, in a murder prosecution, grisly photographs of the victim might constitute favorable evidence on the question of premeditation but neutral evidence on the question of the perpetrator's identity.

As the above discussion has indicated, evaluating an item of evidence as favorable, neutral, or harmful is a fundamental task that the advocate must perform in deciding whether to use the item at trial. It is, however, only a preliminary step. As will be shown below, the second critical step is to evaluate the sponsorship costs in using the evidence. Only after conducting both tasks can an advocate decide whether to use it or omit it.

Categorizing Favorable Evidence as Strong

In addition to the terms harmful, neutral, marginal, and favorable, this book uses a further term — strong — to describe the strength of evidence. That term is used only as a conclusory term. More specifically, it is a label that is applied to an item of evidence only after the circumstances of its introduction by one of the parties are taken into account. An item of favorable evidence is strong only if it is viewed by the jury as enhancing the advocate's case notwithstanding the fact of his introduction of it. To use the terminology introduced in Chapter Two, *favorable evidence is strong only if its probative value outweighs the sponsorship costs incurred by a party's introduction of it.* As a rule-of-thumb, an advocate assessing whether evidence is strong should ask himself whether he has a *persuasive* reply to his opponent's contention that such evidence proves *nothing* of substance. Only if the jury is apt to conclude that the evidence materially advanced the advocate's case will such evidence qualify as strong.

The advocate must consider each cost of sponsorship identified in Chapter Two in assessing whether an item of favorable evidence qualifies as strong when introduced by him. Consider, for example, the decision whether to call a witness. First, the advocate must assess the cost of introduction. As explained in Chapter Two,[13] the jury assumes that witnesses are carefully prepared by the advocate who calls them. It also normally assumes that it is hearing only what the advocate wants it to hear and how he wants it heard. This makes it skeptical and suspicious of the testimony. Moreover, the jury will view the advocate calling the witness as making an implicit concession that the testimony is material. On this point as well, the jury will be skeptical. In the worst case situation, the jury will ask itself, "What does that prove?"

Second, the advocate must assess the cost of any unusual efforts. For instance, any lengthy or complex testimony elicited through the use of elaborate exhibits or demonstrations would result in additional costs.

Finally, the advocate must assess the cost of overtrying. Specifically, he must consider the possibility that the jury will assume that the advocate was forced to call this witness because his other evidence was insufficient. Thus, as explained in Chapter Two,[14] he must consider the extent to which the jury will give less weight to his other evidence because of his own apparently dim view of it. The introduction of the additional witness may trouble the jury and prolong its deliberations. In the worst case scenario, the additional witness could lead to an adverse verdict, as the jury concludes that the witness's testimony is not enough to put an otherwise inadequate case "over the top."

Only after this rigorous analysis will the advocate be able to evaluate the witness as the jury evaluates him. And only then will he know whether the testimony of the witness is truly favorable *as introduced by him.*

---

[13] *See* pages 36-39, *supra.*

[14] *See* pages 41-45, *supra.*

The above-described analysis of how to evaluate a witness is not limited in application to testimonial evidence. Thus, the advocate must conduct a rigorous analysis of the three sponsorship costs in assessing the strength of any exhibit that he is considering for use at trial. For example, a seemingly innocuous document that an advocate initially assessed, on balance, to be favorable may be viewed by the jury as harmful because of his introduction of it. The jury's critical scrutiny of the document may cause it to focus solely on those features that are damaging to the advocate's case. Most experienced trial lawyers are familiar with examples of cases where jurors got sidetracked by — and perhaps even based an adverse verdict on — some aspect of an exhibit that an advocate had carelessly introduced to support his case.

It is important not to be misled by the term "strong" as it is used in this book. In a weak or circumstantial case, many items of seemingly weak evidence may be categorized as strong because the sponsorship costs are so low. This is apt to be true most often where the advocate's other evidence is likewise extremely weak. In such a circumstance, the cost of overtrying is negligible. Since the advocate's other evidence is so insubstantial, his implicit concession that he needs the item in question to win will be essentially harmless. The jury will view the advocate's other evidence as weak even without regard to the additional item of evidence.

An example of this type of strong evidence would be much of the circumstantial evidence used to convict Wayne Williams, the serial child murderer in Atlanta. The government had no eyewitnesses to the murders. Thus, it was forced to rely on, among other things, fibers discovered on the victims' bodies that were similar to fibers recovered from Williams's home and from various automobiles that he had driven.[15] Had there been eyewitnesses,

[15] *See Williams v. State,* 251 Ga. 749, 312 S.E.2d 40 (1983).

much of this circumstantial evidence would have been less-than-strong.

It is critical to reiterate that the initial labeling of evidence along the continuum from favorable to harmful must be done by assuming that the evidence is not associated with either of the parties by having been introduced by one of them. The advocate's final labeling as "strong" involves adjusting for the three costs associated with his having sponsored the evidence. Only after adjusting for these costs can the advocate decide whether he in fact benefits from introducing the evidence.

*****

This chapter provided guidance in identifying the issues in the case that are likely to be disputed. It further introduced a set of definitions that an advocate should use in evaluating the strength of evidence. The following three chapters build on these principles and describe the process for selecting evidence to use at trial.

Part Two
Selection of Evidence

4

Selection of Evidence on Disputed Issues

It has often been said that a trial lawyer should not "overtry" his case.[1] Yet, while this saying is known to virtually every trial lawyer, we have found neither precise guidance on how to avoid overtrying a case, nor an adequate explanation of why this rule is a sound one. Perhaps this explains why so many practitioners fail to follow this advice.

Sponsorship theory provides a simple formula for not overtrying a case. Specifically, when the advocate is selecting evidence bearing on a disputed issue, he should use only strong evidence. This rule acts as a "pruning" device enabling the advocate to eliminate evidence that will detract from his presentation.

Some commentators maintain that in most cases, an advocate is constrained to introduce *all* available evidence if

[1] *See, e.g.,* J. Appleman, *Preparation and Trial* 211 (Coiner Pub., Ltd. 1967) ("[D]on't forget one primary rule. Never overtry a case."); *but cf. ibid.* ("All occupants of an automobile always must be called or accounted for, irrespective of the fact that they may know nothing relating to the events.").

he is to win the case.[2] We reject this position. In our view, virtually every trial involves a selection from available evidence. Even a one-witness case typically presents multiple opportunities to introduce (or refrain from introducing) exhibits or documents. And in such a case, decisions concerning the scope of direct examination require the advocate to exercise judgment in the selection of testimony to elicit. Thus, the question of what, if any, evidence to introduce on a disputed issue is one that every advocate must address, regardless of whether his case is simple or complex.

Despite the old saying, many attorneys deliberately overtry their cases. They are fearful of omitting any favorable evidence, no matter how little their cases are advanced. This fear stems from a concern that the jury will speculate that the evidence not produced would have been harmful. Since such attorneys perceive no cost from introducing evidence that is at least neutral, the very idea of sifting through favorable and neutral evidence to avoid overtrying the case seems unworthy of the effort. These factors often lead attorneys to conclude that, like the "straw that broke the camel's back," *any* item of favorable evidence might be just what the jury needs to clear up a question and render a verdict in his favor. By this reasoning, any item of evidence falling on the "plus" side should be introduced, even if that evidence is only slightly helpful. Ultimately, however, whether the advocate invariably uses all of his evidence because he is afraid to omit anything that is even arguably helpful, or whether he uses it all because he sees no harm in doing so, such a strategy is not warranted.

---

[2]*See, e.g.*, 2 F.X. Busch, *Law and Tactics in Jury Trials* § 290, at 847 (Bobbs-Merrill Co., Inc. 1959) (referring to the "situation in which there are more witnesses available than are ... necessary to establish a claim or defense," the author claims that "[m]ore often than not this situation does not exist; the advocate usually finds himself faced with the hard fact that if he is to make out a respectable case he will have to use every person who can give relevant testimony").

This chapter establishes a framework for enabling the advocate to avoid overtrying his case. The general rule, as we have stated, is to use only strong evidence. The following three sections discuss the use of favorable, neutral, and harmful evidence at trial. The chapter concludes with a discussion of the process of selecting evidence to undermine evidence previously presented by an opponent. Chapter Five discusses two categories for which a different selection rule is required: evidence needed to satisfy a legal burden of proof and evidence that is uniquely associated with one party to the case.

Favorable Evidence

This section discusses issues relating to the selection of favorable evidence for use at trial. It begins by providing the advocate with the theoretical justification for using only strong evidence. It then identifies a number of specific categories of favorable evidence that will rarely qualify as strong. The discussion then focuses on the value that an advocate may obtain through pre-trial disclosure of certain favorable evidence. Finally, the discussion addresses considerations pertinent to the use of marginal evidence.

Theoretical Underpinnings for Using Only Strong Evidence

Because this book defines favorable evidence as evidence which, on balance, makes the advocate's position more probable in the jury's eyes than it would have been without such evidence,[3] it would seem only logical that an advocate should introduce *all* evidence categorized as favorable. Indeed, many advocates, unaware of sponsorship costs, routinely use evidence that does not materially advance their cases out of a fear that the jurors will penalize

[3] *See* Chapter Three, page 52, *supra*.

them if such evidence is omitted. A critical teaching of this book is that such a fear is unjustified as long as the item of evidence in question is equally available for use by the opponent and the jury is aware of that availability. When these conditions are met, the jury will not hold the absence of the evidence against the advocate's case.

This conclusion follows from the jury's assumption that an advocate will put on only evidence that *materially* advances his case. When an advocate fails to introduce an item of evidence, the jury is apt to assume that the evidence would *not* have significantly helped his case. And when the evidence is equally available for use by both advocates and neither advocate introduces it, the jury will assume that it would not have materially aided *either* side's case.

For instance, in a case where the jury knows that a given witness who was not called was equally available to both sides, if one juror suggests during deliberations that the witness may have seriously harmed one side's case, another juror will be apt to respond that if that witness was so harmful, the other side would have called him. As the jurors realize that *neither* attorney considered the witness's testimony material enough for the witness to be called, they will reach the same conclusion as the attorneys did. They will then move on in their deliberations.

If the advocate's fear is that his opponent will exploit in summation the non-production of the less-than-strong witness, such fear is unwarranted and should not cause the advocate to introduce the less-than-strong evidence. The advocate can readily rebut the point by emphasizing the equal availability of the witness. This can be easily illustrated.

Assume that a defendant struck and injured the plaintiff with his automobile and that the defendant is claiming unavoidable accident. Assume further that there were three pedestrian eyewitnesses, that the plaintiff calls only two of them, and that the testimony elicited at trial reveals that the third pedestrian was in a position to have seen the accident. Here, assuming that the defense had learned prior to trial of the identity and address of the third pedestrian, defense counsel would not benefit from highlighting the plaintiff's failure to call the witness. If he were to make such an argument, plaintiff's attorney could respond:

> Ladies and gentlemen, the whole job of a lawyer is to bring in witnesses who have testimony favoring his client's case. My opponent heard the testimony of the two pedestrians who we called and who established overwhelmingly the elements of our case. After he heard them, you can bet that he would have had the third pedestrian up on the stand in a minute if that individual had anything helpful to say for his side.
>
> To illustrate how illogical defendant's argument is, imagine a defendant in a burglary case who had solid fingerprint evidence that the government had the wrong man. No defense lawyer would withhold such compelling evidence and have everything ride on the argument that the government failed to introduce fingerprint evidence implicating the defendant.

This argument of equal availability should satisfy the jury that the witness can give no material testimony.[4]

A final point requires discussion. In most circumstances, the jury will consider evidence to be freely available for introduction by both parties in the case. This is especially true when the evidence at trial indicated that both sides knew the identity of the particular witness or item of evidence. Occasionally, however, this will not be

---

[4] In a criminal case, a prosecutor must exercise great care in making such an argument. He is barred from suggesting that the defendant had any obligation to put on evidence. Nonetheless, he *can* state that the defense was free to put on evidence. *See, e.g., United States v. Sblendorio,* 830 F.2d 1382, 1393 (7th Cir. 1987); *see generally* Chapter Six, page 142, note 7, *infra* (discussing restrictions on prosecutor's arguments).

the case. Some juries may erroneously believe that only one side had the ability to use certain evidence. In that situation, there is a theoretical risk that the jury will penalize one advocate for not introducing evidence that his opponent could have introduced. Nonetheless, our experience has taught us that this risk is insubstantial. As noted above, if the opposing attorney tries to exploit the absence of the witness from the advocate's case, the argument that the opponent could have called the witness should effectively neutralize the point. Where the opponent does not make the point, the jury, acting on the assumption that he is advancing his best arguments, will not be apt to make it for him.[5]

The foregoing discussion has explained how juries treat evidence that is not produced and how they react to arguments of counsel that attempt to exploit an opponent's non-production. As a jurisprudential aside, it should be noted that the argument of equal availability counseled by sponsorship theory corresponds with the principles underlying the so-called "missing witness" doctrine. To understand why this is so, a brief explanation of that doctrine is required.

Under the missing witness rule, if a party fails to call a witness who is peculiarly within his knowledge and power to produce, his opponent may obtain an instruction informing the jury that the failure to produce the witness permits an inference — which the jury can accept or reject — that the witness's testimony would have been unfavorable to that party.[6] Like sponsorship theory, the missing witness rule is premised on the fundamental assumption

[5] As we show in Chapter Five, there is a special category of witnesses — party-associated witnesses — for which the argument of equal availability may not be fully successful and for which one side may be penalized for not calling a witness, even if the other side does not highlight the witness's absence.

[6] *See, e.g.*, W. LaFave & J. Israel, *Criminal Procedure* § 23.3(b), at 876 (West 1985); *see generally* 1 E. Devitt & C. Blackmar, *Federal Jury Practice and Instructions* § 17.19, at 565-566 (West 3d ed. 1977); 3 E. Devitt, C. Blackmar & M. Wolff, *Federal Jury Practice and Instructions (Civil)* § 72.15, at 45 (West 4th ed. 1987).

that an advocate will seek to put on his best evidence.[7] For present purposes, the significant point to note is that a missing witness instruction will not be given, and argument along those lines will not be permitted, unless the attorney seeking the instruction can satisfy the requirement that the evidence was uniquely available to his opponent.[8] This means that where a witness is equally available to both sides, neither side may argue that the missing evidence would have been unfavorable to his opponent's case.[9] This is precisely what sponsorship theory predicts that the jury will conclude from the non-production of an equally available witness.

Generic Examples of Favorable Evidence Outweighed by Sponsorship Costs

Whether favorable evidence qualifies as strong depends, among other things, on the strength of the other evidence in the case. Thus, it is not possible to identify categorically those items of favorable evidence that will be less-than-strong in every case, once sponsorship costs are assessed. Nonetheless, there are various types of evidence that usually do not qualify as strong. Some types are en-

[7] The rule is inapplicable, and no adverse inference may be drawn, unless the missing evidence would have been "superior" to that already produced. *See, e.g.*, II Wigmore, *Evidence* § 287, at 202-203 (Little, Brown & Co. Chadbourn rev. 1979) (terming it "plain" that "possible witnesses whose testimony would be for any reason comparatively ... *inferior* to what is already utilized, might well be dispensed with by a party ... without any apprehension as to the tenor of their testimony.... [T]here is a general limitation ... that the [adverse] inference cannot fairly be drawn except from the non-production of witnesses whose testimony would be *superior* in respect to the fact to be proved.") (emphasis in the original).

[8] *See, e.g., Evans v. Multicon Const. Corp.*, 6 Mass. App. 291, 375 N.E.2d 338 (1978); *United States v. Currier,* 454 F.2d 835, 839 (1st Cir. 1972); *Shurman v. United States,* 233 F.2d 272, 275 (5th Cir. 1956).

[9] *See, e.g., Pointer v. Pointer,* 251 S.W.2d 334, 338 (Mo. App. 1952) ("Either party could have called [the witness] and we find no basis for an inference that [the] testimony would have been unfavorable...."); II Wigmore, *supra* note 7, § 287, at 202-204.

countered with sufficient frequency to merit special mention.

Character Evidence

Character witness testimony often constitutes less-than-strong evidence once sponsorship costs are assessed.[10] Such a witness typically cannot testify to the facts of the case. Rather, the proof of a party's good character is made in the hope that the jury will find that the conduct alleged in the suit would have been so "out of character" that the party could not have committed it.

Juries, however, normally do not view good character as a bar to the commission of bad acts.[11] Moreover, they may be particularly skeptical when the character witness is a relative of the person on whose behalf he is testifying or is otherwise biased in favor of that person. Even in the case of an ostensibly unbiased witness, the jury is likely to think that virtually anyone can find witnesses who will swear to a person's good character.

The message of the advocate who introduces character evidence is apt to be that he lacks confidence that his other evidence, standing alone, is sufficient to prove his case. Once that message is communicated, it is extremely unlikely that the character evidence will bridge the gap in the jury's eyes. Indeed, based on the cost of overtrying alone, the character testimony may be received by the jury as harmful to the overall presentation.

To be sure, character evidence may sometimes be strong. For example, the jury might be persuaded when the character testimony comes from someone who would

[10] The use of character evidence is typically subject to detailed rules governing admissibility. *See, e.g.,* Fed. R. Evid. 404(a).

[11] Courts have recognized that character evidence has only limited probative value. *See, e.g., United States v. Burke,* 781 F.2d 1234, 1239 (7th Cir. 1985) ("People of impeccable reputation may commit crimes, and when they are charged with crime the question is whether they did it, not whether they enjoy a high social standing.").

not be apt to lie, such as a priest or a nun.[12] As a general rule, however, character evidence will rarely qualify as strong and thus should seldom be used.

Corroborative Detail Evidence

Many trial advocates regularly succumb to the temptation of introducing corroborative evidence on a minor detail. The reasoning is that a case will appear stronger to the jury when various collateral details are confirmed by multiple witnesses or items of evidence.[13] For example, in a rape case where the victim has identified the defendant as her assailant, some prosecutors may be tempted to introduce test results showing that foreign pubic hair recovered from her genital area came from a person belonging to the same race as the defendant.[14] In a metropolitan area where a majority of the population belongs to this same race, however, those test results would be an example of favorable evidence that may damage the government's case in light of the cost of overtrying. If the defense is misidentification, even the defense is conceding that he is the same race as the actual assailant. Thus, at the very least, defense counsel will likely belittle this evidence

[12] Similarly, a jury may occasionally believe that someone with high standing in the community would have too much to lose to commit a serious crime. *See generally United States v. Burke, supra* note 11, 781 F.2d at 1240.

[13] *See, e.g.,* Markus, *A Theory of Trial Advocacy,* 56 Tul. L. Rev. 95, 105 (1981). ("The factfinder is more likely to accept [testimony regarding his observations] if the witness can recite [supplemental details] which confirm his ability to make those observations.... [Such] details have no significance to the [issue in dispute], but they confirm the ability of the witness to perceive and recall the recited event.") (footnote and citation omitted); 2 A. Amsterdam, B. Segal & M. Miller, *Trial Manual for the Defense of Criminal Cases* § 395, at 1-536 to 1-537 (Amer. Law Inst. 1984) ("It is vital to corroborate the [client] on every point on which corroboration is possible.... Every matter in which [he] is supported by proof that the trier of fact is likely to believe has a capacity to spread and envelop his ... testimony with an atmosphere of veracity.").

[14] We assume, for purposes of this example, that DNA forensic testing techniques are not available to the prosecutor. *Cf.* N.Y. Times, June 12, 1989, at 1, col. 1 (reporting on FBI's adoption of DNA identification techniques).

by pointing out that it is entirely consistent with his defense.

Ultimately, the only value of the pubic hair test is in eliminating the possibility that the victim was mistaken or lying about the race of her assailant. Yet, such a theory of the case is so unlikely that, before the introduction of the test results by the prosecutor, most defense attorneys would not have thought to bring it to the attention of the jury. By introducing the test results, the prosecutor has raised theories of innocence that were not even espoused by his opponent. Because the test results are completely consistent with the defense in the case, the prosecutor has done nothing to persuade the jury on the disputed issue, namely, whether the defendant is actually the assailant.

Informant and Accomplice Testimony

Informant and accomplice witnesses are frequently favorable to the government before sponsorship costs are taken into account. After such costs are considered, however, the testimony of such witnesses is more often than not less-than-strong.[15] Thus, the prosecution should normally be very reluctant to call informant and accomplice witnesses, especially in the case-in-chief. The testimony of such witnesses is virtually always encumbered by one or more motives to fabricate. For instance, informants have often received payments from the government, and accomplices are often seeking to satisfy the obligations of a plea bargain or to avoid harsh punishment (if they are awaiting sentencing).

Because of the cost of introduction, some juries would evaluate such a case as if the accomplice or informant testimony did not exist at all. They might suspect that

[15] *Cf.* 1 Devitt & Blackmar, *supra* note 6, § 17.02, at 524; *id.* § 17.06, at 531 (model jury instruction that jurors should view informant and accomplice testimony with great caution); *see also United States v. Bernard,* 625 F.2d 854, 857 (9th Cir. 1980) (describing accomplice testimony as "unreliable").

such a witness is apt to say anything to advance his own interest. Moreover, because of the cost of overtrying, some juries might go even further. Rather than simply ignoring the accomplice/informant testimony, they might actually give *less* weight to the remainder of the government's evidence in light of the prosecutor's apparent concern that he needed that testimony to win. Thus, the prosecutor is often better off omitting the accomplice or informant testimony from his case-in-chief, since he avoids this appearance of reliance.[16]

Strong Evidence the Opponent Will Introduce or Enable the Advocate to Introduce in Rebuttal

Previous portions of this chapter instruct that the advocate should use all "strong" evidence, that is, favorable evidence that outweighs sponsorship costs. This section provides a somewhat high risk strategy that the advocate may wish to consider in the appropriate case. The strategy is for the advocate to refrain from introducing some of his strong evidence if he is virtually certain that his opponent will be introducing it.

Such a strategy may be warranted for two reasons. First, as predicted by the cost of introduction, an advocate gains more from an item of evidence if his opponent introduces it. Specifically, while the advocate avoids the jury's tendency to discount the strength of evidence that he introduces, he capitalizes on its inclination to give enhanced weight to any evidence introduced by his opponent that is unfavorable to the opponent's case.[17]

---

[16] As we explain in Chapter Six, however, *see* page 150, *infra*, the use of such testimony may be warranted as rebuttal evidence.

[17] The trial tactics literature contains observations consistent with this advice. For example, one writer, in counseling against calling a witness one's adversary will be compelled to call, notes that calling such a witness "render[s] everything unfavorable said by the witness doubly operative against the party calling him, [and] also deprive[s] that party of the power of counteracting the effect of the testimony." J. Reed, *Conduct of Lawsuits* § 383, at 270-271 (Little, Brown 2d ed. 1912) (citations omitted). *Accord, e.g.*, R. Keeton, *Trial Tactics and Methods* § 2.2,

Second, as we have seen, the act of introducing an item of favorable evidence is often tantamount to a concession that such evidence is essential to the advocate's case. The effect, as predicted by the cost of overtrying, may be to reduce the probative weight given to the advocate's other evidence. The advocate is therefore much better off if he can tell the jury that the evidence helps his case but that the case does not depend on it. The fact that he did not introduce the evidence will lend credence to that claim. This technique only works, however, when the advocate can credibly claim that he is entitled to prevail without the evidence and therefore had no need to go to the effort of marshaling it. So long as the advocate can make this claim, he does not risk the jury concluding from his lack of sponsorship of the favorable item that it is not entitled to any weight.

Accordingly, a defense counsel whose strong evidence is introduced in his opponent's preceding case generally should not seek to reintroduce such evidence in his own case. Thus, he generally should not elicit points favorable to his case on cross-examination when such points have already been elicited on direct examination. The only exception is if he is not sure that the jury fully comprehended the point. In that situation, he should seek a clarification. For example, he might ask on cross-examination:

> Let me just get this straight, Mr. Jones. You testified on direct examination that ... ?

---

at 14 (Little, Brown & Co. 1973) (urging the advocate to consider the strategy of not calling a witness with both favorable and unfavorable testimony in the hope that his opponent will call him, thus giving the advocate "the opportunity of obtaining the testimony [he] desire[s] ... without the disadvantages of calling him"). *Cf.* F. Bailey & H. Rothblatt, *Successful Techniques for Criminal Trials* § 22.3, at 498 (Lawyers Co-op. Pub. Co. 1985) ("Anything that [a] witness [called by your opponent] says for your side can be argued as beyond question."); *Trial Preparation: An Interview with Louis Nizer,* 2 Trial Dip. L.J. 6, 11 (1979) (prominent trial lawyer remarking on the value of being able to prove his case "out of the mouths of [his] very adversaries, the witnesses on the other side").

Having done so, he should immediately move on to another topic. This strategy enables him to minimize his apparent reliance on those points to win the case.

This might seem to be a strategy dilemma that would almost never arise in practice. In fact, however, an advocate's introduction of evidence supporting his opponent's case is not unusual. Indeed, many trial manuals urge advocates to introduce *all* relevant evidence.[18]

Plaintiff's attorneys and prosecutors should also consider the same strategy. Thus, if such an attorney believes that a witness with strong testimony will be called by his opponent, he should consider not calling the witness himself. When his opponent calls the witness, the advocate can elicit the information in cross-examination. The opponent may even elicit the advocate's strong evidence himself.

This strategy, however, is hazardous. To begin with, the judge may rule that the planned cross-examination to elicit the favorable testimony is beyond the scope of the direct examination and is thus impermissible. Moreover, the judge may bar the advocate from later introducing the evidence in rebuttal.[19] Accordingly, the advocate must

---

[18] *See, e.g.,* A.E. Morrill, *Anatomy of a Trial* 108 (C.P.I. 1968) ("[I]n the situation where the lawyer has three occurrence witnesses ... [t]he temptation is to use one good, strong witness to nail down the liability issue and avoid the risks involved in using [the others].... Despite what he would like to do, he must use them all...."). *See also* 1 S. Schweitzer, *Cyclopedia of Trial Practice* § 260, at 675 (Lawyers Co-op. Pub. Co. 2d Ed. 1970) (recommending that plaintiff's counsel in a civil case call the defendant as a witness on the theory that "you can state on summation that you were so confident of the truth of the plaintiff's story that you took the liberty of offering the defendant as your own witness, knowing you would be bound by what he testified"); Appleman, *supra* note 1, at 215 ("I like to call, with great frequency, the opposing party as an adverse witness.... This takes a lot of sting out of the defendant appearing in his own case, at a later point in the trial."). *Cf.* H. Spellman, *Direct Examination of Witnesses* 88 (Prentice Hall 1968) ("[I]t is better to have an unfavorable matter exposed through one's own witness...."); A.E. Morrill, *supra* at 96 (section entitled, "Bring Out The Bad Stuff In Your Own Case."). *See also* page 96, note 42, *infra.*

[19] *See* Chapter Six, *infra,* pages 149-150 (discussing standards governing use of evidence in rebuttal).

evaluate the judge in the case. Pertinent considerations include whether the judge normally gives attorneys wide latitude in conducting cross-examination and whether he is permissive in his approach to rebuttal.

A further problem is that the advocate can never be positive that the other side will call a witness or offer a particular piece of evidence. If he does not, the jury will never hear the evidence in question unless the advocate is permitted to bring it out in rebuttal.

There is a further danger that stems from the jury's assumption that an advocate is committed to presenting all evidence that materially favors his case. If the other evidence in the case has pointed to that item of evidence, and the advocate withholding it is not permitted to bring it out later in the trial, the jury may assume that the item would *not* have materially advanced the advocate's case, even though it actually would have done so.

Nonetheless, in many circumstances, the advocate will have a fairly good idea whether his opponent plans to call a particular witness. One situation where a prosecutor or plaintiff's counsel can be all but certain that his opponent will call a witness is where the defense opts to make an opening statement at the outset of the trial and announces that the witness in question will definitely be called in the defense case.

A case tried by one of the authors illustrates the value in having the opponent introduce one's strong evidence. The defendant was charged with an armed assault with intent to kill. At the scene, the defendant's girlfriend, an eyewitness, told the police that the defendant had acted in self-defense, an account contradicted by other eyewitnesses. Later, however, the girlfriend testified before the grand jury that from what she had seen of the incident, the defendant had *not* acted in self-defense. She also revealed to the grand jury that the defendant had called her shortly after the incident and had confided that he had picked a fight with the victim and was disappointed that the victim had not died.

At trial, the prosecutor decided not to call the girlfriend, even though his only other evidence of the defendant's intent to kill, namely, the gravity of the injury, was purely circumstantial. He chose to take the risk because defense counsel had revealed his plan to call her. As expected, the defense called the witness, who testified on direct examination that the defendant had acted in self-defense. On cross-examination, the prosecutor confronted the witness with her grand jury testimony. The witness ultimately admitted that her grand jury testimony had been correct. Even if the prosecutor had believed that the girlfriend, on balance, would have been a strong witness in his case because of her willingness to repeat the defendant's confession, he was almost certainly better off letting the defense call the girlfriend. Because the defense called the witness, the prosecutor was able to point out that his case was bolstered by a key *defense* witness. By contrast, had the prosecutor called her, the defense could have scored points by emphasizing the witness's statements in support of the defendant at the scene of the crime.

The foregoing illustrates the benefits to the advocate from having his opponent introduce the advocate's favorable evidence. Because of these benefits, the advocate may wish to consider tendering his favorable evidence to his opponent in the hope that he will use it in his case.[20]

Moreover, as explained in Chapter Eight,[21] even if the advocate decides that he must call a witness to prove a specific point, there is still a method that can result in his opponent eliciting other points from that witness that bolster the advocate's case. That method is for the advocate to omit selected strong points and conduct a very brief

[20] A detailed discussion of the concept of tendering evidence is contained on pages 77-79, *infra*. It should be noted that in the criminal context, a prosecutor has a constitutional duty to tender exculpatory evidence. *See generally Brady v. Maryland*, 373 U.S. 83 (1963).

[21] *See* pages 176-179, *infra*.

direct examination of his witness after thoroughly preparing him for the questions anticipated on cross-examination. In many such cases, the opponent will elicit the advocate's strong evidence that the advocate himself elected not to bring out. Such evidence will be far more helpful to the advocate's case than it would have been had the advocate himself brought it out.[22] The chances of an opponent eliciting the advocate's strong evidence are even greater in a consolidated trial, where there may be several opponents. In that situation, one opponent may be happy to elicit points that are damaging to another.

Another circumstance in which the advocate should consider not introducing strong evidence is where he is virtually certain that his opponent will afford him the opportunity to use the evidence in his rebuttal case. As we explain in Chapter Six,[23] the advocate is normally better off presenting a given item of evidence in rebuttal than in the case-in-chief.

In sum, the advocate should not assume, merely because he has strong evidence, that he should always introduce it. His opponent may be planning to introduce it if the advocate does not do so. In that circumstance, the advocate may want to forego introducing it himself. Finally, if the advocate is confident that his opponent will afford him with the opportunity, he should consider saving the evidence for rebuttal. For the reasons previously discussed, however, these strategies entail serious risks and should not be undertaken lightly.

---

[22] *See, e.g.*, Bailey & Rothblatt, *supra* note 17, § 11.20, at 308 (acknowledging this technique as one employed by the government in criminal trials, and characterizing it as a "prosecution trap").

[23] *See* page 150, *infra*.

The Value of Tendering Favorable Evidence to One's Opponent

Tender for the Purpose of Having the Opponent Use the Evidence

If the advocate has decided not to use an item of favorable evidence in his own case, he should consider making it available for his opponent's use at trial. By doing so, the advocate stands to gain if his opponent introduces it, since the costs of sponsorship would then be operating in the advocate's favor.

The opponent will frequently be unaware of an item of evidence that is favorable to the advocate's case. In a criminal case, a prosecutor is under no general obligation to tender inculpatory evidence to the defense. Tendering of evidence to the defense is mandatory only where the evidence is exculpatory or is otherwise subject to disclosure pursuant to an applicable rule of evidence or procedure.[24] In the typical civil case, if extensive discovery has been conducted, it is much more likely that the opponent will have learned of such evidence. Even in civil cases, however, discovery may not have uncovered everything.

Where the opponent is not aware of an item of the advocate's favorable evidence, the question of whether to tender such evidence initially depends on whether the advocate foresees a use for it anywhere in his own case, including rebuttal.[25] This is frequently difficult to assess. If the evidence relates to a fact that at the outset seems collateral, there is always the chance that opposing counsel, unaware of the advocate's evidence, will introduce evidence that can be disproved or discredited by evidence that the advocate had previously categorized as less-than-strong. In these circumstances, if the advocate tenders

---

[24] *See, e.g., Brady v. Maryland,* 373 U.S. 83 (1973); Fed. R. Crim. P. 16.

[25] This analysis assumes that the favorable evidence in question is not subject to mandatory disclosure pursuant to any court decision or rule of procedure.

such evidence, he will have unwittingly educated his opponent on the existence of such a "surprise" witness or item of evidence. Thus, while the decision to tender must be made early enough for the opponent to act on it, it should generally be postponed until the advocate fully comprehends his opponent's factual theory of the case.

Tender to Avoid the Opponent's Criticism for the Advocate's Non-Use of the Evidence

Where the evidence in the case has pointed to the existence of evidence that is not equally available to the opponent, and the advocate has decided against using such evidence himself, then he must tender it to his opponent or run the risk that the opponent will criticize him in summation for failing to produce it. A tender eliminates any argument that the advocate's failure to introduce the evidence indicates that it would have harmed his case. This is because a legal requirement for such an argument — lack of equal availability — will not be met.[26]

The advocate should be aware that, although a tender will preclude the opponent from suggesting to the jury that the missing item would have *harmed* the advocate's case, it will not prevent the opponent from noting that the advocate's case is not as strong as it would have been had that witness or item of evidence been favorable to his case.[27] Thus, even where opposing counsel does not estab-

[26] *See* page 67, note 9, *supra* (citing authorities). For the same reason, a tender precludes the opponent from establishing the requirements for a missing evidence jury instruction. *Cf.* 3 Devitt, Blackmar & Wolff, *supra* note 6, § 72.16, at 46 (model jury instructions providing that if a party fails to produce evidence in his control that was not reasonably available to his opponent, then the jury "may infer that the evidence is unfavorable to the party who could have produced it and did not"). The requirements of the missing witness rule are discussed on pages 66-67, *supra*. It should be noted, as explained in Chapter Five, that a tender may not serve the above-mentioned purposes with respect to evidence that is uniquely associated with one party.

[27] *Cf. Arnold v. United States*, 511 A.2d 399, 416 (D.C. 1986) (permitting comment on absence of witness or evidence but requiring advance clearance to do so).

lish the requirements for the missing witness instruction, he may attempt to score points by highlighting the absence of the item from the advocate's presentation. Moreover, the trial court's general instructions may lend weight to such an argument.

For example, juries are often instructed that in evaluating the testimony of a witness, they may consider whether and to what extent he has been corroborated by other evidence.[28] Thus, where the advocate has called a witness to establish a point, and where the evidence shows that there were other available witnesses with material testimony on the same point whom the advocate did not call, his opponent may be able to refer to such an instruction and ask the jury to consider that his witness was not corroborated by other evidence. Although a tender will not preclude opposing counsel from making this argument, it will at least enable the advocate to argue to the jury that his opponent could have called the witness if that witness had anything adverse to say concerning the advocate's case.

Marginal Evidence: A Shortcut to Identifying Less-than-Strong Evidence

In a previous section,[29] we described the basic "pruning" device for the advocate to use in selecting evidence bearing on disputed issues: use only strong evidence. As we have seen, although the rule is simply stated, it involves a series of calculations, beginning with the evaluation of the evidence and ending with an assessment of the three separate costs of sponsorship. The concept of marginal evidence relieves the advocate from the need to consider the costs involved in the use of much of his evidence.

[28] *See, e.g., Criminal Jury Instructions, District of Columbia,* §§ 2.11, at 50 (3d ed. 1978).

[29] *See* pages 63-67, *supra.*

By definition, favorable evidence that is "marginal" is so weak that, when considered with the advocate's other evidence, it has no realistic chance of swaying an otherwise adverse jury to vote in his favor. As a practical matter, it is neutral. Thus, given the certainty that at least some sponsorship costs will be incurred by using that evidence, such evidence — and, *a fortiori,* neutral and harmful evidence as well — can be presumptively eliminated from the advocate's presentation.[30] The reason should be clear: if the evidence cannot sway the jury prior to adjusting for sponsorship costs — that is, even if introduced by a neutral source — then it cannot possibly help the advocate's case once such costs are taken into account. Indeed, it is generally safe to assume that such evidence will be harmful once those costs are assessed.

For example, assume that plaintiff is suing for injuries suffered as a result of a dog bite and has two unbiased eyewitnesses who maintain that they are certain that it was the defendant's dog, not someone else's, who attacked the plaintiff. Assume further that a third eyewitness, who was farther away from the scene than the other two witnesses, can say only that the dog "resembled" the defendant's dog. The third witness is clearly marginal. Although he technically supports the plaintiff, thereby making his testimony "favorable," he is substantially inferior to the other two witnesses. If the other two are not enough, then the third plainly will not make the difference. Indeed, because of the cost of overtrying alone, the third might actually reduce the weight given to the other two. The critical point to recognize for present purposes, however, is that in such a situation, the advocate can safely eliminate the third witness without even considering the costs involved.

[30] Occasionally, however, the influence of the cost of apparent efforts to omit will dictate the use of less-than-strong evidence. This exceptional situation is addressed below (pages 88-94, *infra*). Also, if the less-than-strong evidence is uniquely associated with the advocate's case (*see* Chapter Five, *infra,* pages 121-137), its use may be warranted.

In sum, the advocate should select his evidence using the rule of thumb that he will not introduce marginal evidence. This is true for both witnesses and tangible evidence.

Neutral Evidence

The general rule of using only strong evidence also counsels elimination from the advocate's presentation of neutral evidence, namely, evidence that is immaterial to the jury's determination of the issues in dispute. The sections below analyze the costs that can be incurred by the use of neutral evidence and provide trial examples illustrating such costs.

The Sponsorship Costs of Using Neutral Evidence

As we have seen, the cost of introduction warns of the risk that the jury's scrutiny of evidence initially labeled as neutral might result in an adverse impact on the advocate's case. Unlike favorable evidence, however, which may give rise to a cost of overtrying, the jury will not normally assume that the advocate is trying to "win" his case with that neutral item of evidence.

Nonetheless, the jury is apt to reason that the advocate himself deemed it significant that the evidence is neutral. Why else would the advocate have introduced it? The jury will thus be inclined to search for a reason motivating the advocate's desire to demonstrate that the item was neutral. As we shall show, any reason that the jury decides upon will be apt to damage the advocate's case.

Although the cost of overtrying is not strictly applicable, the jury, casting about for a motivation, may conclude that the advocate used it in the hope that the jury would view it favorably. If the jury reaches this conclusion, the use of neutral evidence is apt to reduce the weight of the advocate's other evidence in a manner similar to that incurred by the cost of overtrying.

Illustrations of Dangers from Use of Neutral Evidence

As noted, because of the cost of introduction, the jury is apt to assume that the advocate introducing neutral evidence deems it important to his case. Since the evidence is not favorable, the jury will generally have no firm theory explaining why the advocate used it. The following examples illustrate some of the damaging theories upon which the jury may decide.

One type of harm from using neutral evidence is that the jury might view such evidence as "padding" by a nervous attorney seeking to bolster an otherwise shaky case. For example, eliciting excessive details concerning a lay or expert witness's biographical background — such as place of birth or education — might cause the jury to wonder why the advocate deemed such an elaborate line of questions necessary. The only rational explanation is that he thought that such questions might help the jury in assessing the witness's credibility. Once the jury dwells on whether it does, the advocate will be harmed if it does not.

There are other possible motivations that the jury can ascribe to an advocate's use of neutral evidence. For instance, it may assume that he is concerned that, without the benefit of seeing such evidence, the jury might render a verdict against him if it speculates that the item would have been harmful. This is the equivalent of communicating a concern that the jury would not find his other evidence of sufficient weight to overcome that speculative harm. In the worst case situation, the jury will conclude that the advocate himself believes that his other evidence is enough to win *only* because the item is neutral. Put another way, the logical conclusion is that the advocate views his other evidence as just barely enough to prevail.

A trial known to the authors illustrates the latter point. A police officer stopped a man on the street and, after briefly conversing with him, observed that he began fidgeting in an odd manner. Moments later, the officer noticed a pistol on the ground only inches from the man's feet. The man was arrested, and the pistol was recovered by the officer. The arresting officer later submitted the weapon for fingerprint tests, but no prints were obtained that could be used for purposes of comparison. The defendant was later brought to trial on charges of unlawful possession of a pistol.

During the government's case-in-chief, the arresting officer testified concerning the defendant's fidgeting and the recovery of the pistol. He further testified that he was sure that there had been no pistol anywhere near the defendant's feet before the stop. The question faced by the prosecutor was whether to elicit the absence of fingerprint evidence. His concern was that the jury might speculate about whether a fingerprint examination of the gun was conducted and, if so, what results were obtained. Fearing that such speculation could potentially harm his case, the prosecutor decided to elicit from the officer the fact that no usable fingerprints were recovered. The prosecutor, who was unaware of the principles of sponsorship, reasoned that (1) he would benefit from foreclosing any risk of jury speculation that the pistol had fingerprints belonging to someone other than the defendant, and (2) there was no cost in introducing the neutral results.

The jury ultimately acquitted the defendant. The error in the prosecutor's strategy was in assuming that his introduction of neutral evidence carried no cost and would be beneficial. At best, the introduction of such evidence merely highlighted for the jury the fact that the prosecutor's case could have been stronger. At worst, the jury may have speculated that the evidence was introduced because the prosecutor thought it important that the defendant had not been ruled out as a suspect by the recovery of prints that matched someone else. In either case, the implicit message was that the prosecutor thought it important that no one else's fingerprints had been recovered, a message that could not have advanced his case. The prosecutor was tacitly suggesting that had the test disclosed fingerprints belonging to someone other than the defendant, the other evidence would not have been sufficient to warrant a conviction.

Significantly, the prosecutor had tendered the inconclusive fingerprint results to the defense in discovery. Had the prosecutor opted not to raise the fingerprint issue at trial, the defense could not have persuasively accused him in summation of "hiding" potentially exculpatory fingerprint results. If he had, the prosecutor could have pointed out that all pertinent fingerprint evidence was tendered to defense counsel and that *he* could have introduced it if there had been anything exculpatory.[31]

This is not to say that a defense counsel in the foregoing situation should refrain from eliciting testimony on cross-examination regarding the failed recovery attempt. After all, police department personnel made efforts, in anticipation of litigation, to recover the fingerprints. As such, a defense counsel might conceivably benefit from making the jury aware of the government's concern — and failed attempt — to locate more favorable evidence.[32] The critical point, however, is that the prosecutor magnified the problem by eliciting the testimony himself.

Even aside from the foregoing, the introduction of neutral evidence will serve only to highlight how much better the advocate's case could have been. This is true, for example, where the plaintiff in an automobile accident case calls a witness who was in the plaintiff's automobile at the time of the accident but who cannot offer relevant testimony because his attention was focused elsewhere or be-

[31] *See* page 65, note 4, *supra* (noting need for the prosecutor to remind jury that defense is not required to put on evidence).

[32] *Cf.* S. Turow, *Presumed Innocent,* at 168-169 (Farrar Straus Giroux 1987) (reflecting concern of fictitious defense counsel to avoid criticism for failed efforts to marshal evidence).

cause he was asleep. Such a witness may serve to underscore to the jury that the plaintiff lacked important corroborative evidence.

Conclusion

The central lesson regarding neutral evidence is clear: the cost of using such evidence will outweigh any risk of adverse jury speculation concerning the missing evidence.[33] For that reason, the advocate should delete neutral evidence from his presentation. As we have stated, because the jury assumes that the advocate's opponent will introduce any evidence that materially advances his case, it will be apt to accept the advocate's argument that if the evidence was harmful to his case, his opponent would have introduced it.

Harmful Evidence

This section describes the considerations involved in whether to use harmful evidence. As will be seen, the general rule is that an advocate should not use such evidence because it is usually rendered considerably more damaging if he is the one who elicits it. There are, however, limited circumstances in which the apparent efforts to omit the evidence are so substantial that the advocate is harmed less by bringing out a weakness himself than by letting his opponent do so.

In contrast to the approach counseled by sponsorship theory, virtually every trial manual urges the wholesale introduction of harmful evidence. As we will show, such advice is unsound and, if followed, can result in serious harm to the advocate's case.

---

[33] Chapter Five addresses special considerations relating to less-than-strong evidence that is not available to the advocate's opponent.

The General Rule Against Use of Harmful Evidence

As indicated in Chapter Two, sponsorship theory dictates, as a general rule, that attorneys should *not* introduce harmful evidence. An analysis of the two sponsorship costs that are pertinent to the use of harmful evidence — introduction and efforts — indicates why this is so.

To begin with, the cost of introduction normally acts to magnify the harmful impact of such evidence. As explained in Chapter Two, the jury assumes that the advocate has packaged the harmful matter in the light most favorable to its case.[34] Thus, it will be inclined to believe that the matter is worse than it appears when presented by the advocate whose case is harmed by it. Moreover, the introduction of such evidence amounts to an implicit concession that the harmful matter is material to the resolution of the case. Finally, the use of such evidence relieves opposing counsel from the costs of having to introduce it himself.

To illustrate the foregoing, consider a case in which a plaintiff is suing his employer, claiming that he was wrongfully terminated. Assume that the plaintiff's attorney has decided to bring out the fact that his client had been fired from his previous job as well, which involved the same line of work. Assume further that the attorney did so because, in his jurisdiction, such evidence is admissible and he wanted to bring out the evidence first to "take the sting out of it." If the witness states that the earlier termination was simply a personality clash and, contrary to what his employer said, had nothing to do with job performance, the jury is apt to be highly skeptical. It will assume that it has heard only the employee's best case scenario for the firing. It therefore may be apt to specu-

[34] The jury's assumption is confirmed by the advice of the trial literature, which counsels attorneys who introduce harmful evidence to present that evidence "in its least damaging light." T. Mauet, *Fundamentals of Trial Techniques* § 3.3, at 51 (Little, Brown & Co. 2d ed. 1988).

late that poor job performance was the real reason behind the firing. In addition, by eliciting such testimony, plaintiff's lawyer will have implicitly conceded that his client's past job history bears heavily on the merits of his present claim. By contrast, if he waits for his opponent to bring out the prior firing, he will be able to argue credibly that the prior employment incident is totally irrelevant.

It is important to recognize that when an attorney volunteers a weakness, his adversary can capitalize on the cost of introduction. For example, by bringing out his witness's prior criminal record, he enables his adversary to argue in summation:

> The witness's prior conviction is critical to the assessment of his credibility. Even my opponent went out of his way to make sure that you knew about it.

By the same token, the attorney who brings out a weakness robs himself of the opportunity to highlight that his opponent was so lacking in meaningful grounds for impeachment that he had to rely on a collateral matter, such as a prior conviction.

In addition to the cost of introduction, if unusual efforts are required to bring out the harmful matter, even greater costs will be incurred. To be sure, as we explain in the following section, exceptional circumstances might warrant bringing out a weakness in order to avoid costs of unusual efforts to omit it. In general, however, the advocate is likely to be harmed, not helped, by volunteering a weakness.

It is important to emphasize that we are not urging an advocate to ignore weaknesses once his *opponent* has put them in issue. The foregoing discussion is concerned simply with the issue of which side should introduce evidence of the weakness in the first place. Once his opponent has brought out a weakness, the advocate plainly should — and must — advance any strong arguments to show why it is not material to the verdict. Since the advocate did not bring up the weakness first, his argument will carry far more weight than it would have carried had he initially volunteered the weakness.[35]

Exception — When the Cost of Apparent Efforts Outweighs the Competing Considerations

This section identifies a narrow category of harmful evidence for which the *failure* to introduce it carries even greater costs than those resulting from introducing it. In this situation, a tender of the evidence to one's opponent does nothing to alleviate the problem.

This exception comes into play only if the jury is apt to conclude that the evidence would normally have been included as part of the advocate's case, and was not presented only because the advocate, by seeming to take unusual efforts, went *out of his way* to omit it.[36] More generally, the advocate must conclude that the jury is more apt to view the *omission* of the evidence as a concession of materiality than it is to view the *introduction* of it as such a concession.

Even if the above condition is satisfied, however, the advocate may incur costs of introduction from the tendency of the jury to assume that he packaged the harmful evidence in its best possible light. Accordingly, he must

---

[35] It should not be assumed that the general rule against volunteering weaknesses automatically applies in the context of a legal submission to a court, such as a brief or a statement of points and authorities. An advocate is *required* to bring to the court's attention case law that is "directly adverse" to his position. Model Code of Professional Responsibility, DR 7-106(B)(1). Significantly, the Model Code of Professional Responsibility contains no similar requirement that a trial attorney present to the jury evidence that is harmful to his case.

[36] *Cf.* K. Hegland, *Trial and Practice Skills,* at 18 (West 1978) (in discussing the question of whether harmful matter should be elicited on direct examination, the author states: "When should you anticipate your opponent's cross? Only where the failure to do so will leave the jury with the feeling that you were trying to sneak one by."); *but cf. id.* at 19 ("If the story on direct holds together as a unit, if the attack you foresee rests on collateral evidence or on the demented mind of your opponent, then you may either anticipate or ignore.").

satisfy himself that the cost that he would incur from appearing to have undertaken efforts to omit the harmful matter is sufficient to outweigh as well the alternative cost stemming from the suspicion that he packaged the evidence in its best light.

Even if both of these factors are outweighed, the advocate must consider the degree to which his use of the harmful evidence will relieve his opponent from incurring sponsorship costs. Here, the advocate must conclude that his own failure to elicit a weakness looks so bad that he is better off introducing it, even though his opponent gets the benefit of having the evidence before the jury without having to incur any costs of his own.

Finally, there is an additional consideration that the advocate should understand. In rare cases where the jury believes that the advocate went out of his way to hide a weakness, it may view the advocate's *entire* case with greater skepticism because it views the full presentation as untrustworthy. That is, the advocate may incur an increased cost of introduction with respect to every piece of his evidence. This will arise, however, only when the advocate's omission is so egregious that it exceeds all bounds of best case advocacy. As a rule, this will be true only when the costs of apparent efforts to omit are extremely high. In that situation, the advocate will have already decided to elicit the weakness himself. For that reason, as a practical matter, the advocate need not consider the possible across-the-board increase in his costs of introduction in deciding whether to elicit a weakness.

Given all of the foregoing points, the rule of sponsorship applicable to harmful evidence is that *an advocate should not introduce an item of harmful evidence unless the cost of apparent efforts undertaken in omitting it exceeds the combination of the costs that the advocate incurs in using the evidence and the costs that he saves his opponent from incurring because the opponent no longer has to introduce it.*

Our experience has shown that, as a practical matter, occasions in which such apparent efforts to omit will justify the introduction of harmful evidence will be rare. Use of harmful evidence will typically be required only in the case of a witness whom the advocate has already decided to call to the stand in order to elicit strong evidence. The dilemma for the advocate in this situation is whether to ask questions in his direct examination to elicit a harmful point. Rarely, if ever, will the advocate be warranted in calling an *additional* witness or introducing an exhibit for the sole purpose of bringing out a harmful matter. The act of calling a witness or introducing an exhibit is so significant in the jury's eyes that the cost of introduction from doing so will almost always outweigh any costs of apparent efforts involved in omitting the harmful matter.

It is important for the advocate to understand that the question of whether to elicit harmful evidence will arise only if his opponent would in all probability bring out the harmful evidence himself if he did not do so. It would obviously be irrational for the advocate to introduce such evidence unless he believes that his opponent will introduce it if he omits it.

In our experience, the assumption that an opponent will introduce an advocate's harmful evidence is often questionable. The advocate frequently cannot be certain (or even confident) that his opponent will do so. Since the advocate's knowledge of his side of the case is generally greater than his opponent's knowledge, it is quite possible that his opponent has not identified many of the weaknesses of the advocate's case. Moreover, in the heat of trial, the opponent may forget to bring out certain weaknesses. Finally, as the lineup videotape case in Chapter One illustrates, the opponent may decide for tactical reasons not to elicit the weakness. The opponent may, for example, conclude that the weakness is not serious enough from his perspective to warrant its inclusion in cross-examination. In these situations, if the advocate whose case will be harmed by a weakness chooses not to bring it out, it will never be heard by the jury. Thus, the advocate should not assume, merely because there is a weakness in his case, that his opponent will bring it out if he does not do so.

The foregoing discussion has provided analytical guidance in determining when the introduction of harmful evidence is warranted. It is not possible to offer a definitive list of the types of evidence falling within this category. Nonetheless, such evidence will typically fall into one of the three classifications described in the following sections.

Filling a Conspicuous Gap

Where items of evidence fall naturally into a series or other grouping, omitting one item from the series because it is harmful may result in very high costs of apparent efforts to omit. An illustration of this category drawn from common experience is the preparation of a resumé. In keeping with the principles of sponsorship, the job-seeker might wish to purge his resumé of all less-than-strong qualifications, neutral verbiage, and harmful information.

In some circumstances, however, the applicant would suffer more harm than good by deleting certain less-than-strong entries. Assume, for example, that he is seeking a position as a Professor of Medicine at Harvard Medical School. He has an undergraduate degree from Stanford, did his residency at Johns Hopkins Medical School, and did further research — for which he obtained numerous awards — at Cornell Medical School. His only weak credential is that he received his medical degree from a mediocre medical school outside the United States. The job-seeker might be tempted to omit any mention of his medical school on the resumé. The attempt to do so, however, is nearly certain to harm him. Plainly, an applicant for a faculty position at a medical school will be expected to submit a resumé showing where he received his medical degree.[37] In these circumstances, omission of the item from the resumé will attract greater attention to the item than it would otherwise have merited. The reader of the resumé will conclude that the applicant took pains to omit any reference to his medical school.

By the same token, if an advocate qualifying an expert at trial is permitted to use a resumé to summarize his expert's credentials, the advocate may be warranted in avoiding the conspicuous omission described in the foregoing example. If, instead of using a resumé, the advocate decides to elicit the expert's qualifications by questioning him, the advocate should likewise avoid the foregoing omission.

A Witness's Relationship to the Parties

When an advocate calls a witness who has a significant personal relationship to one of the parties, it may be wise for that advocate to elicit that relationship. For instance, if a defendant's relative or close friend testifies as a character witness,[38] the advocate should elicit that relationship.[39] If he fails to elicit it, the jury may assume that the witness was coached to conceal this fact. The jury's perception that the advocate took pains to conceal the fact might only highlight its significance.

In the case of a character witness, the omission of the fact might leave the jury asking itself: Who is this witness? How does he know the party? How is he qualified to offer

---

[37] *Cf.* T. Jackson, *The Perfect Resumé* 86 (Anchor Press Doubleday 1981) (advising that a chronological resumé must be "without major gaps").

[38] As we have noted (*see* pages 68-69, *supra*), character evidence will usually not constitute strong evidence. We assume here that the advocate concluded that, in his particular case, the character evidence qualified as strong.

[39] *Cf.* 1 Schweitzer, *supra* note 18, § 191, at 515 (advising the direct examiner to elicit any "natural relationship between a witness and the party for whom he is testifying ... [including] the relationship of a close friend of many years' standing, employee-employer, blood relationship or one created by marriage of next of kin").

the opinion in question? Obviously, the jury must be given such information regarding a character witness.

This does not mean, of course, that an advocate should volunteer all harmful facts regarding a character witness. For instance, in the above example, the advocate should not elicit the fact that the defendant's character witness has an impeachable conviction.[40] The advocate would not appear to have gone out of his way to avoid eliciting such information.

The decision whether to elicit the relationship between the party and other types of witnesses requires a more difficult judgment. For example, where one of plaintiff's witnesses to an automobile accident is acquainted with plaintiff because they work together at a factory, it is not clear whether the advocate should bring out that fact. He must consider, at a minimum, whether the jury would conclude that the witness was coached to avoid that fact and whether, by eliciting it, he would substantially undermine his ability to claim in summation that the work relationship is not significant.

The Brief Narrative

If a witness would almost certainly include a harmful fact when candidly describing an incident in everyday conversation with a close friend or relative, then the advocate should consider disclosing such a fact in direct examination. In our experience, this is a narrow category. The advocate should not allow it to swallow the general rule against introducing harmful evidence.

To illustrate the difficulty of applying this test, if a prostitute looking for customers was forced at gunpoint into a car and raped, the prosecutor may be justified in eliciting, during direct examination, the fact that the victim was streetwalking. A prostitute who is candidly recounting the

[40] *See, e.g.*, Fed. R. Evid. 609(a) (providing circumstances where a prior conviction can be used to impeach a witness).

events of the rape to a relative or close friend might well include some mention of what she was doing immediately prior to the rape. If that fact is omitted and comes out only on cross-examination, the jury might conclude that the witness had to be coached to sidestep that fact in her testimony. The advocate's effort to avoid mention of that fact might highlight its significance in the jury's eyes.

Notwithstanding this, the prosecutor might choose not to bring out the fact. If his opponent brought it out, the *opponent* would have to convince the jury of its relevance. Depending on the defendant's theory, the prosecutor might be able to express outrage at his opponent's implicit suggestion that exceptions can be made to the armed rape laws of the jurisdiction. Thus, the costs that the advocate would relieve his opponent from incurring might justify omitting a weakness even though the jury perceives that the advocate took pains to do so.

In the above example, there are at least arguable reasons to elicit the harmful matter. If, however, the victim had simply been a prostitute several years ago and had a prior conviction for prostitution (and assuming *arguendo* that such evidence is admissible), eliciting that conviction in direct examination would clearly *not* be warranted under the "brief narrative" test. Such a fact would not normally be included as part of a candid narrative to a relative or close friend concerning the rape, and the jury therefore would not view the advocate as having purposefully avoided it.

Manner of Exposing Weaknesses

If the advocate decides that he must elicit a factual weakness, he should do so in a natural and logical manner in order to minimize the emphasis given to it. For example, in the above case of a character witness who is related to the defendant, the approach *not* to take would be as follows:

> Mr. Smith, let's get something out of the way right up front. You're the defendant's uncle, aren't you?

This approach would send a signal to the jury that the witness's bias is critical and had to be conceded at the outset. A better line of questioning would be as follows:

> Q: Please state your name.
> A: Thomas Smith.
> Q: Where do you reside?
> A: 119 East 64th Street.
> Q: Are you employed?
> A: Yes.
> Q: Where?
> A: At the local Post Office.
> Q: Do you know the defendant in this case?
> A: Yes, I do.
> Q: How?
> A: He's my nephew.

The examination would then proceed into the facts establishing the alibi.

As the above example shows, the advocate should not give the potentially harmful fact undue prominence. At the same time, however, he must not present it in such a way as to appear that he is trying to hide it. Thus, in the above example, it would be counterproductive to try to "slip in" the relationship in the middle of the examination. Because such a fact identifies the witness, it belongs at the beginning of the testimony. Accordingly, although it is sometimes tactically beneficial for an advocate to "bury" a weakness,[41] it is essential that he not be perceived as having deliberately done so.

The Conventional Wisdom on Harmful Evidence

As the foregoing discussion reveals, sponsorship theory counsels that, except in rare instances, harmful evidence

---

[41] *See* Mauet, *supra* note 34, § 4.2, at 86 (noting that an advocate should "bury [a weakness] in the middle of the direct examination").

should not be elicited by the advocate whose side is harmed by it. In contrast to this approach, virtually every leading trial manual takes the opposite position and urges the wholesale introduction of harmful evidence.[42] These commentators do not base their view on any purported ethical or legal duty of an advocate to expose his weaknesses to the jury.[43] To the contrary, the advice urged by these commentators is based solely on the premise that revealing one's weaknesses before the other side does so is tactically sound and helps win trials.[44] Since we have al-

[42] *See, e.g.*, Mauet, *supra* note 34, § 4.2, at 86 (referring to view of the "conventional wisdom" that an advocate should "volunteer weaknesses"); S. Goldberg, *The First Trial: Where Do I Sit? What Do I Say?* at 204 (West 1982) ("Weak spots in the case are usually mentioned in opening statement. Not your opponent's weak spots, but your own."); Bailey & Rothblatt, *supra* note 17, § 9:11, at 249; P. Bergman, *Trial Advocacy* 137 (West 1979); L. Decof, *Art of Advocacy: Opening Statement* § 1.18, at 1-43 (Matthew Bender 1987); 1 S. Gazan, *Encyclopedia of Trial Strategy and Tactics* 92 (Prentice-Hall, Inc. 1962); J. Sonsteng, R. Haydock & J. Boyd, *The Trial Book — A Total System for the Preparation and Presentation of a Case* § 5.5(d), at 193 (West 1984); R. Carlson & E. Imwinkelried, *Dynamics of Trial Practice* § 5.5(D), at 73 (West 1989); A. Julien, *Opening Statements* § 1.03, at 1-4 (Callaghan & Co. 1980) (referring to technique of volunteering a weakness as "[w]orkshopping" the weakness). Even the fictional literature takes this approach. *See e.g.*, Turow, *supra* note 32, at 241 ("A smart prosecutor usually seeks to defuse defense evidence by mentioning it first, demonstrating from his own mouth that his case can stand the defense's strongest blows."). *But cf.* K. Hegland, *Trial and Practice Skills* 16-19 (West 1978) (urging caution in bringing out weaknesses, noting that "most beginners overdo it — their entire case becomes one long apology").

[43] It should be noted that some jurisdictions require prosecutors to introduce *all* available eyewitnesses to a crime (*see generally* LaFave & Israel, *supra* note 6, § 23.3, at 876). Such a rule will occasionally compel introduction of harmful evidence as a matter of law. Aside from this, we know of no law or ethical rule requiring the introduction of such evidence. *Cf. Brady v. Maryland,* 373 U.S. 83 (1973) (establishing a rule of *tender,* not introduction at trial, of evidence exculpating a criminal defendant); Fed. R. Crim. P. 16 (mandating discovery and inspection, but not introduction at trial); Fed. R. Civ. P. 16(b) (authorizing discovery but not requiring introduction of any specific evidence); Model Code of Professional Responsibility, DR 7-103(B) (requiring prosecutor's "disclosure," but not introduction of, evidence favorable to a criminal defendant); *id.,* DR 7-106(B)(1) (requiring disclosure to court of adverse case law but not containing similar requirement of disclosure of evidence to juries at trial).

[44] Significantly, the conventional wisdom suggests eliciting a weakness only if the advocate believes that his opponent will elicit it if he fails to do so. *See, e.g.,*

ready explained why the wholesale use of harmful evidence is not sound in light of sponsorship analysis,[45] we now focus on the reasoning underlying the conventional wisdom.

It is difficult to pinpoint precisely the rationale for the conventional wisdom's recommendation that an advocate should volunteer his harmful evidence. Although virtually every manual gives this advice, there is little detailed analysis of the underlying reasoning. Apparently, the advice is considered so obviously correct that an extended discussion of the merits of the tactic is unnecessary and can be omitted.[46] Although we can find no comprehensive explanation of the conventional wisdom's reasoning, the commentators have offered two general rationales.

The First Rationale

One of the two main justifications advanced in support of volunteering weaknesses is that the advocate who discloses his weak evidence enhances his credibility with the jury.[47] The hope is that the jury will view the advocate not

---

Keeton, *supra* note 17, § 2.20, at 54-55 (urging an advocate to bring out a weakness if it "is directly related to the issues in the case and is a matter that in all probability your opponent will inquire about on cross-examination"). *See* pages 70-91, *supra* (noting difficulty in determining whether an opponent will bring out a weakness).

[45] *See* pages 86-88, *supra.*

[46] The assumed obviousness of the rationale for the strategy is somewhat puzzling in light of the fact that the practice of impeaching one's own witness was actually *prohibited* under the common law. *See, e.g.,* Thomas, *The Rule Against Impeaching One's Own Witness: A Reconsideration,* 31 Mo. L. Rev. 364 (1966); *cf.* Fed. R. Evid. 607 (reflecting modern rule permitting impeachment of one's own witness).

[47] *See, e.g.,* Sonsteng, Haydock & Boyd, *supra* note 42, § 5.5, at 194 ("An open and candid disclosure of [weaknesses] will usually increase the sincerity and credibility of the attorney...."); 1 Gazan, *supra* note 42, at 92 ("Candor, absolute candor, should be the guiding consideration. Tell the jury frankly not only the strength of your case but also its weaknesses."). The debate over the wisdom of using the credibility of the speaker as a means of persuasion has ancient antecedents. *See, e.g.,* G. Kennedy, *The Art of Rhetoric in the Roman World* 42 (Prince-

as a "hired gun" but as a fair and impartial arbiter striving to present a balanced and unbiased picture of the evidence. In this manner, the advocate's objective is to have the jury view him as presenting not just the client's best case but also his *worst* case.

Using the terminology of sponsorship theory, the hope is that the advocate's costs of introduction will be reduced across the board. Thus, the "packaging" component of that cost might be reduced if the jury thinks that the advocate is too impartial to prepare his witnesses to give testimony that puts his client's case in the best possible light. In addition, there might be less of a concession of materiality regarding each item of his evidence if the jury — contrary to the assumption of best case with minimum effort — accepts the notion that the advocate will go out of his way to present the "whole picture," and not merely the evidence that he needs to win.

In our view, this rationale is misplaced, since the jury simply will not embrace the proposition that an interested advocate can be relied upon to present his case impartially.[48] The assumption that the advocate is biased will be confirmed for the jury when, in summation, he tells the jury — as he inevitably must — that the weakness is not fatal to his case. Once he makes that argument, the jury will realize that his admission of weaknesses was harmless and, ultimately, self-serving. As long as the jury knows that an advocate will never confess that he should lose the case, it will be skeptical of his attempts to gain credibility by exposing weaknesses.[49]

---

ton Univ. Press 1972) (contrasting the "[ancient] Greek orator [who] tends to argue his audience into believing something [with the] Roman [who] by his authority convinces the audience that something should be believed because he says so").

[48] *Cf. Inglett & Co. v. Everglades Fertilizer Co.*, 255 F.2d 342, 349 (5th Cir. 1958) (Brown, J.) ("[W]e think it an unnatural, if not virtually impossible, task for counsel, in his own case, to drop his garments of advocacy and take on the somber garb of an objective fact-stater.").

[49] We agree, of course, that as a general proposition, the credibility of the speaker may influence the decision-maker. *See generally* Aristotle, *The Rhetoric*

An example from common experience illustrates the fallacy in the credibility rationale. Assume that a diner has asked the waiter at a restaurant for his recommendations concerning the entrées on the menu. Assume further that in response, the waiter admits that some customers have been complaining about the chicken curry, but that the filet mignon has garnered rave reviews. Once the diner notices that the filet mignon costs twice as much as the chicken curry, the waiter's appearance of candor will be undermined. Because the diner will view the waiter's recommendations as motivated by a desire to increase the gratuity, he will not feel safe in relying on anything the waiter says about the quality of the filet mignon. The chances are high, however, that he will avoid the chicken curry.

The jury behaves no differently. Its tendency to question the reliability of statements favoring the advocate's case is reflected in evidentiary principles relating to the reliability of hearsay declarations against interest. Under the hearsay rule, such a statement is considered reliable only if, *on balance,* it is disserving.[50] Ultimately, the jury will view as *unreliable* statements that on balance are self-serving. This is contrary to the conventional view, which posits that if the advocate is willing to acknowledge the bad in his case, he can be relied upon in his assessment of its good aspects. The flaw in this reasoning is that the jury will not view both statements — the bad and the good — *taken together* as a statement against interest. Because of this, it will credit his negative statements regarding his evidence but will view with suspicion his positive state-

---

1358a1, *translated in The Complete Works of Aristotle* 2155 (Barnes ed. Princeton Univ. Press 1984) (discussing the importance of a speaker's credibility). For example, politicians correctly recognize the value of obtaining endorsements from prominent and well-regarded figures, such as actors and noted scholars. Our point is simply that in the case of an *interested advocate,* such a speaker generally gains little by trying to bolster his credibility.

[50] *See, e.g.,* R. Lempert & S. Saltzburg, *A Modern Approach to Evidence* 489 (West 2d ed. 1982) (noting that "[i]f [a] statement seems on balance self-serving, it will be excluded").

ments. The credibility rationale, which is based fundamentally on an effort to curry favor,[51] thus provides no basis for volunteering one's weaknesses.

The credibility rationale suffers from a further impediment. As noted previously, the very fact that an interested advocate has gone out of his way to introduce evidence harmful to his case will, at a minimum, ratify the significance of that evidence to the verdict. Given this, we find it puzzling that the very writers who instruct attorneys to volunteer their harmful evidence also urge those attorneys to tell the jury that such evidence "really has no bearing" on its decision.[52] How one's credibility can survive this disparity between words and deeds is difficult to perceive.

The commentators are correct in recognizing that if an advocate is to prevail, he will have to argue that the harmful matter is not verdict-dispositive. This being so, we fail to see why the advocate would want to be the one to highlight the matter in the first place. In our view, the better approach is for the advocate to ignore the weakness and address it only if his opponent raises it. At least under the latter strategy, when the advocate asserts that the matter "really has no bearing" on the verdict, his words will be consistent with his deeds.[53]

A variant of the credibility rationale is the suggestion of some commentators that an attorney must disclose his harmful points or he will appear unfair.[54] The reasoning

[51] *Cf.* Fed. R. Evid. 804, Adv. Comm. Note (b)(3) ("a statement admitting guilt and implicating another person, made while in custody, may well be motivated by a desire to curry favor with the authorities and hence fail to qualify as against interest").

[52] Decof, *supra* note 42, § 1.18[2], at 1-44.

[53] Even if an advocate actually believes that the weakness is *fatal* to his case and is contesting the matter only because his client has insisted on a trial, he does not benefit from ratifying the significance of the harmful evidence.

[54] *See, e.g.*, Decof, *supra* note 42, § 1.18, at 1-43 ("[Y]ou must not present your case in a totally one-sided fashion, leaving out some critical weakness you know the defense will raise, lest you dispel the notion of fairness you have worked so hard to establish.").

appears to be that the jury may rule against the advocate's client for the simple reason that it finds the advocate's tactic of presenting a one-sided case to be unsavory. Even assuming that a jury would rule against a client because it disapproves of the lawyer, this rationale does not withstand scrutiny.

Unless the advocate has taken unusual efforts to conceal a weakness, he will not be viewed negatively for failing to volunteer it. This is because, as we have suggested,[55] the jury does not expect an advocate to go out of his way to present evidence harmful to his case. Put another way, it does not expect him to portray his client's case in its worst light. For that reason, it will not view him as unfair if he fails to do so. In any event, an advocate who volunteers weaknesses in an effort to seem fair is probably defeating his purpose. As explained above,[56] the jury is apt to conclude that the advocate's case is even worse than he has stated and that his weak presentation is actually his *best* case scenario.

Some advocates may take satisfaction in volunteering the weaknesses in their cases and may feel morally superior to those who practice best-case advocacy. Unless, however, such an advocate would volunteer the weakness in question even where he is *certain* that his opponent would not introduce it himself, then he has no basis for any feeling of moral superiority. In this regard, we are not aware of a single trial commentator or practitioner who would recommend volunteering weaknesses in the absence of an expectation that his opponent will introduce the item if he does not.[57] If such an advocate did exist, we believe that he would be betraying his client, since he would be presenting damaging evidence that even his opponent would not have used.

Alternatively, an advocate may derive personal satisfaction from believing that the jury holds him in high esteem

[55] *See* page 20, *supra.*

[56] *See* page 86, note 34, *supra.*

[57] *See* note 44, *supra.*

for volunteering his weaknesses and views him as a balanced and eminently fair lawyer. In our experience, however, this high esteem rarely increases the likelihood of a favorable verdict. If such an advocate is liked by the jury, it is because he has acted against his client's interests by making important admissions and concessions. Not surprisingly, therefore, the trial lawyers we have known who were most ardent in their efforts to achieve an image of fairness by parading their weaknesses had the least impressive trial records. Indeed, the authors' own early — and unsuccessful — experimentation with that strategy confirms that an advocate's image of fairness does not translate into victories.

Ultimately, the fairness strategy fails for the same reason as the credibility strategy: the effort is self-serving. The jury knows that the advocate is volunteering weaknesses in an effort to *win* the case and that he will never be so "fair" as to suggest that his client should *lose*.[58]

The Second Rationale

The second rationale for the conventional wisdom is that the advocate who discloses his harmful evidence will take out the "sting" that would otherwise result from its introduction by his opponent.[59] Consistent with this book,

[58] We are not rejecting fairness as a worthwhile goal. Rather, we are simply pointing out that introducing harmful evidence in an effort to appear fair will generally be counterproductive. An advocate should by all means try to appear as fair as possible, for example, by treating the court, the witnesses, and the jurors with respect.

[59] *See, e.g.*, Bergman, *supra* note 42, at 137 ("One of the oldest pieces of advice is to remove some sting from your opponent's cross examination by revealing negative matter that will come out anyway."); Mauet, *supra* note 34, § 4.2, at 86 (noting strategy of volunteering weaknesses to "take the sting out" of them); Bailey & Rothblatt, *supra* note 17, § 9:11, at 249 (advising criminal defense lawyers that "[n]o matter how damaging the evidence against the accused is, expose it ... [T]he evidence sounds a lot less damaging if it comes from you"); 1 *Goldstein Trial Techniques* § 10.48, at 10-42 (Callaghan & Co. 3d ed. 1984) (advising advocates to bring out weaknesses in opening statement in order to "soften the blow"); Carlson & Imwinkelried, *supra* note 42, § 5.5(D), at 73

this analysis posits that the impact of harmful evidence is influenced by who introduces it. The impact posited, however, is precisely the opposite of that predicted by the cost of introduction. Employing the materiality graph depicted in Chapter Two (figure 2-1), the conventional view posits a rightward shift on the graph representing a lessened impact on the jury. In essence, it posits a benefit, not a cost, of introduction.[60]

Two noted commentators provide a concise explanation for why they believe that the harm is reduced when an advocate volunteers his weaknesses: "The jury will feel that it cannot be too bad if the [party's] own attorney reveals it."[61] In our view, this rationale is erroneous. When an attorney goes out of his way to present evidence that is harmful to his case, the jury is far more apt to conclude that he himself thought it was so bad that he felt the jury would penalize him for *not* introducing it. Moreover, the harm is magnified because the jury thinks that it is seeing the harmful item packaged in the light most favorable to the advocate's case.[62]

By contrast, if the advocate's opponent introduces a harmful fact, the jury is apt to believe that it is seeing the same item of evidence in the light most favorable to the *opponent's* case. Furthermore, the opponent must convince the jury of its materiality — a job that the advocate relieves his opponent of by introducing it himself.

An example illustrates the point. Assume that an eyewitness to an automobile accident was not wearing his glasses at the time of the incident. Assume further that the

("[W]eaknesses may strike the jurors as far more damning if they learn of them for the first time [from the opponent]").

[60] *See, e.g.,* Mauet, *supra* note 34, § 3.3, at 50-51 ("Where ... [a] weakness is apparent and known to the opponent, you should volunteer it as soon as possible. If you don't, your opponent will, with twice the impact.").

[61] Bailey & Rothblatt, *supra* note 17, § 9:11, at 249; *accord, e.g.,* M. Berger, J. Mitchell, & R. Clark, *Trial Advocacy: Planning, Analysis, & Strategy* 206-207 (Little, Brown & Co. 1989) ("By presenting [a weakness] yourself and mentioning the problem throughout trial ... jurors may begin to think that, if you are willing to keep talking about it, it can't be that bad.").

[62] *See* page 86 and note 34, *supra.*

witness has adequate but not perfect vision without his glasses. It is difficult to see how the plaintiff's attorney would be better off bringing out this adverse fact himself. If he chose to do so, the jury would likely conclude that *he* thought it significant that the witness was not wearing his glasses, and it would be skeptical of the witness's claim that his vision was adequate.

Moreover, plaintiff's attorney could not later argue with any credibility that the fact that the witness was not wearing glasses is immaterial and that the adequacy of the witness's vision should not concern the jury. If that is so, the jury will wonder, then why did the attorney go to the trouble of eliciting the testimony in the first place?

By contrast, if defense counsel brings out the fact that the witness was not wearing glasses, plaintiff's attorney would be on solid ground in arguing the lack of materiality of that fact during summation.[63] Thus, by bringing out the harmful evidence himself, plaintiff's attorney deprives himself of an otherwise persuasive argument. Moreover, he will have focused the jury's attention on an issue that cannot possibly advance his case.

For its part, sponsorship theory offers a clear basis for the conclusion that, on rare occasions, the impact of an item of harmful evidence will be magnified by an opponent's later introduction of it.[64] In contrast, the precise basis for the conventional wisdom's conclusion that the impact is *always* magnified by the opponent's later introduction is not clear. It is enough to note, however, that if the conclusion were generally applicable, the asserted "benefit" of introduction would counsel an advocate's introduction of *all* evidence in the case. Thus, for example, a prosecutor in a rape case would relish the opportunity to call the defendant's alibi witnesses and character witnesses, such as a priest who has known the defendant

[63] Methods for handling an opponent's criticism for not introducing harmful evidence are addressed in Chapter 12, *infra*, pages 284-286.

[64] *See* pages 88-94, *supra*.

through the defendant's charity work. By the same token, the defendant might welcome the opportunity to call as his own witnesses the victim and the doctor who examined her after the attack. If there were admissible other "bad acts" committed by the defendant,[65] such as prior similar rapes committed by him in the same neighborhood, he would want to introduce these facts himself as well.

A review of the conventional literature reveals that, with few exceptions,[66] the manuals urging attorneys to volunteer their weaknesses recommend that approach only with respect to witnesses whom the attorneys have already decided to call.[67] They do not recommend calling a witness solely to bring out a weakness. Because of this limitation, neither the "sting" rationale nor the credibility/fairness rationale can survive scrutiny. If either rationale were correct, then there would be no principled reason to so limit the advice. For example, an advocate would presumably be the *most* credible by calling a witness for the single purpose of eliciting a weakness. The only basis for the distinction is a recognition of the prohibitively high sponsorship costs that would be incurred by calling a witness only to elicit a harmful matter. Once the proponents of the conventional wisdom concede the costs of bringing out a weakness, then both the credibility and "sting" rationales are undermined.

In sum, an advocate errs in proceeding on the assumption that he normally benefits by eliciting harmful evidence. In most situations, he will be better off limiting his presentation to his best evidence, which is what the jury expects of him in the first place.[68]

---

[65] *See, e.g.,* Fed. R. Evid. 404(b) (permitting, *inter alia,* evidence of prior bad acts to prove identity).

[66] *Cf.* Appleman, *supra* note 1, at 215 (urging plaintiffs' attorneys to call the defendant).

[67] *See, e.g.,* Mauet, *supra* note 34, § 4.2, at 86.

[68] Since the conventional wisdom posits a benefit of introduction of harmful evidence, it might also posit a corresponding benefit of overtrying. *Cf.* Turow, *supra* note 32, at 241 (pertinent excerpt quoted at note 42, *supra*). Any theoretical "benefit of overtrying", however, suffers from the same defect as the as-

Selecting Evidence to Undermine Evidence Previously Presented by the Opponent

The foregoing sections of this chapter have addressed the topic of selecting evidence to put on one's best case. By contrast, this section addresses the topic of selecting evidence to undermine evidence previously presented by one's opponent. Here, the advocate is not seeking to use the evidence to bolster his own case. Rather, he is seeking to demonstrate that the evidence presented by his opponent fails to advance the opponent's case.[69]

In these circumstances, the advocate's selection of evidence focuses primarily on the harm to his opponent's case rather than on the benefit to his own case. Specifically, the rule for selecting evidence to undermine the opponent's evidence is simply the mirror image of the rule of using only strong evidence: *an advocate should use evidence to undermine his opponent's evidence only where the amount by which he can reduce the probative value of the opponent's evidence outweighs the sponsorship costs incurred by the advocate in doing so.* In applying this test, the advocate should recognize that reducing the probative value of an item of the opponent's evidence will cause his opponent to incur costs of overtrying. This reduction in the probative value of the opponent's *other* evidence must be taken into account when deciding whether the advocate's own sponsorship costs are outweighed.

Under the foregoing rule, the advocate will occasionally be warranted in using evidence that, when analyzed with-

---

serted "benefit of introduction": it would counsel the advocate to seek to introduce *all* evidence in the case, including his *opponent's* best evidence. Both asserted benefits fly in the face of the classic image of the advocate as someone striving to put forward *his* client's best case. *See, e.g.,* G. Kennedy, *The Art of Persuasion in Greece* 139 (Princeton Univ. Press 1962) (noting that in ancient Greek rhetoric, "[t]he necessity of fairness in presenting both sides of the case [was] forgotten and immediate persuasion [became] the sole object, divorced from all considerations of the subject which might detract from persuasion").

[69] As previously noted, the jury looks to each advocate not only to present his own best case but also to undermine his opponent's best case. *See* page 33, *supra.*

out regard to the opponent's evidence, is *unfavorable* to the advocate's case. This will be true so long as the reduction in the probative value of the opponent's evidence outweighs the advocate's costs in using it. In this situation, the jury will understand that the advocate is using such evidence solely to reduce the value of his opponent's evidence, not to bolster his own case.[70]

For example, assume an accident involving two eyewitnesses. The first is called by the plaintiff in the case-in-chief and gives testimony favorable to that side. He acknowledges that he cannot see well without glasses but maintains that he was wearing his glasses at the time of the accident. The second witness, who has favorable substantive testimony for the defense, is called by the defense not only to provide that testimony but also to testify that the first witness, who was standing next to him, was *not* wearing glasses at the time of the incident. The latter testimony is not "favorable" to the defense in a substantive sense, since the first witness's testimony, however much undermined, can still serve only to support plaintiff's version of the events. Nonetheless, defense counsel's decision to elicit such testimony will be warranted as long as the reduction in the probative value of the witness's evidence exceeds the defense's sponsorship costs in eliciting it.

A common situation in which the mirror image test will apply is in the decision whether to ask questions on cross-examination in order to discredit a witness. The advocate's purpose in doing so is not to present affirmative substantive proof, but rather to impeach or otherwise un-

[70] Strictly speaking, such evidence is "favorable" as that term is defined in this book. *See* Chapter Three, *supra,* at 52. When viewed together with the opponent's evidence, the item of evidence increases the likelihood of the advocate's position in the jury's eyes. *See* pages 34-36, *supra* (benefit of the attack). Given this, the rule of using only strong evidence would be sufficient, as a formal matter, to guide the selection of such discrediting evidence. This book employs the mirror image rule for the selection of such evidence, however, because that rule does not require the advocate to characterize evidence as "favorable" or "strong" when that evidence, standing alone, would in fact be *unfavorable.*

dermine the probative value of the opponent's evidence.[71] For example, consider again the automobile accident case in Chapter Two in which the plaintiff's expert testified, based on skid marks, to the speed that the defendant was driving. Assume that the expert testified that the defendant was traveling 40 mph in a 30 mph zone. Assume further, however, that the figure was in fact based on a mathematical error and should have been 31 mph. The defense counsel who has detected that error would almost certainly be warranted in forcing the expert to admit that his own figures revealed a speed of only 31 mph. This is so even though testimony that the defendant's speed was 31 mph is not, standing alone, "favorable" to the defendant.

Similarly, it is common for prosecutors to impeach defendants with inconsistent exculpatory statements. For example, if a defendant testifies at trial that he was with his girlfriend at the time of the crime, his testimony will be substantially discredited if he is shown to have made a prior statement to the police that he was at home asleep at the time of the crime. Obviously, the prosecutor, in bringing out the prior statement during cross-examination or rebuttal, is not asking the jury to accept the statement as true. Rather, he is using it to show that the defendant must be guilty since he cannot keep his alibi straight.

For the same reason, an advocate may occasionally be justified in bringing out a neutral fact where it substantially undercuts the testimony of an opponent's witness. For instance, if a nurse in a medical malpractice case testifies for the plaintiff that the treating physician appeared tired on the morning of surgery, the defense would be

[71] *Cf. People v. McKee,* 235 N.E.2d 625 (Ill. 1968) (noting that purpose of impeachment is to destroy credibility, not to prove facts stated in impeaching statement); 1 Devitt & Blackmar, *supra* note 6, § 17.16, at 562 (sample jury instruction providing that a prior inconsistent statement "may be considered by the jury for the sole purpose of judging the credibility of the witness" and not "as evidence or proof of the truth of any such statement").

warranted in eliciting that the nurse did not even work on the day in question and therefore had the wrong day in mind. The defense is not using the nurse to provide evidence favorable to his own case. Nonetheless, he will have succeeded in substantially reducing the probative value of the nurse's testimony for the plaintiff, thus increasing the plaintiff's costs of overtrying, while incurring only minimal costs himself.

The critical condition that permits an advocate to gain by using evidence that does not favor his own case is that his opponent, by calling a witness or introducing an item of evidence, has conceded the materiality of that evidence to his case. The advocate would not benefit by delving into these points without his opponent first having put them in issue. Thus, in the above automobile accident example, had the plaintiff not called the witness, the defense would have severely damaged his case by putting on that witness to testify that defendant was driving 31 mph. Similarly, in the malpractice example, had the plaintiff not called the nurse, there would have been no reason for the defendant to have called him to elicit that he was not working on the day in question.

*****

This chapter has introduced sponsorship theory's general rule of evidence selection on disputed issues: use only strong evidence. This rule enables an advocate to avoid overtrying his case by eliminating favorable evidence that is outweighed by sponsorship costs. This chapter has also explained why an advocate should avoid burdening his case with weaknesses unless such a strategy is warranted by the cost of apparent efforts to omit the weakness. Finally, this chapter has introduced a mirror image rule to the rule of using only strong evidence. The mirror image rule applies when an advocate is attempting to undermine evidence previously presented by his opponent.

The rule of using only strong evidence, while fundamental, must occasionally yield to other considerations. The following chapter describes two categories of evidence to which the rule does not apply.

5

Selection of Evidence: Undisputed Issues and Party-Associated Evidence

As Chapter Four demonstrated, a significant contribution of sponsorship theory is its prescription of the rule, applicable to disputed issues, of using only strong evidence. There are, however, two special categories of evidence selection decisions to which different rules apply.

The first category is limited to certain selection decisions faced by advocates who must sustain a legal burden of proof, namely, plaintiffs' attorneys, prosecutors, and defense attorneys asserting affirmative defenses. Here, the task for the advocate is to determine the quantity of evidence that he must introduce on those elements of his claim or defense that are undisputed by his opponent. The second category relates to the use of what we term "party-associated evidence." Briefly stated, party-associated evidence is evidence that the jury preconceives to be uniquely associated with one of the parties to the case. The foremost examples include the plaintiff, the complainant in a criminal case, and the defendant. This chapter sets forth and applies the rules of evidence selection for undisputed issues and for party-associated evidence.

Undisputed Issues

In any lawsuit, civil or criminal, the party suing for relief must satisfy a legal burden of proof. Thus, plaintiffs' attorneys and prosecutors will always be faced with having to satisfy such a burden. By contrast, the party sued — the defendant — will have *no* legal burden of proof except in cases where he opts to present an affirmative defense.

Any legal burden of proof consists of one or more elements, each of which must be satisfied by the party required to meet such a burden. In any trial, the party's opponent will be disputing one or more of those elements. At the same time, the opponent will typically be conceding the merits of the party's position on other elements, rendering them undisputed.

The focus of this section is on the evidence that an advocate facing a legal burden of proof must introduce to sustain his burden on undisputed elements. As this section will demonstrate, the jury does not expect an advocate to concern himself with introducing evidence on those elements of his claim that his opponent does not dispute. For those elements, the jury will tend to give full credit to the opponent's concession.[1] Notwithstanding this, the advocate must still introduce at least a minimum amount of evidence to satisfy the judge that the legal burden has been met.

The first section that follows elaborates on the need for a separate rule of evidence selection on undisputed issues. The second section provides guidance in ascertaining the legal elements applicable to the claim or defense at issue. The third section addresses the quantity of evidence nec-

[1] As will be shown in the second part of this chapter, however, this conclusion does not apply with respect to party-associated evidence.

essary to establish those elements. Finally, the fourth section specifies the general rule dictated by sponsorship theory for the selection of evidence on undisputed issues: use only that amount of evidence required to satisfy the applicable legal burden.

The Need for a Separate Evidence Selection Rule on Undisputed Issues

As we explained in Chapter Four, when the advocate's position on an issue is *disputed* by his opponent, the jury expects the advocate to put on his best case on that issue. That task can be accomplished only by following the rule of using only strong evidence.

By contrast, where the advocate's position on an issue is *not* disputed, the jury does not expect the advocate to put on his best case on that issue. Here, the jury will not be apt to detain itself on the sufficiency of the evidence introduced with respect to that issue. To be sure, the jury is instructed by the court that it must find that the advocate has satisfied every element of the claim or defense before it can rule in the advocate's favor.[2] Since the opponent himself does not contend that the evidence is inadequate, however, the jury will not be apt to reach such a conclusion. This follows from the jury's assumption of best case. As a general rule, the jury will rely more heavily on the failure of the opponent's lawyer to dispute a point than it will on any evidence that the advocate can introduce. To persuade the jury on the undisputed issue, the advocate need only point out in summation his opponent's lack of disagreement.[3]

---

[2] *See, e.g., Criminal Jury Instructions, District of Columbia* § 2.08, at 44 (3d ed. 1978).

[3] Non-courtroom examples of the use of this technique are not difficult to find. *See, e.g.,* Wash. Post, June 9, 1989, at A18, Col. 1 (after the resignation of a Republican National Committee staffer who authored an allegedly malicious memorandum concerning the Democratic Speaker of the House of Representa-

Even though the jury does not expect an advocate carrying a legal burden of proof to preoccupy himself with introducing evidence on undisputed issues, such an advocate is nonetheless required by law to introduce evidence on each such issue, unless the opponent's decision not to dispute the issue is formalized in a stipulation. Since, as will be seen, the standard for satisfying the legal burden of proof on undisputed issues is different than the standard for persuading the jury on disputed issues, the advocate must apply two different evidence selection rules.

The advocate must recognize that satisfying the legal burden of proof on undisputed issues has nothing to do with persuading the jury to render a verdict in his favor.[4] Satisfaction of such burdens is purely a legal requirement that must be met before the jury is even allowed to deliberate on the merits of his case. The purpose of the requirement is merely to ensure that the advocate's case is substantial enough to warrant its submission to the jury for a decision.[5] Accordingly, as a practical matter, the judge is the only person in the courtroom who must be satisfied that these minimum legal requirements are met.

Identifying the Requirements for Satisfying the Legal Burden of Proof

The requirements for satisfying a legal burden of proof are determined solely by reference to law. In identifying the essential elements of his case, the advocate can consult

---

tives, President Bush, when asked whether the resignation was sufficient to consider the matter closed, responded: "[The Speaker is] the one who says the matter should be closed and he's right.").

[4] Even where the opponent *disputes* the element in question, the legal burden of proof is irrelevant to the selection of evidence to persuade the jury. The advocate cannot assume, merely because his evidence is sufficient to satisfy his legal burden of proof, that his evidence will be sufficient to convince the jury to rule in his favor.

[5] *See, e.g.,* 8A *Moore's Federal Practice* ¶ 29.02, at 29-7 (Matthew Bender 2d ed. 1989) (citations omitted) (noting that the reason for a legal standard "is that a defendant is entitled to protection against an improper or irrational verdict of the jury").

a variety of sources for guidance. For instance, he can examine the jury instructions applicable to a particular claim or offense.[6] He can also examine the statute governing the claim at issue as well as the cases construing that statute. In addition, he can consult various secondary sources.[7]

Quantity of Evidence Necessary to Satisfy the Legal Burden

The term often used to describe the quantity of evidence sufficient to meet a legal burden of proof is the "*prima facie* case."[8] The advocate's task in introducing evidence sufficient to establish a *prima facie* case is generally not a substantial one. In a federal civil case, for example, a motion for a directed verdict against the plaintiff will be denied so long as reasonable men could reach different conclusions based on the evidence introduced.[9] In a federal criminal case, a motion for judgment of acquittal will be granted only if there is no evidence upon which a reasonable mind might fairly conclude guilt beyond a reasonable doubt.[10]

---

[6] *See generally* E. Devitt & C. Blackmar, *Federal Jury Practice and Instructions* (West 3d ed. 1977) (containing model jury instructions for numerous civil and criminal actions).

[7] *See, e.g.,* D. Drussel & J. Wade, *Plaintiff's Proof of a Prima Facie Case* (Callaghan & Co. 1982).

[8] *See, e.g., id.;* J. Nolan, *Trial Practice: Cases and Materials* 133, 134 (West 1981).

[9] *See, e.g., Onufer v. Seven Springs Farm, Inc.,* 636 F.2d 46, 48 (3d Cir. 1980) (citation omitted); *Edward J. Sweeney & Sons, Inc. v. Texaco, Inc.,* 478 F. Supp. 243, 254 (E.D. Pa. 1979), *aff'd,* 637 F.2d 105 (3d Cir. 1980); *compare* Nolan, *supra* note 8, at 133 ("[P]laintiff . . . must 'get across the rail' by producing a prima facie case. This attainment consists of producing some evidence beyond a mere scintilla in support of every element in the case.").

[10] *See, e.g., Curley v. United States,* 160 F.2d 229, 232-233 (D.C. Cir.), *cert. denied,* 331 U.S. 837 (1947); *United States v. Lumpkin,* 448 F.2d 1085, 1093 (D.C. Cir. 1971); *Austin v. United States,* 382 F.2d 129, 138 (D.C. Cir. 1967); *compare* Nolan, *supra* note 8, at 134 ("A prima facie case [in a criminal matter] is one in which the government has introduced *some* evidence on every required element of the crimes for which the defendant is being tried. . . .") (emphasis in original).

If the advocate's legal burden of proof has already been satisfied during his opponent's presentation, the advocate is relieved from satisfying that burden in his own case. This can occur, for instance, where defense counsel in a contract case establishes his affirmative defense of duress through the cross-examination of his opponent's witnesses.

Similarly, one or more elements of the advocate's legal burden of proof will frequently be stipulated to by the opponent. In such a circumstance, as long as the record for appeal is clear, there is no need to introduce evidence to satisfy the uncontested element.

Often, the opponent who opts not to dispute an element of the advocate's burden of proof will nonetheless refuse to formalize his decision in a stipulation. In these circumstances, the advocate is required to introduce evidence to satisfy the undisputed element. For instance, in a prosecution for distribution of heroin, the government must offer evidence that the substance in question is in fact heroin even if the defendant does not dispute the chemical analysis of the substance showing that it is heroin, but claims instead that he is not the person who sold the drugs. Likewise, in a federal prosecution for extortion under the Hobbs Act,[11] the prosecutor must demonstrate that the alleged extortion affected interstate commerce even if the defense does not contest that aspect of the case. Similarly, in a breach of contract suit, the plaintiff must show that a contract was formed even if the defense is asserting accord and satisfaction and does not dispute the formation of the original agreement.

Satisfying an undisputed element will not help an advocate persuade the jury. As noted, the only purpose is to prevent the court from summarily rejecting the claim or defense without letting it reach the jury. This point can be illustrated in the context of an appellate brief. The body of the brief is designed to convince the judges to rule in

[11] 18 U.S.C. § 1951(a).

the advocate's favor. Other technical portions of the brief, however, while necessary under court rules, are not concerned with persuading the court. For instance, in the federal system, even if the appellee does not dispute the appellate court's jurisdiction, the appellant's brief must nonetheless contain a statement of the course of proceedings and the disposition in the lower court.[12] Such a statement will not help the advocate win the case except in the narrow sense that a failure to submit such a statement will cause the court of appeals to reject the brief for violation of the applicable rule.

One final comment is in order on the mandatory nature of the legal burden of proof. Chapter Four, in setting forth the pertinent evidence selection rule where the element of the claim or defense is *disputed,* demonstrated that persuading the jury requires an advocate to balance the sponsorship costs of introducing an item of evidence against its inherent probative value. Under the principles set forth in that chapter, the advocate may conclude, for instance, that a piece of favorable evidence should not be introduced because the costs are too high.

When evidence is necessary to sustain a legal burden of proof, however, the advocate does not have the luxury of considering the omission of the item from his presentation. The failure to introduce evidence on every element of the claim or affirmative defense will result in a summary rejection of that claim or defense.[13] Thus, if the advocate determines that the introduction of an item of evidence is required to sustain a legal burden, he need not detain himself with the question of whether sponsorship costs are incurred by its use. His use of the item will be mandatory.

---

[12] *See* Fed. R. App. P. 28(a)(3).

[13] *See, e.g.,* Fed. R. Crim. P. 29(a) (court "shall order the entry of judgment of acquittal ... if the evidence is insufficient to sustain a conviction"); Fed. R. Civ. P. 50(a) (motion for directed verdict in civil case).

The Rule for Selecting Evidence on Undisputed Issues

Chapter Four provided the rule, applicable to disputed issues, of using only strong evidence. Since the quantity of evidence required to satisfy a legal *prima facie* burden is a minimal one, it should be clear that as a practical matter, the use of this rule will invariably result in the satisfaction of any legal *prima facie* burden applicable to a disputed issue. The only real question facing the advocate concerns the appropriate rule of evidence selection to apply at trial on *undisputed* issues. This section sets forth that rule and the reasons underlying it.

It should be clear that the introduction of even the minimum amount of evidence necessary to satisfy the legal burden on an undisputed issue may entail sponsorship costs. Most significantly, the jury might view the advocate as putting on undisputed evidence in an effort to bolster his weak evidence on the disputed issues.[14] Any such costs, however, are unavoidable since the advocate must satisfy the legal burden just to get his case to the jury. Thus, the advocate need not even consider the sponsorship costs incurred by the use of such minimum evidence.

By contrast, once his legal burden has been satisfied, the advocate is free to evaluate whether to introduce *additional* evidence on the undisputed issue. Such an approach is warranted only if the benefits exceed the costs incurred. With respect to undisputed issues, there is generally no reason to risk incurring the costs of putting on more than the minimum amount of evidence. As we explained,[15] the jury will tend to give full credit to an opponent's failure to

[14] Of course, if the opponent directly criticizes the advocate for putting on evidence bearing on undisputed issues, the advocate can simply respond that he is required to introduce minimal evidence on all elements of the claim or charge, including those that are not in dispute. Because the use of such evidence is mandatory, the advocate's costs of overtrying are apt to be low or nonexistent.

[15] *See* page 113, *supra.*

dispute an issue. Accordingly, the advocate, in not introducing more than the minimum amount of evidence on an undisputed issue, runs no significant risk that the jury will rule against him on that issue.[16]

While there is no real value in putting on more than the minimum amount of evidence on undisputed issues, there is a serious disadvantage in doing so. The jury is likely to speculate that the advocate focused so heavily on the undisputed facts because he had very little to offer on the matters in dispute.[17] For this reason, the rule for selection of evidence on undisputed issues is that *the advocate should introduce no more than is necessary to satisfy the legal burden.*[18] Any additional evidence will not benefit the advocate and might result in considerable sponsorship costs.

To illustrate, consider a murder case where defense counsel delivers his opening statement immediately after the prosecutor's opening statement and announces unequivocally that, while his client concedes that the crime occurred, he maintains that someone else committed it and that he was erroneously identified as the perpetrator. Although the prosecutor in such a case has the legal burden of proving that the murder actually took place, he

---

[16] As we show in the next section, however, this conclusion does not apply with respect to party-associated evidence.

[17] *See, e.g.,* R. Traver, *Anatomy of a Murder* 466 (Dell 1958) (closing argument by fictional defense attorney criticizing the prosecutor in a murder trial for "spen[ding] hour after hour and witness after witness — and incidentally dollar after public dollar" on the "gory details" of the murder at issue even though the defendant, who was claiming temporary insanity, had "never denied" the shooting).

[18] In evaluating evidence as it bears on *undisputed* issues, there is no need for the advocate to consider whether an item is "strong." This consideration relates only to persuading the jury on disputed issues. In addition, in assessing whether an item of evidence is "favorable" on an undisputed issue for purposes of satisfying his legal burden, the advocate need not consider whether it is "favorable" in the jury's eyes as that term was defined in Chapter Three (*see* page 52, *supra*). This follows from the fact that the legal burden of proof has no relevance to the jury. The advocate need only determine whether the item of evidence "[has] any tendency to make the existence of [the] fact [to be proved] more probable ... than it would be without the evidence." Fed. R. Evid. 401.

should not concern himself with that issue, since his opponent has conceded that there was a murder.

Thus, although the prosecutor must tender at least minimal evidence showing that the crime occurred in order to establish the *prima facie* case, he should not introduce multiple grisly photographs of the slain victim. Highlighting the seriousness of the offense will do nothing to help the jury resolve any doubts it might otherwise have about whether the defendant is the murderer. Indeed, the very seriousness of the offense may provoke the opposite reaction.[19] The jury, knowing that a harsh penalty is certain upon conviction, may be even more reluctant to convict what may be the wrong man. Indeed, such reluctance could be magnified when the jurors realize that an erroneous conviction would not only punish the wrong man, it would close the case as well, leaving the real perpetrator free to commit similar ghastly crimes, perhaps in a juror's own neighborhood.[20]

Of course, such photographs may be relevant in defeating a claim of self-defense. In that situation, a photograph showing multiple stab wounds would be highly probative. Similarly, if the defendant is convicted, the photographs might be useful at the sentencing hearing.

In contrast to the rule governing undisputed issues, if the element in question is *disputed,* the advocate will not want to use simply the minimum amount of evidence necessary to satisfy his *prima facie* burden. For disputed issues, the advocate must *persuade* the jury of the merit of his position. As reflected in Chapter Four, sponsorship is the key to persuasion for the interested advocate. For this

---

[19] *But see State v. Vincent,* 24 Iowa 570 (1868) (prosecutor secured victory after exhibiting severed head of victim, preserved in jar of alcohol, to establish victim's identity).

[20] *Cf. Manson v. Brathwaite,* 432 U.S. 98, 127 (1977) (Marshall, J., dissenting) ("[I]f the police and the public erroneously conclude ... that the right man has been caught and convicted, the real outlaw must still remain at large. Law enforcement has failed in its primary function and has left society unprotected from the depredations of an active criminal.").

reason, the advocate should resort to the basic rule of using only strong evidence.

Party-Associated Evidence

As we have previously demonstrated, an advocate's usual insurance policy in refraining from introducing evidence is the argument that the *opponent* could have introduced the evidence. As will be seen, for evidence that is party-associated, such an argument will not be apt to satisfy the jury. The reason is that the jury preconceives party-associated evidence to be unavailable to the opponent and thus does not expect him to use it. Accordingly, a different rule of evidence selection is necessary where the evidence is party-associated.

Identifying Party-Associated Evidence

This section provides guidance on identifying party-associated evidence. It first describes common characteristics of witnesses and tangible evidence falling within that category. It then provides a basic test — grounded in the fundamental concept of unique availability — that an advocate can employ with respect to any piece of evidence that he believes may be party-associated to aid him in making a reliable determination.

Practical Unavailability as the Key Characteristic

Party-Associated Witnesses

The key characteristic of party-associated evidence is the jury's preconception that it is not fully available to the opponent despite the opponent's physical access to it. For witnesses, the jury preconceives such witnesses to be in the advocate's "camp" or to be known prior to trial only to the advocate's side.

A typical characteristic of a party-associated witness is that he is likely to be heavily biased in favor of one side and would, in the jury's mind, be likely to go out of his way to help that side. The jury is apt to assume that such a witness is not likely to have submitted to pretrial interviews with the opponent's investigators. It is further apt to believe that, even if the witness were to have granted such an interview, he probably would have been uncooperative. For these reasons, the jury's assumption that the opponent will present all of his best evidence is suspended. The jury does not expect him to make efforts to overcome these obstacles and subpoena him for trial without knowing what his testimony will be, even if he has reason to suspect that the witness could have materially advanced his case.

On occasion, even a completely unbiased witness may qualify as party-associated. This will be true where the jury preconceives that information concerning the witness is in one party's exclusive custody. An example is where a party reveals at trial that someone known only to him witnessed the incident in question and could corroborate his version of it. Such a witness is considered uniquely available to that party unless the jury is informed that the witness's name and address had been disclosed to the opponent prior to trial.

Party-Associated Tangible Evidence

For items of tangible evidence to qualify as party-associated, the jury must ordinarily preconceive the item to be in the possession, custody, or control of one of the parties or in some other manner uniquely available to him.[21] When this is so, the jury will assume that his opponent would have been impeded in his inspection of the item as

[21] *Cf.* 3 E. Devitt, C. Blackmar & M. Wolff, *Federal Jury Practice and Instructions (Civil)* § 72:16, at 46 (West 4th ed. 1987) (missing evidence instruction limited, *inter alia,* to evidence "under [a party's] control").

a potential exhibit. It will thus tend to excuse him for not introducing it even if he had reason to suspect that it might materially advance his case. Here, too, the jury's assumption of best case is suspended.

Even where the jury learns that the opponent had the opportunity to inspect the item, its preconception of unique availability may sometimes not be eliminated. This comports with actual conditions that often hamper an attorney's inspection of his opponent's physical evidence. For example, in civil discovery, where opposing counsel is permitted to inspect voluminous business records at the company's offices, the corporation's custodian and attorney will often be hovering close by and noting those documents that opposing counsel finds significant. Similarly, when a criminal defense lawyer seeks to examine the government's photographic evidence, his consideration of that evidence will sometimes be hindered by the impatience of the watchful police custodian. Despite the foregoing phenomena, however, it will be rare for a jury to continue to preconceive of an item of tangible evidence as uniquely available to an advocate where he affords his opponent a formal opportunity to inspect it.

The Basic Test

The test for identifying party-associated evidence consists of determining whether the tender argument set out in Chapter Four[22] will be fully persuasive. Specifically, the advocate should assume that neither side has introduced an item of evidence at trial. He should further assume that the opponent does not raise the issue of non-production in his summation, but that a juror raises the issue during deliberations and suggests that an adverse inference should be drawn against the advocate's case because he failed to produce the evidence. The test is whether the members of the jury will be satisfied with the observation

[22] *See* page 65, *supra*.

of another juror that the *opponent* could have introduced the evidence and that *no* adverse inference should be made in either direction.

It should be clear that the pivotal factor for the deliberating jury in resolving this issue will be whether the other evidence at trial has revealed that both sides had access to the missing item or whether such evidence was available only to the advocate. If the other evidence has given no clue concerning the availability of the missing item, then the jury's preconceptions concerning availability will almost certainly be controlling.

Analogy to the Missing Witness and Missing Evidence Doctrine

The task of identifying party-associated evidence is similar to a court's task in deciding whether to permit an advocate to urge the jury to draw an adverse inference from his opponent's failure to introduce evidence, even where it is physically available for the advocate's use. Under basic missing witness principles, an advocate is permitted to urge such an adverse inference from the non-production of evidence that is uniquely available to the opponent.[23] Moreover, the doctrine also allows an advocate to urge an adverse inference from missing evidence *notwithstanding* the advocate's ability to secure the evidence himself by subpoena, so long as there is a legally sufficient relationship between the missing evidence and the non-producing opponent.[24] A court's decision as to what con-

[23] *See, e.g.,* II J. Wigmore, *Evidence* § 285, at 192 (Little, Brown & Co. Chadbourn rev. 1979).

[24] *See, e.g., Kean v. Comm'r of Internal Revenue,* 469 F.2d 1183, 1188 (9th Cir. 1972) ("The determination of the question of equal availability depends upon all the facts and circumstances bearing upon the witness's relationship to the parties and not merely upon his physical presence at trial or accessibility for service of a subpoena."); *Pointer v. Pointer,* 251 S.W.2d 334, 338 (Mo. App. 1952) (noting that "if the relationship of the witness to a party is such that the witness would reasonably be expected to testify in favor of that party and against the other, such a witness is not equally available"). *See generally* Annota-

stitutes such a legally sufficient relationship is analogous to the trial lawyer's determination of whether the relationship between an item of evidence and his opponent's side is sufficiently exclusive as a practical matter to constitute party-associated evidence. Typically, a court making such a determination for purposes of the missing witness doctrine — like the trial lawyer — will find the relationship to be sufficiently exclusive where the advocate's claim of lack of practical availability is a reasonable one.

For this reason, much of the case law under this aspect of the missing witness doctrine is pertinent to the question of whether a given item of evidence is party-associated. This should not be surprising: under both sponsorship theory and the missing witness doctrine, the assumption that the advocate will use all of his best evidence is suspended where the evidence is not fully available to the advocate because of party association.

The trial advocate, however, should exercise caution in seeking guidance from this body of case law. We have found that this book's category of party-associated evidence is generally a narrower one than the corresponding category under the missing witness doctrine. For example, many courts apply a general rule that an employee is not available to the employer's opponent, notwithstanding the opponent's knowledge of and physical access to the witness.[25] A trial attorney, however, would be remiss in mechanically treating an employee as party-associated with his employer based on the fact of that relationship alone.

---

tion, 5 A.L.R. 2d 893 (1949) (collecting cases under the topic of "Relationship between party and witness as giving rise to or affecting presumption or inference from failure to produce or examine witness"); II Wigmore, *supra* note 23, §§ 285-291, at 192-229 (detailed discussion of missing witness and missing evidence rules).

[25] *See, e.g., Kean v. Comm'r of Internal Revenue,* 469 F.2d 1183, 1187-1188 (9th Cir. 1972); *Illinois Central Railroad Co. v. Staples,* 272 F.2d 829, 834 (8th Cir. 1959) ("[W]here witnesses are employees of one of the parties, they are not equally available to the other party...."); *see generally* Annotation, 5 A.L.R.2d 893, *supra* note 24, at 897-913 (collecting cases); Note, *Drawing an Inference From the Failure to Produce a Knowledgeable Witness: Evidentiary and Constitutional Considerations,* 61 Cal. L. Rev. 1422, 1424 (1973).

Ultimately, in determining whether a particular employee is a party-associated witness, the advocate should apply the test set out earlier in this chapter.[26]

The Rule for Selecting Party-Associated Evidence for Use at Trial

In Chapter Four, we discussed a risk that may arise when an advocate omits evidence from his presentation.[27] The risk is that the jury, not having seen the evidence, will speculate that such evidence would have harmed the advocate's case. This risk does not arise where the evidence is also available for the opponent's use. Where evidence available to both sides is introduced by neither, the jury will be apt to assume that such evidence would not have materially advanced or harmed *either* side's case. In sum, given equal availability, the advocate need not concern himself with any risk of adverse jury speculation from his omission of evidence.

This is not true in the case of party-associated evidence. Here, the jury has no logical basis for inferring from the opponent's omission of the evidence that it would have failed to benefit his case. Accordingly, because the jury preconceives that party-associated evidence is not equally available, the rule of evidence selection must take into account the risk of adverse jury speculation that arises when an advocate omits such evidence.

On the other hand, any rule for party-associated evidence must also assess the harm from the alternative of *using* it. Specifically, where the evidence bears on a disputed issue and is not strong, the advocate must evaluate the sponsorship costs incurred by using it. Where it bears on an undisputed issue, the advocate must likewise evaluate whether he incurs any costs by using it. Given these competing concerns, the rule of evidence selection for

[26] *See* pages 123-124, *supra.*

[27] *See* pages 63-68, *supra.*

party-associated evidence is as follows: *use only that party-associated evidence for which the risk of adverse jury speculation from omitting it outweighs the harm from introducing it (with sponsorship costs considered).* It should be clear that this rule involves a comparison of alternative adverse consequences.

As we explain below, the application of this rule will vary depending on whether the issue upon which the evidence bears is disputed or undisputed. The following sections focus separately on the alternative adverse consequences of omitting the evidence and using the evidence in these contexts.

Disputed Issues

The Risk from Non-Use of Less-than-Strong Party-Associated Evidence on Disputed Issues

As a preliminary matter, it should be clear that no issue arises with respect to whether *strong* party-associated evidence should be used. Since the need for a special rule of evidence selection arises only from the *omission* of such evidence, and since the use of any strong evidence will, by definition, benefit the advocate's case, he should plainly use all strong party-associated evidence.

Where the evidence is less-than-strong, however, the advocate must consider whether its use is nonetheless warranted. He cannot rely on the general rule to the contrary, which depends on equal availability of the evidence in question, a condition that is not satisfied in the case of party-associated evidence. Where evidence is party-associated, the advocate must understand that, even though the evidence harms his case, that harm may be outweighed by the risk that the jury will speculate that the omitted evidence is *more* harmful. Specifically, if the opponent criticizes the advocate for not producing such evidence, the advocate cannot persuasively respond that his opponent could have introduced it. Thus, the jury may speculate that it could have helped the opponent's case, perhaps significantly.

Assume, for example, a lawsuit arising out of an automobile accident in which the plaintiff's brother, a passenger in his car, was asleep and thus could not testify for his brother. Defense counsel may decide to argue:

> You heard, ladies and gentlemen, that the plaintiff's brother was in the car at the time of the accident. But did you hear him come in here to lend any support to the complainant's unusual account of how this accident occurred? No, you didn't. And I suggest that you recall that fact in your deliberations when you consider, as the judge will instruct you to do,[28] the extent to which the plaintiff's version is supported by other evidence in the case.[29]

As suggested in Chapter Four,[30] the danger to the plaintiff from such an argument is that the jury, not having heard the witness, may speculate that the brother's testimony would have *harmed* the plaintiff's case. The advocate must assess the likelihood of such speculation and the extent to which it could be reduced by reminding the jury that his opponent was free to call the brother.

The failure to introduce less-than-strong party-associated evidence on a disputed issue will not always risk such consequences. The risk arises only where such evidence, in the jury's eyes, would materially bear on a disputed issue.[31] Whether it does will depend on the other evidence

---

[28] *See generally* 1 Devitt & Blackmar, *supra* note 6, § 17.01, at 519-520.

[29] If the court finds that the close family relationship rendered the brother not equally available to the defendant, then it would permit the defendant to urge an even stronger point: that the jury should draw an adverse inference from the plaintiff's failure to produce the brother. *See generally* Annotation, 5 A.L.R.2d 893, *supra* note 24, at 928-937 (collecting pertinent authorities).

[30] *See* pages 63-67, *supra*.

[31] The analogous missing witness rule requirement is that the witness must "elucidate[]" the transaction. II Wigmore, *supra* note 23, § 285, at 192. As defined in the case law under that rule, the phrase "elucidate the transaction"

presented. Only where the other evidence indicates that the less-than-strong party-associated evidence might materially bear on the issue will there be a risk of adverse speculation. Returning to the above example, if the evidence conclusively revealed that the brother was asleep, the risk of adverse jury speculation would be non-existent.

Occasionally, even the testimony of the party-in-interest will not materially bear on the disputed facts. For example, where a homeowner who loses his home in a fire sues an insurance company to recover on his policy, and the only disputed issue is whether he deliberately set the fire to defraud the company, it is unlikely that a company representative can say anything that will bear on the issue.

The Harm from Use of Less-than-Strong Party-Associated Evidence on Disputed Issues

The harm from using less-than-strong party-associated evidence should by now be obvious. By definition, evidence is less-than-strong because the three sponsorship costs of using it outweigh its favorable value. When the evidence is favorable, the most significant cost will generally be the cost of overtrying, since the jury is apt to assume that the advocate introduced the party-associated evidence because he viewed his other evidence on the disputed issues as insufficient.

For example, assume a rape prosecution in which the victim's twelve-year-old daughter was a witness. Assume further that the defense is misidentification. If the daughter can testify only that defendant was about the same height as the rapist, the jury might conclude that the prosecutor thought that he needed such testimony to win. A defense suggestion that proof of defendant's guilt hinged on the testimony would be hard to rebut.

---

means that the evidence is material to a *disputed* issue in the case. *See, e.g., Thomas v. United States,* 447 A.2d 52, 57 (D.C. 1982); *United States v. Young,* 463 F.2d 934, 940 (D.C. Cir. 1972); *Cooper v. United States,* 415 A.2d 528, 533 (D.C. 1980); *Dent v. United States,* 404 A.2d 165, 170 (D.C. 1979).

Where the evidence is neutral or unfavorable, the most significant cost to consider will generally be that of introduction. The jury will give the evidence enhanced weight because of the advocate's concession of materiality and because the jury will seek to "unpackage" the evidence.

For example, assume that in the foregoing rape case, the rapist left his belt behind at the victim's house. Assume further that, prior to trial, the prosecutor had advised defense counsel of the existence of the belt and allowed it to be inspected pursuant to an applicable criminal discovery rule,[32] that defense counsel opted against its use as an exhibit at trial, and that the prosecutor likewise opted against using it, since he could not be certain that it would fit the defendant. Finally, assume that during the cross-examination of the complainant, defense counsel inadvertently elicits testimony about the belt having been left behind and recovered by the police. With testimony now before the jury indicating that an item of evidence in the government's custody might materially bear on the case, the prosecutor would now be faced with the decision of whether to use the exhibit to foreclose adverse jury speculation. If, once introduced, it fits the defendant but only tightly, the prosecutor will incur sponsorship costs. Among other things, he will have communicated a message that he thought it important for the jury to see it. Ultimately, because the *prosecutor* introduced the belt, the jury will be more inclined to view the belt as ruling the defendant out, not in.

The Presumption Against Use

An advocate who concludes that an item of his less-than-strong evidence bearing on a disputed issue is party-associated should not assume that he will necessarily be

[32] *See, e.g.*, Fed. R. Crim. P. 16(a)(1)(C) (requiring, upon defense request, that the government permit inspection of, *inter alia*, objects "belong[ing] to the defendant").

better off introducing it than not doing so. In our experience, it will be exceedingly rare for the risk of adverse jury speculation resulting from the omission of the evidence to outweigh the harm from using it.

For example, in a criminal prosecution following an arrest on a busy street corner, the jury's common experience may tell it that the police usually take the names and addresses of witnesses at the scene. And the jury might not assume that such names and addresses are made available to the defendant.[33] Thus, there is at least a theoretical risk of the jury speculating that the eyewitnesses not called by the government would have harmed its case.[34] We have found, however, that the harm from use in such a case will almost invariably outweigh the risk of omission. Most significantly, the jury will be apt to think that the attorney calling these witnesses deemed them necessary to his presentation on the disputed issue. The attorney will normally have no means of dispelling his opponent's criticism for calling such witnesses. Accordingly, the advocate considering the use of less-than-strong party-associated evidence should adopt a general presumption against use when applying the rules for selecting such evidence.

Before an advocate ever decides to use such evidence to foreclose adverse jury speculation, he should consider his alternatives. Above all, he should consider what steps he can take to dispel the jury's preconception of unique availability short of introducing the evidence himself. Introduction of such evidence should be viewed as a last resort.

---

[33] Indeed, the law often prevents criminal defense counsel from obtaining the identities of such witnesses from the prosecutor unless the witnesses are exculpatory. *See, e.g., United States v. Dreitzler,* 577 F.2d 539, 553 (9th Cir. 1978) (noting that Fed. R. Crim. P. 16 does not require government to disclose witnesses), *cert. denied,* 440 U.S. 921 (1979); *see generally Brady v. Maryland,* 373 U.S. 83 (1963) (discussing government's constitutional duty to disclose exculpatory evidence).

[34] Presumably, this is the rationale behind the advice of those commentators who suggest that a prosecutor must call *all* available eyewitnesses or suffer adverse tactical consequences. *See, e.g.,* A.E. Morrill, *Anatomy of a Trial* 107-108 (C.P.I. 1968).

Undisputed Issues

The Risk from Non-Use of Party-Associated Evidence on Undisputed Issues

Earlier in this chapter, we explained why an advocate seeking to satisfy a legal burden on an undisputed issue should use no more than the minimum amount of evidence necessary to satisfy that burden.[35] Where evidence bearing on an undisputed issue is not equally available to the opponent, however, the jury may not be satisfied that the opponent had the information necessary to make a reliable determination of whether the issue was capable of dispute. Moreover, in these circumstances, the jury will not be apt to expect the opponent to go out on a limb by making an issue of the matter where he is handicapped by a lack of information. When this is true, the advocate's failure to introduce evidence on an undisputed issue that was not fully available to his opponent might cause the jury to hold it against the advocate.

Here, as with party-associated evidence relating to a disputed issue, the advocate should be aware that the failure to introduce party-associated evidence on an undisputed issue will not always give rise to a risk of adverse jury speculation. Indeed, the risk from non-production is apt to be non-existent unless the testimony relates to a factual matter at the very foundation of an element of the claim or defense. The reason is that the jury will not view the opponent's failure to dispute an issue as unreliable unless it believes that the evidence that was unavailable to him could have been verdict-determinative. For this reason, the risk of adverse jury speculation on undisputed issues is limited to evidence that goes to the foundation of an element of the claim or defense.

The two sections that follow set forth the considerations pertinent to the use of party-associated witnesses and tan-

[35] *See* pages 118-121, *supra.*

gible evidence going to the foundation of an element of the claim or defense. As will be seen, even though such evidence does not bear on disputed issues, the advocate's failure to consider the use of such evidence can lead to grave consequences.

Party-Associated Witnesses on Undisputed Issues

The above discussion made clear that the advocate should not call a party-associated witness to provide testimony on an undisputed issue unless the testimony bears on a factual matter going to the foundation of the claim or defense. The need to call such a witness can be illustrated by using a paradigm party-associated witness — the injured complainant.

In both criminal and civil cases, where an injured victim is not produced to testify about his injury, a matter which obviously goes to the foundation of his claim, he incurs a risk even where the defense does not dispute the fact of the injury. Clearly, the jury will not be convinced by the argument that the defendant could have called the victim, since it views the victim, as a practical matter, to be unavailable to the defense. Consequently, the non-production of the victim will encourage the jury to speculate about the fact of the injury, and such speculation may result in an adverse verdict.[36]

The armed robbery trial recounted in the first chapter, with one factual change, illustrates the foregoing point. Assume that the good samaritan actually had witnessed the holdup and had seen the perpetrator take the purse. As a technical matter, the victim's testimony would be unnecessary to establish the prosecutor's legal burden. The eyewitness could establish both the fact that the robbery occurred and the identification of the assailant.

---

[36] The failure to produce the defendant, which raises similar issues, is treated in Chapter Six.

Nonetheless, a prosecutor who failed to bring on the complainant to testify that she was robbed would be taking an unwarranted risk. In the worst case scenario, the jury might conclude that the complainant would have testified that the defendant was *not* the assailant. Alternatively, it might conclude that the whole case was a setup and that the government could not find an elderly woman willing to fabricate the role of victim. The prosecutor would score no points by observing that the defendant could have called the complainant. Because the jury preconceives the complainant as not being fully available to the defense, it will not assume that defense counsel is able to present his best case regarding her testimony. Furthermore, it may not expect the defense attorney to go out on a limb by urging it to acquit because of the victim's absence when he is also urging misidentification as the reason for acquittal. As a result, the jury might decide that the absence of the complainant makes an acquittal the only fair verdict. In this limited circumstance, it might render its verdict based on grounds not even urged by the attorney. Accordingly, under such circumstances, the prosecutor should call the victim and elicit brief testimony concerning the fact of the injury.

Of course, the mere fact that the advocate has decided to call a party-associated witness to testify on an undisputed issue does not mean that he should elicit whatever testimony the witness has on the *disputed* issues. Each point elicited must be independently justified under the rule applicable to the selection of party-associated evidence.

Moreover, it is important not to overdo the examination of the witness on an undisputed issue. This can only result in sponsorship costs being incurred. Returning again to the armed robbery case recounted in Chapter One, it will be recalled that the defendant did not deny the occurrence of an armed robbery, but claimed instead that someone else committed the crime. At the actual trial, the prosecutor elicited testimony of the elderly victim for the purpose of covering the undisputed elements of the armed robbery. Nonetheless, knowing that the victim had been unable to make an identification, the prosecutor did not elicit the fact that she could not identify defendant. Such a question would have amounted to eliciting evidence that was at best neutral on the disputed issue, thereby highlighting how much stronger the case could have been.

Party-Associated Tangible Evidence on Undisputed Issues

As with party-associated witnesses bearing on undisputed issues, the only occasion in which the advocate will need to consider introducing party-associated tangible evidence bearing on such issues is when the evidence goes to the foundation of an element of his case. When the party that the jury preconceives as having custody of such evidence does not introduce it at trial, the jury will not attach significance to his opponent's failure to do so. Specifically, because of its preconception of unequal access to the evidence, the jury will not be apt to rely on the opponent's failure to dispute the issue. For this reason, it may conclude that the advocate did not satisfy his burden, even on an issue that his opponent did not dispute.

Some examples will illustrate the point. In a counterfeiting prosecution, the jury preconceives the counterfeit money seized to be maintained in the custody of the government. Thus, unless there is something troublesome about the exhibit[37] — or the advocate otherwise has reason to believe that he will incur high sponsorship costs by using it[38] — the government should normally produce it *in specie,* rather than through testimony, unless its absence is somehow explained. In such a case, even if the defense asserts a claim of misidentification and does not dispute

[37] *See* Chapter Nine, *infra,* pages 208-210 (discussing occasional need to use substitutes for tangible evidence).

[38] This will be very rare. *See* page 137, *infra.*

that *someone* used counterfeit money, and even if the introduction of the counterfeit is not legally required, the jury may indulge in adverse speculation if the prosecutor omits the evidence.

Similarly, in a bank robbery prosecution, the government should normally introduce the note that the robber passed to the teller. If the robber retrieved the note and it was never recovered, the fact of the robber's retrieval should be brought out through testimony. Likewise, in a prosecution for receiving stolen property, the prosecutor should normally introduce the stolen goods or account for his failure to do so.

The jury's unfavorable response to the omission of such evidence is not based on any legal obligation that certain physical evidence be produced. As we have noted, the standards for a legal burden of proof have no relevance to the jury. For example, in a bank robbery case, the production of the note is not legally required for the government to prove its case. The jury may conclude, however, that the absence of such basic evidence masks a fatal defect in the evidence. For instance, it might speculate that the handwriting on the note did not match the defendant's handwriting. It might even conclude that there was no note at all and that the government's whole case is fabricated. Obviously, it is important for the advocate to avoid such speculation.

The Harm from Use of Party-Associated Evidence on Undisputed Issues

An advocate considering the use of party-associated evidence bearing on undisputed issues must evaluate the potential harm from such use. Specifically, he must assess the possibility that the jury will view his use of that evidence to prove an undisputed issue as an attempt to conceal the inadequacy of his evidence on *disputed* issues.

As the foregoing sections revealed, the only party-associated evidence that the advocate should consider using on undisputed issues is evidence going to the foundation of an element of the claim or defense. Where the evidence is so fundamental to the case, the cost of overtrying incurred by its use is generally negligible. The jury will not be apt to view the use of such evidence as an effort to mask the inadequacy of evidence on the disputed issues. If the advocate is criticized for using such evidence, the jury will be apt to accept his response that it is his job to prove all elements, even undisputed ones. In sum, the harm from the use of such fundamental evidence on undisputed issues will normally be insubstantial.

The Presumption in Favor of Use

In general, there is a considerable risk of adverse jury speculation from the failure to introduce party-associated evidence bearing on an undisputed issue where that evidence goes to the foundation of the claim or defense. At the same time, the sponsorship costs of using such evidence are apt to be very low. Accordingly, although he should not overdo it,[39] an advocate should generally follow a presumption in favor of using such evidence.

*****

The following chapter focuses on whether to put on a defense case and whether to put on rebuttal evidence. As will be seen, the decision whether to defend is complicated considerably by the fact that the defendant is a party-associated witness.

---

[39] *See, e.g.*, pages 119-120, *supra* (illustrating excessive use of evidence bearing on an undisputed issue).

6

Selection of Evidence: Defense and Rebuttal

The defendant is being tried for murder, and the prosecutor has just rested after presenting a compelling case against him. Defense counsel must now decide whether to put on a case. His client denies any involvement in the murder and has two witnesses who say that he was elsewhere when the crime occurred. The problem, however, is that his client has a prior armed robbery conviction, and the two alibi witnesses are not very credible. Does the advocate call the defendant to the stand to deny the charges? Should the alibi witnesses be used? How will the jury react if the advocate decides not to put on any evidence? These are some of the most difficult tactical decisions a trial lawyer will face.

This chapter explains how sponsorship theory bears on resolving such questions. More generally, the chapter focuses on the evidence selection decisions involved when the opponent has already presented his case. For defense attorneys, the question is whether to put on a defense; for plaintiffs' attorneys and prosecutors, the question is whether to follow a defense case with a rebuttal case. We consider first the decision to defend and then discuss the decision to rebut.

The Decision to Defend

A number of factors bear on the question of whether to put on a defense.[1] In large part, the rule of using only strong evidence, set forth in Chapter Four, along with its mirror image rule of using only strong discrediting points, will govern the decision. As will be seen, however, the decision to defend is greatly complicated by special considerations involving whether the defendant — a party-associated witness — should be called as a witness.

A critical cost to consider in putting on a defense is the cost of overtrying. Specifically, the advocate may be viewed as acknowledging that his opponent's preceding case is substantial. In the extreme case, defense counsel's decision to defend will send a message to the jury that, in his view, his opponent established a sufficient case that must be rebutted.

There is a further dimension to putting on a defense case stemming from the jury's assumption of best case. Because of this assumption, the jury will view any presentation as the defendant's best case. It will not be inclined to seek out and evaluate alternative theories that defense counsel himself did not view as worthy of advancing. If the theory advanced by the defense is unpersuasive, the jury may settle on the opponent's presentation for the sole reason that it presents the only viable alternative. In this worst case scenario, the plaintiff's or prosecutor's burden of persuasion is essentially lifted.

---

[1] This section addresses only the threshold decision whether to defend. Once that decision is made, the question of what evidence to use should be resolved by reference to the guidance provided in Chapters Four and Five.

This burden shifting is not a legal one, but a practical one.[2] Simply put, the jury's focus is no longer on whether the plaintiff or prosecutor has met his legal burden. Instead, the jury's focus is on comparing the *relative* strengths of the two cases. The risk is that the contest will collapse into a "battle of competing theories." Other things being equal, this shift harms the defense. Before the defendant puts on a case, the plaintiff's attorney or prosecutor is largely limited to impressing the jury with the merits of his own case.[3] Once the defendant puts on evidence, however, the plaintiff's lawyer or prosecutor can attack his opponent's case.[4]

The practical consequence of shifting the burden by putting on a defense ultimately reflects the cost of overtrying. Specifically, by putting on a defense, defense counsel enhances the weight that the jury will be apt to attach to his opponent's evidence.

Not putting on a defense, however, also carries considerable disadvantages. Because the jury assumes that defense counsel will put forward his client's best case, it will normally infer from the lack of a defense case that the client has no respectable case whatsoever. Furthermore, as we explain below,[5] even when a defense is presented, the decision not to call the defendant as a witness in his own case may severely prejudice his chance of victory.

---

[2] Of course, where defense counsel puts on an affirmative defense, he himself assumes a legal burden of proof. *See, e.g.,* 3 E. Devitt, C. Blackmar & M. Wolff, *Federal Jury Practice and Instructions (Civil)* § 75.01, at 89 (West 4th ed. 1987) (model instruction on affirmative defense of statute of limitations); *id.,* § 75.03, at 95-96 (model instruction on affirmative defense of accord and satisfaction).

[3] As we note below, however, he is not prevented from attacking defense counsel's *theory* of the government's or plaintiff's evidence. *See* Chapter Twelve, *infra,* pages 279-281.

[4] One experienced defense attorney has recognized that putting on a defense has serious burden-shifting costs, and she therefore generally prefers not to do so. *See* J. Nelson, *Her Life is Her Job,* Wash. Post, June 12, 1988 (Magazine), at 35 ("[P]utting on defenses ... ultimately shifts the burden.... I'd much rather have the prosecutor try to explain away the weaknesses in his case than have him point out the weaknesses in ours.") (quoting former District of Columbia public defender Michele Roberts).

[5] *See* pages 144-145, *supra.*

It should be noted that the impact of resting without calling the defendant or otherwise putting on a defense may be greater in a civil case than in a criminal case. The reason stems from a criminal defendant's Fifth Amendment right not to testify or otherwise put on a case. In civil cases, an attorney is free to comment on the significance of the failure to present a defense case.[6] In the criminal context, however, such comments are largely prohibited.[7]

The following sections discuss the considerations pertinent to whether to defend (and whether to call the defendant) when favorable defense evidence is available and when it is not. Each is treated separately.

The Decision to Defend When Favorable Defense Evidence is Available

This section assumes that the defendant has favorable evidence available. The initial question here, as elsewhere,

[6] *See, e.g.*, 3 *Goldstein Trial Techniques* § 23.11, at 23-13 (Callaghan & Co. 3d ed. 1984) (citing authorities).

[7] The Supreme Court has held that comment on a defendant's failure to testify is generally prohibited. *See generally United States v. Robinson,* 108 S. Ct. 864 (1988); *Griffin v. California,* 380 U.S. 609 (1965); *but cf. United States v. Robinson,* 108 S. Ct. 864, 869 (1988) (comment on defendant's silence permissible when it is "a fair response to a claim made by defendant or his counsel," such as a claim that the government prevented the defendant from telling his side of the story). Indeed, the defendant is entitled to an instruction, upon request, that his silence may not be used against him. *See Carter v. Kentucky,* 450 U.S. 288 (1981); 1 E. Devitt & C. Blackmar, *Federal Jury Practice and Instructions* § 17.14, at 556 (West 3d ed. 1977) (model instruction); *cf. Lakeside v. Oregon,* 435 U.S. 333 (1978) (court may instruct jury to ignore a defendant's silence even where defendant objects to such an instruction). There is, however, authority for the proposition that comment on the lack of defense *evidence* is generally permissible so long as no adverse inference regarding the *defendant's* silence can be drawn. *See, e.g., United States v. Sblendorio,* 830 F.2d 1382, 1392 (7th Cir. 1987); F. Bailey & H. Rothblatt, *Successful Techniques for Criminal Trials* § 25.24, at 580-581 (Lawyers Co-op. Pub. Co. 1985) (noting, based on case law, that it is generally permissible for the prosecutor to state that his evidence is uncontradicted, unless such statement can be construed as comment on defendant's failure to testify). *Cf. Lockett v. Ohio,* 438 U.S. 586, 594-595 (1978) (prosecutor's reference to government's case as "unrefuted" and "uncontradicted" not reversible error where defense counsel had outlined defense case in opening statement but then offered no evidence to rebut government's case).

is whether the favorable evidence outweighs the three sponsorship costs. Although determining this requires the advocate to perform the analysis outlined in Chapters Three and Four, further discussion is needed to explain the assessment of the cost of overtrying.

Two variables will bear on the cost of overtrying incurred by the use of an item of favorable defense evidence: the strength of that defense evidence and the strength of the opponent's preceding case. In general, as common sense would indicate, the more compelling the defense evidence, the lower will be the cost of overtrying. Because the jury expects an attorney to put on all evidence that materially favors his case, he will lessen costs of overtrying when his evidence comports with that expectation. Similarly, the stronger the *opponent's* case, the more apt the advocate should be to use a given item of favorable defense evidence. This is because the acknowledgment of the strength of the opponent's preceding case resulting from putting on defense evidence will not be as likely to "shore up" the opponent's case where that case is already strong. If, on the other hand, the opponent's case was weak, putting on a defense may significantly enhance the opponent's evidence. In this latter circumstance, therefore, the advocate should be less inclined to put on a defense, other things being equal.

Returning to the murder case example at the beginning of this chapter, assume that the government has rested. If the government's case is compelling, a given favorable alibi witness will be more apt to qualify as strong, since the costs of overtrying will be minimal. By contrast, where the government's case is weak, it will be less likely that the same witness should be called, since those costs will be greater. Of course, even where the government's case is weak, calling an extremely favorable alibi witness is apt to be warranted, notwithstanding the high costs of overtrying incurred by his use, because of the high probative value of the evidence.[8]

It should be apparent that before defense counsel presents a case, he must assess not only the cost of overtrying but also the costs of introduction and efforts. Setting aside party-associated evidence, defense counsel should present evidence on a disputed issue only if the evidence is still favorable after applying all three costs.

The status of the defendant as a party-associated witness complicates the foregoing analysis. If the defendant provides favorable evidence outweighing sponsorship costs, then he plainly should be called for the reasons stated above. Obviously, the defendant should also be called even if he is the *only* strong witness. By contrast, however, if his testimony, standing alone, would be considered less-than-strong after applying sponsorship costs, and if there is other defense evidence available that qualifies as strong, defense counsel must consider whether to put on such other evidence without calling the less-than-strong defendant.[9]

As we indicated in Chapter Five, the defendant is a party-associated witness. Where the evidence indicates that the defendant would have something material to say, defense counsel who is considering not calling his client must take into account the risk of adverse jury speculation about what the defendant would have said had he been called. This is because the jury does not expect the defen-

---

[8]Some commentators recommend that a criminal defendant put on no evidence after a weak government case, apparently without regard to the strength of the defense evidence available. *See, e.g.,* Bailey & Rothblatt, *supra* note 7, § 15.1, at 392 ("If the prosecution has put in a poor case and there is an excellent chance that the jury may completely ignore and disregard the flimsy evidence presented, you should rest and rely upon this lack of evidence."). In our view, such advice goes too far. If the defense has compelling evidence available to it, the benefit of putting on a defense may outweigh the sponsorship costs, even when the government has put on a weak case.

[9]The same consideration must be made with any party-associated evidence, not just the defendant. For simplicity, we address only the problem posed by the less-than-strong defendant.

dant to be called by his opponent even if his testimony would have advanced the opponent's case. Indeed, in a criminal case, the jury is normally instructed that the defendant cannot be compelled to testify against his will under any circumstances.[10] Given these factors, where defense counsel decides to present other evidence but not to call the defendant, the risk of adverse speculation will be at a maximum, since the absence of the defendant's testimony will be magnified. The jury will recognize that calling the defendant would have required little effort, since he is sitting in the courtroom, only feet from the witness stand. For example, if the defense calls an alibi witness who testifies that he was out-of-town with the defendant at the time of the murder, the jury is likely to view the defendant's failure to take the stand more negatively than it would have if the alibi witness not been called.[11] This problem is apt to be even greater in a civil case, where the opponent is permitted to comment on the defendant's failure to testify.[12]

Thus, for the foregoing reasons, as well as for the reasons set forth more generally in Chapter Five, it will sometimes be tactically sound to call the defendant even though his testimony cannot be characterized as strong. Nonetheless, the advocate should not conclude from the above analysis that the defendant should *always* be called when a defense case is being presented. In some circumstances, the harm from calling the defendant will outweigh its value in foreclosing adverse jury speculation concerning his testimony. Thus, in the foregoing murder example, if the defense is presenting strong alibi wit-

---

[10] *See* note 7, *supra* (citing authorities); 1 Devitt & Blackmar, *supra* note 7, § 17.14, at 556 (model instruction that the law does not force the defendant to testify).

[11] This example recognizes the inclination of some juries in criminal cases to give weight to a defendant's failure to testify, notwithstanding instructions to the contrary. *Cf. Lakeside v. Oregon,* 435 U.S. 333, 340 n. 10 (1978).

[12] *See, e.g.,* 3 Goldstein, *supra* note 6, § 23.11, at 13 (citing authorities).

nesses, defense counsel would normally be justified in *not* calling the defendant where he would have to admit to a prior murder conviction. As with any party-associated evidence, defense counsel must balance the risks incurred by not calling the defendant against the harm from the jury actually hearing his less-than-strong testimony.

Finally, if defense counsel is considering putting on a defense case but omitting the defendant, he must ensure that his other evidence — which he has assessed to be strong, standing alone — actually results in a net benefit to his case given the enhanced risk of adverse jury speculation incurred by the defendant's conspicuous absence. Defense counsel must satisfy himself that there is such a net benefit before he opts in favor of presenting a defense that does not include his client.

The Decision to Defend When No Strong Evidence is Available

If defense counsel finds himself without any strong evidence, he should not automatically conclude that no defense case should be presented. He should first consider whether he is warranted in introducing evidence solely for the purpose of undermining evidence introduced by his opponent.[13] For example, in the videotape case in Chapter One, it was shown that defense counsel might have been warranted in introducing the videotape to demonstrate the hesitancy of the government's star witness in identifying the defendant. This is true even though the videotape could not possibly have been considered beneficial to the defense, had the government not called the witness appearing in the videotape.[14]

Even if no such discrediting evidence is available, defense counsel should consider whether a less-than-strong

[13] *See* Chapter Four, pages 106-109, *supra.*

[14] This might have been the case, for example, had the government been able to locate another eyewitness.

defendant should be introduced where no other defense evidence is being presented.[15] Where the defense does not put on other evidence, defendant's absence is not highlighted to the same degree as it is where other defense evidence is presented. Thus, the risk of adverse jury speculation from not calling the defendant is apt to be less in circumstances where no other evidence is being presented. Nonetheless, the need to consider the risk of not calling the defendant obviously cannot be overlooked. The rule for whether he should be called, as with any party-associated witness, is whether the risk of adverse jury speculation from non-use outweighs the harm from use.

To illustrate, assume that in the foregoing murder example, the defense has no available evidence except the defendant's own uncorroborated — and not very credible — alibi. Employing the above test, if the defendant has a prior narcotics conviction, the defense may be justified in calling him. On the other hand, if the defendant has a prior conviction for murder, calling him would in most cases be tactically unwise. In the latter situation, calling him would probably be at least as damaging as the adverse speculation from not calling him.

If the use of less-than-strong evidence cannot be justified under either rationale discussed above, and the advocate has no strong evidence available, then he should not present a defense case. By doing so, he would be incurring costs of overtrying by signaling a concern about the strength of his opponent's case. Where the defense evidence is not strong, the advocate, by definition, would not be reaping any benefit to counterbalance those costs.

---

[15] We note that the use of other party-associated defense evidence raises equivalent considerations. As in the foregoing section, however, the presentation in this section is simplified by limiting the discussion to the case of the defendant.

General Observations on the Decision to Defend

Because the jury is apt to view a defendant's failure to put on any evidence as an indication that he has *no* defense, it might appear logical to conclude that there should be a strong presumption in favor of putting on a defense. We believe that any such presumption would be unwarranted. Each case must be analyzed on its own merit, based on the above considerations, with no presumption either way. As former prosecutors, the authors recall many cases that were lost by defense lawyers who, instead of resting without putting on a case, followed a thin government case with a weak defense case.

A case tried by one of the authors illustrates this danger. Two police officers observed packets of narcotics being thrown out of the windows of an automobile containing five occupants. The officers retrieved the narcotics and then stopped the vehicle. A search of the vehicle uncovered no more drugs, but various items of drug paraphernalia were recovered. Although the officers could not specifically link any one individual to the packets or paraphernalia, a heavy aroma of phencyclidine-laced marijuana permeated the automobile. Accordingly, the officers arrested all five defendants. At trial, after the government rested, the prosecutor felt certain that the defense would put on no evidence and that the jury, after hearing arguments and instructions, would quickly return from its deliberations with five not guilty verdicts. To his surprise, however, each of the five defendants opted to testify. Each stated that he was certain that no one had tossed drugs from the vehicle. Some of the defendants had prior convictions, and their testimony, viewed jointly, was very unpersuasive. The jury rapidly returned guilty verdicts against all five defendants. The consensus of those viewing the trial was that they would have won had they not put on a case.

The Decision Whether to Rebut

The purpose of rebuttal is to present evidence to refute evidence previously presented by an opponent.[16] Specifically, rebuttal evidence is said to be evidence used to "'explain, repel, counteract, or disprove the evidence of the adverse party.'"[17] When the advocate is considering use of rebuttal evidence for any of these purposes, he should employ the rule that counsels the use of discrediting evidence that outweighs sponsorship costs.[18]

In assessing his costs of overtrying, he should analyze all of the evidence previously presented in the case — his own as well as that of his opponent — to determine the impact of his rebuttal evidence. This requires two principal inquiries. The first involves the strength of the defense case in light of his own preceding case. If the defense case was comparatively weak, a given item of discrediting rebuttal evidence is less apt to qualify for use. The jury will wonder why the advocate went to the effort to rebut a seemingly weak case and will be apt to find it significant that he felt a need to do so. Moreover, the advocate may lose the ability to assert with credibility that the defense case was so weak that no rebuttal evidence was necessary.

The second inquiry involves the strength of the rebuttal evidence. The greater its impact in undermining the defendant's evidence, the less likely it is that the advocate will suffer costs of overtrying. As previously indicated,[19] an advocate is *expected* to marshal evidence that significantly undermines his opponent's case.

---

[16] *See, e.g.*, M. Graham, *Handbook of Federal Evidence* § 611.13, at 539 (West 1986); 4 S. Gard, *Jones on Evidence* § 24:1, at 74 (Lawyers Co-Op. Pub. Co. 6th ed. 1972); VI J. Wigmore, *Evidence* § 1873, at 678 (Little, Brown & Co. Chadbourn rev. 1979).

[17] *United States v. Mallis*, 467 F.2d 567, 569 (3d Cir. 1972), *quoting Luttrell v. United States*, 320 F.2d 462, 464 (5th Cir. 1963).

[18] *See* Chapter Four, page 107, *supra*.

[19] *See* Chapter Two, page 33, *supra*.

It should be noted that where the rebuttal evidence actually *favors* the advocate's own case and does not simply undermine an item of the opponent's previously presented evidence, the advocate can benefit from the favorable value of the evidence without incurring the higher sponsorship costs of using that evidence in his case-in-chief. A case tried by one of the authors illustrates the point.

An accomplice to a bank holdup had plea-bargained for lenient treatment and had identified the defendant as the "wheelman" or getaway-car driver in the incident. At trial, the prosecutor opted to call the accomplice in his case-in-chief. The case ended in a mistrial when the jury, after several days of deliberations, was unable to reach a verdict.

On retrial, a different prosecutor (the author) tried the case. Even though the other evidence of guilt was not substantial, the new prosecutor chose not to call the accomplice in his case-in-chief. After the defendant testified and denied any role in the holdup, the prosecutor determined that the ability of the accomplice's testimony to undermine the defendant's version outweighed the cost of using him and thus called him as a rebuttal witness.

In summation, defense counsel, who had vigorously cross-examined the accomplice, argued at length that the accomplice's testimony could not be trusted. The prosecutor responded in his rebuttal argument that his case did not depend on the accomplice, but only on the evidence in the case-in-chief, and that the accomplice was called only because he so effectively undercut defendant's testimony.

A guilty verdict was returned in under an hour. Defense counsel, in discussion with the prosecutor, attributed the verdict to the fact that the previous prosecutor, by calling the accomplice in the case-in-chief, had made his whole case depend on whether the jury credited that witness. Thus, while defense counsel's focus on the accomplice in his summation was effective in the first trial, it appeared weak and desperate in the second trial.

This case illustrates that an advocate who calls a witness in his case-in-chief is apt to incur higher costs of overtrying than when he calls that same witness in rebuttal. In the above case, although the second prosecutor incurred sponsorship costs, those costs were less than those incurred by the first prosecutor. Specifically, when the second prosecutor called the accomplice in rebuttal, the jury might have given less weight to the prosecutor's case-in-chief, reasoning that the prosecutor was concerned that the defendant's testimony had rendered his evidence-in-chief inadequate. Nonetheless, this was still a lesser cost than the first prosecutor's implicit concern, reflected in his decision to call the accomplice in his case-in-chief, that his other evidence was insufficient to convict even *prior to* the negative impact of the defendant's testimony. The second prosecutor, by holding the accomplice for rebuttal, was still able to argue with some credibility that his other evidence, standing alone, was sufficient to convict.[20]

It will be recalled that in Chapter Four, we set forth a high risk strategy of withholding strong evidence in the expectation that the advocate will be able to use it in rebuttal.[21] While the benefits of such a strategy may be substantial, the advocate must realistically assess the likelihood that the court will rule that the evidence in question does not qualify as rebuttal evidence. Many courts are reluctant to permit the advocate to use evidence in rebuttal that would have qualified for admission in the advocate's case-in-chief.[22] Thus, the advocate who withholds evidence for use in rebuttal should assure himself that he

[20] The advocate must, of course, recognize that in holding a witness for rebuttal, he incurs the risk of not being able to use the witness at all if his opponent decides not to put on a case or if the judge rules that the withheld witness's testimony does not qualify as rebuttal evidence.

[21] *See* pages 71-76, *supra.*

[22] *See, e.g., Jones on Evidence, supra* note 16, at § 24:1, at 75 (citing authorities for "[t]he rule ... that a party may not withhold part of his proof and introduce it as rebuttal instead of offering it as part of his case in chief").

will have a supportable rationale for how such evidence will qualify as rebuttal evidence.

Finally, the advocate must not use less-than-strong evidence in rebuttal where he lacks a rationale for its use based upon undermining his opponent's evidence. On the other hand, if the advocate finds at the end of the defense case that he has *strong* evidence for his own case that cannot be said to undermine his opponent's evidence, he should consider whether he can use such evidence in rebuttal. Some courts are liberal in allowing the use of evidence in rebuttal, even though it could have been used in the case-in-chief.[23]

*****

The Five Steps of Sponsorship Theory for Evidence Selection

This chapter and the three preceding it have discussed the issues involved in the evaluation of evidence and in the selection of what, if any, evidence to introduce. The following chapters turn to a discussion of the relevance of sponsorship theory to each phase of the trial, from jury selection and opening statement to closing argument. Before doing so, however, we believe it useful to summarize the process of evidence selection. The various decisions that must be made can be summarized in five steps:

1. Identify the disputed and the undisputed issues.
2. For undisputed issues, use only the minimum evidence necessary to satisfy *prima facie* legal burdens, if any, unless the evidence bearing on the undisputed issue is party-associated with your side, goes to the foundation

[23] *See, e.g., Weiss v. Chrysler Motors Corp.*, 515 F.2d 449, 457-458 (2d Cir. 1975) (noting that the trial court's discretion to exclude evidence that could have been offered in the case-in-chief "should be tempered greatly where the probative value of proffered evidence is potentially high and where such evidence ... was unnecessary for the plaintiff to establish its *prima facie* case").

of the case, and the risk of adverse jury speculation from omitting the evidence outweighs the harm in using it (with sponsorship costs considered).

3. Evaluate the strength of available evidence on the disputed issues to identify your strong evidence, namely, your favorable evidence that outweighs the costs of introduction, efforts, and overtrying.
4. Use all strong evidence on disputed issues except in rare instances where you opt in favor of the high-risk strategy of omitting evidence in reliance on the expectation that your opponent will later use it or enable you to use it in rebuttal.
5. Use no less-than-strong evidence on disputed issues unless:
   a. the cost of apparent efforts in omitting the evidence would outweigh the sponsorship costs of its use plus the opponent's saved sponsorship costs,

   or

   b. the evidence is being used to undermine evidence previously presented by your opponent and the resulting reduction in the probative value of the opponent's evidence outweighs the sponsorship costs of its use,

   or

   c. the evidence is party-associated with your side, would be viewed by the jury as materially bearing on the disputed issue if omitted, and the risk of adverse jury speculation from omitting the evidence outweighs the harm in using it (with sponsorship costs considered).

Utilizing the foregoing five steps will enable the advocate to avoid a common fault of many trial lawyers: using too much evidence. In our experience, many practitioners select evidence using a different set of assumptions. Those assumptions are: (1) there are no costs associated with the use of evidence, or at least none significant enough to affect the decision whether to use it; (2) the jury might rule against the advocate if the evidence is not used, even where such evidence does not relate to any disputed issue; (3) an argument that the opponent could have used the evidence will not relieve the advocate from the need to introduce it; and (4) given the foregoing, there is no need for a precise evaluation of the strength of available evidence bearing on the disputed issues. This strategy results in an approach to evidence selection that is far more inclusive than the above rules counseled by sponsorship theory. As a result, cases are overtried and unnecessary burdens are assumed.

We must confess the source of our familiarity with this alternative approach to evidence selection. The approach is consistent with the one that we applied rigorously in a number of our early trials — strong cases that we believe were unnecessarily lost for the reasons set forth in this book.

Part Three
The Trial

7

Jury Selection and Opening Statement

This chapter addresses two topics: jury selection, commonly known as voir dire, and opening statements. These portions of the trial are the first exposure that an advocate will have to the jurors who will be deciding the case. As the foregoing chapters of this book have made clear, the jurors will be monitoring the advocate's every word and deed from the moment they file into the courtroom for jury selection. This chapter provides guidance on how, during these early parts of the trial, the advocate can advance his prospects for obtaining a favorable verdict. It also emphasizes how the advocate can harm those prospects by ill-considered and careless statements and actions.

Voir Dire

Voir dire is that portion of the trial where the jury is selected from a panel of prospective jurors drawn from the community in which the court is located. From the perspective of the administration of justice, the purpose of voir dire is to ensure, to the extent possible, that the individuals ultimately selected to hear the case will be able to render a fair and impartial verdict. The mechanism for accomplishing this goal is to place the entire panel of prospective jurors under oath and to examine them on matters bearing on their ability to decide the case impartially. The foremost example of such examination is questioning designed to identify those individuals who are personally acquainted with one of the parties to the case or who have knowledge of the dispute and have formed preconceptions concerning it.

The perspective of the advocate is a different one. His job is *not* to ensure that his opponent's side of the dispute is sympathetically heard; that is his opponent's job. The advocate's responsibility is to ensure that *his* client's side of the dispute is given fair consideration. Thus, the most critical task for the advocate to accomplish in voir dire is to eliminate from the panel those individuals who are apt to be unsympathetic to his client's contentions.[1] In order to accomplish this critical screening task, the advocate must be alert to gather whatever information he can about the prospective jurors. Accordingly, he should avail himself of any opportunity to collect information on such matters as a potential juror's age, location of residence, and occupation.

To illustrate the foregoing, assume that an advocate represents a discharged employee claiming wrongful termination. The advocate might conclude, for example, that

[1] Some commentators have suggested an additional goal for the advocate to pursue during voir dire: To impart selected information to the potential jurors in the hope that they will be favorably "indoctrinated" to the advocate's position in the case. *See, e.g.*, J. Jeans, *Trial Advocacy* §§ 7.19-7.22, at 191-195 (West 1975). Because such indoctrination involves "communicat[ing] information rather than collect[ing] it," J. Tanford, *The Trial Process: Law, Tactics and Ethics* 240 (The Michie Co. 1983), the propriety of such an undertaking is questionable. *See generally* M. Berger, J. Mitchell, & R. Clark, *Trial Advocacy: Planning, Analysis, & Strategy* 180 (Little, Brown & Co. 1989) (discussing legislative efforts to curtail the practice). In our view, opening statement, not voir dire, is the proper time for the advocate to educate the jury concerning his position in the case.

his client will receive a more sympathetic hearing from a juror who is an employee rather than an employer.[2] If he reaches this conclusion, he should seek to identify potential jurors who are employees.

In some jurisdictions, basic biographical data concerning the jurors is supplied to the advocates in written form at the outset of the jury selection process. More often than not, however, the advocate must rely on answers to specific questions posed to the entire panel and to questions posed to individual jurors. Questions of this nature may include, in the appropriate case, such things as whether the prospective juror was ever a party to a civil suit (and if so, the circumstances of the case); whether he has any close relatives in the law enforcement field; and whether he has ever been a victim of or witness to a crime.

In sum, it is important for an advocate to screen jurors for basic sympathies regarding the nature of the dispute, such as whether a prospective juror is likely to be "pro-defense." Beyond this, the advocate concerned about a specific weakness in his case may want to eliminate jurors based on how they are apt to react to that weakness once it is brought out at trial. The trial tactics literature generally encourages the advocate to question jurors about the weaknesses of his case.[3] The advocate, however, should

---

[2] Substantive guidance on determinations of this sort is beyond the scope of this book. The reader, however, may consult the extensive body of literature providing advice on selecting the optimal jurors for a particular case. *See, e.g.*, 1 *Goldstein Trial Techniques* §§ 9.44-9.48, at 9-55 to 9-58 (Callaghan & Co. 3d ed. 1984) (discussing the preferred sex, marital status, age, nationality, physical make-up, and occupation of jurors for plaintiffs and defendants in personal injury and criminal cases); *id.*, § 9.30, at 9-42 (similar discussion from standpoint of defendants in personal injury cases); Suggs & Sales, *Using Communication Cues to Evaluate Prospective Jurors During the Voir Dire,* 20 Ariz. L. Rev. 629 (1978); Frederick, *Jury Behavior: A Psychologist Examines Jury Selection,* 5 Ohio No. U. L. Rev. 571 (1978).

[3] *See, e.g.*, Tanford, *supra* note 1, at 216, 227-230 (quoting authorities on the benefits of bringing out in voir dire, *inter alia,* a client's criminal record, the accident record of a plaintiff in a negligence case, and various other unfavorable matters); Berger, Mitchell & Clark, *supra* note 1, at 206-207 (noting the importance of screening jurors by exposing them to weaknesses in the advocate's case).

recognize the dangers involved in such a strategy. It is obviously in the advocate's interest to eliminate prospective jurors who would be inclined to give a weakness in his case undue weight. The tactical dilemma faced by the advocate is whether his case will be harmed if the weakness is raised during voir dire. The risk is that the weakness will be given such prominence that the advocate will later have difficulty arguing at trial that it is not significant and does not bear on the verdict.

The resolution of this dilemma involves a difficult weighing process. On the one hand, the advocate must consider the benefit that he will derive from identifying and eliminating potential jurors who will be more apt to hold the weakness against his case. On the other hand, he must consider the detriment to his case from parading his weakness before the potential jurors.

With respect to the potential benefit of disclosing a weakness, the advocate must be realistic about his prospects for identifying potential jurors who are most apt to hold the weakness against his case. In our experience, the effectiveness of voir dire as a mechanism for detecting such predispositions is questionable. It is certainly the case that direct and pointed questions about a person's ability to render a fair verdict are unlikely to identify potentially biased jurors. Unless they are deliberately trying to be excused from jury service, few people will directly admit in front of a large group of strangers that they hold any biases or prejudices or that they could not decide a case fairly. Occasionally, however, an advocate can craft a question in a more subtle way, so that he can identify individuals who are likely to be unsympathetic to his case.

To illustrate the foregoing, assume a criminal prosecution in which the victim was shot while trying to collect on a debt owed by the alleged assailant's thirteen-year-old brother. Assume further that the reason for the debt was that the victim had supplied narcotics to the brother. Finally, assume that the victim has a long record of drug arrests and convictions. The prosecutor must decide whether he will benefit from having the panel of prospective jurors examined regarding their attitudes about convicted drug dealers. Plainly, many of the potential jurors are apt to be sympathetic to the defendant for his understandable anger at the victim's having supplied the defendant's younger brother with narcotics. Nonetheless, few potential jurors will be apt to come forward when asked in voir dire whether they would be unable to render a fair verdict given the circumstances surrounding the shooting.

A more indirect question might achieve better results. For example, the potential jurors could be asked simply whether they have very strong feelings against narcotics dealers. The advocate can make note of those with affirmative responses. Of course, with a question that broad, the advocate might elicit an affirmative response from the majority of the panel members. A follow-up question of whether those holding such strong feelings would be unable to render a fair verdict in a case involving a drug dealer might yield few or no affirmative responses. Thus, it is unclear whether voir dire concerning the unsympathetic victim will yield useful information.

In sum, in the appropriate circumstances, it may be possible for an advocate to make some headway in identifying persons on the jury panel who are predisposed to hold a weakness against his case. The task is a difficult one, however, and will depend on the nature of the weakness and on the advocate's ability to craft a question that will yield useful information.

Even if an advocate believes that he might be able to identify some potentially biased jurors by highlighting a weakness, this does not necessarily mean that such a strategy should be followed. The advocate must be alert to the fact that whether he or the judge asks the questions implicating the weakness,[4] that weakness will have been given

[4] Jurisdictions vary in their approaches to whether the judge or the attorney is responsible for conducting voir dire examination. In a small number of jurisdic-

prominence at a very early stage of the proceedings. The advocate's later attempts to downplay the significance of that weakness will be hampered by this fact.

If the advocate himself conducts the examination concerning the weakness, he makes the implicit concession that the weakness is a matter of such importance that it must be addressed even before his opponent has raised it. This is the same dilemma faced by an advocate who volunteers a weakness during the trial itself. In the above drug case, for example, a prosecutor who highlights the victim's criminal background and his involvement in a drug transaction with the defendant's brother is apt to convey the message that those facts bear on the defendant's guilt or innocence. Since the prosecutor himself singled out those facts even during the voir dire, he will have difficulty arguing later that such facts are irrelevant and have nothing to do with the case.

Furthermore, even if the judge conducts the examination raising the weakness, the advocate suffers from the fact that his opponent is thereby relieved from raising it for the first time. As noted in Chapter Two,[5] an attorney, by introducing evidence that is favorable to his case, makes an implicit statement that he is relying on that evidence to win. Thus, in the foregoing murder example, if defense counsel is the first to raise the weakness, such as during the cross-examination of the victim, *he* will have to convince the jury that the fact is somehow relevant. Put another way, *he* will suffer the sponsorship costs. If the *judge* highlights the weakness during voir dire, the oppo-

---

tions, the attorneys have complete control over the questioning. In others, including many federal courts, the judge conducts the entire voir dire, although he will consider asking written questions submitted by the attorneys. Still other jurisdictions have a practice in which the judge conducts general interrogation and then turns the questioning over to the attorneys. *See generally* Tanford, *supra* note 1, at 192-194 (discussing the various voir dire practices); T. Mauet, *Fundamentals of Trial Techniques* § 2.3, at 25-27 (Little, Brown & Co. 2d ed. 1988) (same).

[5] *See* page 37, *supra.*

nent will likewise be relieved of some of the burden of showing that the weakness bears on the verdict.

To summarize, there may be a considerable cost in bringing out a weakness in one's own case during voir dire. Unless the advocate foresees a substantial likelihood that he will be able to eliminate jurors likely to be predisposed against his case, he should avoid highlighting a weakness during voir dire. Instead, he should let his opponent bring out the weakness during the trial.

Opening Statement

Opening statement represents the advocate's first chance to give the jury a detailed overview of his case. From the jury's perspective, it provides the opportunity to hear a summary of the *best* case supporting the advocate's position. As will be seen, sponsorship theory is fully applicable to opening statements, and the content of the remarks must be planned with the utmost care. The first part of this section provides guidance in crafting an effective opening statement.

Although plaintiffs' attorneys and prosecutors have no choice over *whether* to give an opening statement (they must), or *when* to do so (it must be at the outset of the trial), defense attorneys are not subject to the same restrictions. The second part of this section addresses the questions of whether, and when, a defendant's opening statement should be given.

Content of the Opening Statement

The content of an opening statement is very important for several reasons. To begin with, as noted above, this is the jury's first real introduction to the advocate's case, and it will be listening carefully to hear his best case scenario. It will assume that the case is no better — and perhaps much worse — than he has stated it. Moreover, opening statement provides the advocate with the opportunity to identify his theory of the case. This will assist the jury in following the evidence that he later introduces.

The jurors may not be the only ones listening carefully to the advocate's opening statement. If his opponent is savvy, he will be paying attention for any alternative or inconsistent theories that the advocate may have mentioned. He will also be listening to the advocate's promises, and will later take the advocate to task for any shortcomings in his evidence.

The following sections provide specific guidance in crafting an opening statement. The principles are straightforward and follow directly from sponsorship theory.

Organization Based on the Case Theory

An advocate should organize his opening statement around his interpretation of the facts, namely, his theory of the case. His theory should be highlighted early in his presentation, and he should attempt to show how each witness and each piece of evidence advance that theory.[6] For example, defense counsel in a contract case should know at an early time — well before his opening statement — whether his theory is mistake, duress, accord and satisfaction, incapacity, failure of consideration, or some other defense. His opening statement should link each key piece of evidence to that defense.

Discussion of the Evidence

The plaintiff's attorney or prosecutor who has learned his opponent's defense should not identify it for him in

[6] *Accord, e.g.,* R. Carlson & E. Imwinkelried, *Dynamics of Trial Practice* § 5.5(C), at 68 (West 1989). As we explained in Chapter Two, page 50, *supra,* an advocate who presents inconsistent theories is inviting trouble. There may also be dangers in advancing alternative theories, even though they are not inconsistent. *See* Chapter Two, pages 50-52, *supra.*

opening statement. Rather, he should simply highlight the *facts* that weigh in his own favor on the disputed issues. He should also provide at least some discussion of evidence on each element of his *prima facie* legal burdens, even if his opponent is not likely to dispute a particular element. The jury, which is unfamiliar with the case, expects to hear from the plaintiff's attorney or prosecutor about the entire incident, not just about the parts in dispute. The plaintiff's attorney or prosecutor who focuses selectively on the facts of the case that bear on the issue that he expects to be disputed would be delivering a disjointed presentation that the jury would have difficulty following. Indeed, in some jurisdictions, the court will enter a directed verdict against an advocate who has a burden of proof if his opening statement does not include a discussion of the evidence supporting each element of the claim or defense, whether disputed or not.[7] By contrast, defense counsel should forcefully highlight only those facts that advance his specific defense.

When discussing evidence bearing on disputed issues, the advocate must be attentive to the need to describe all of the strong evidence that he plans to introduce. This is important, since the jury expects to hear a summary of his case in its best light.[8]

At the same time, the advocate should obviously not identify any testimony or piece of evidence unless he is certain that he *can* and *will* introduce it. Indeed, it is improper for an advocate to refer in opening statement to evidence that he does not intend to introduce or that will be ruled inadmissible.[9] From a tactical viewpoint, the ad-

[7] *See generally* Tanford, *supra* note 1, at 274 (citing authorities).

[8] *Accord, e.g.,* R. Aron, J. Fast & R. Klein, *Trial Communication Skills* § 21.04, at 243 (Shephard's/McGraw-Hill, Inc. 1986) (discussing importance of stressing strengths in opening statement).

[9] *See, e.g.,* 1 *A.B.A. Standards Relating to the Prosecution Function and the Defense Function* (1971), § 5.5, at 119 (providing that it is improper to refer to evidence in opening statement "unless [the advocate has] a good faith and reasonable basis for believing that such evidence will be tendered and admitted in evidence"); *see also id.,* § 7.4, at 165-166.

vocate's later failure to introduce such evidence will almost certainly be highlighted during the opponent's summation.[10]

With regard to less-than-strong evidence, since sponsorship theory holds that the advocate generally should not introduce such evidence during his own case, he obviously should not discuss such evidence in his opening statement.[11] An opening statement is designed to outline evidence that the advocate plans to introduce, not evidence that he has decided to omit. Even if he decides, however, that he must introduce less-than-strong evidence, he should avoid highlighting such evidence in opening statement. The jury will tend to place exaggerated weight on such evidence and will, as a result, pay insufficient attention to his discussion of the strong evidence.

Highlighting any harmful matter is destructive to the advocate's presentation. To illustrate the point, picture twelve newly empaneled jurors in a stabbing case involving a claim of self-defense. Assume that the prosecutor, during his opening statement, tells them: "You will hear evidence that the defendant stabbed the victim with all his

---

[10] Techniques for highlighting an opponent's failure to keep his promises in opening statement are discussed in Chapter Twelve, *infra,* pages 273-274.

[11] Virtually all commentators take the opposite approach and uniformly urge advocates to identify their weaknesses in opening statements. *See, e.g.,* S. Goldberg, *The First Trial: Where Do I Sit? What Do I Say?* at 204 (West 1982) (pertinent excerpt set forth in Chapter Four, page 96, note 42, *supra*); Mauet, *supra* note 4, § 3.3 at 50-51 (urging advocates to volunteer weaknesses in opening statement if such weaknesses are known to the opponent); J. Sonsteng, R. Haydock & J. Boyd, *The Trial Book — A Total System for the Preparation and Presentation of a Case* § 5.5, at 193-194 (West 1984) ("An open and candid disclosure of [weaknesses during opening statement] will usually increase the sincerity and credibility of the attorney and will often reduce the impact of the opposition's tactics."); S. Schweitzer, *Cyclopedia of Trial Practice* § 181, at 493 (Lawyers Co-op. Pub. Co. 2d ed. 1970) (providing sample opening statement showing how to bring out weaknesses); 1 S. Gazan, *Encyclopedia of Trial Strategy and Tactics* 93 (Prentice-Hall, Inc. 1962) (advising the advocate to "take the jury into your confidence by telling them that the proof will show that your client is a gambler or a bartender or a race track tout (or any other occupation against which a juror may have a prejudice) ..."); Aron, Fast & Klein, *supra* note 8, § 21.04, at 243; *id.,* § 21.10, at 248.

might," and "you will hear as well that the victim was a pretty mean guy." At the outset of the presentation of evidence, the jury will not have made up its mind about whether the defendant used all his might to stab the victim. One fact, however, will already have been established beyond all doubt: The victim was "pretty mean" and perhaps more vicious than the prosecutor has suggested. Moreover, because the jury will be apt to view the two statements together as, on balance, self-serving,[12] the prosecutor's attempt to gain credibility by disclosing the weakness will most likely backfire.[13]

The advocate's opening statement should also be screened to eliminate all neutral matter. Thus, the advocate should avoid *all* remarks that do not bear directly on why the evidence supports his version of the facts.

Many advocates devote considerable attention to discussions of neutral legal principles, involving subjects such as the purposes of an opening statement and the lack of evidentiary value in the advocates' remarks. For example, one leading commentator[14] provides the following sample of how to begin an opening statement:

> As the court has told you, this part of the trial is called the opening statements. Often the evidence in a case is presented in little bits and pieces and it's sometimes difficult to understand how each piece fits into the case. For that reason we are permitted to tell you what the overall picture will be now, so that each piece of evidence you hear will make sense when you hear it.

---

[12] *See* Chapter Four, *supra*, page 99.

[13] For this reason, contrary to the suggestion of one commentator, Schweitzer, *supra* note 11, § 181, at 493, if the advocate is concerned, for example, about the fact that his witness's ability to observe was affected by his having had three drinks, it is counterproductive to disclose the drinking and then assert that the witness was *not* intoxicated. The jury will fully credit the fact that the witness had at least three drinks, but it will be highly skeptical of the advocate's claim that the witness was sober.

[14] Mauet, *supra* note 4, § 3.5, at 65.

Contrary to the numerous trial manuals that urge such an approach,[15] our view is that such discussions generally serve no useful purpose and should ordinarily be avoided. Remarks of this sort in no way explain why a verdict should be rendered in the advocate's favor. In fact, there is at least a theoretical risk that the jury will view such discussion as "filler" to disguise the lack of evidence supporting the advocate's position. It follows *a fortiori* that an advocate should never undermine his opening statement by self-effacing statements concerning his own bias or lack of personal knowledge.[16] The jury already views the advocate as a "hired gun," and such statements only heighten the problem.

In sum, the focus of the opening statement should be on the strong evidence that the advocate plans to introduce at trial. Introductory and generalized remarks should be avoided. Similarly, the advocate should not understate his case or highlight his bias as an advocate. Finally, while the opening statement must not be argumentative,[17] the advocate should nonetheless strive to show the jury why his side plainly deserves to win the case.

---

[15] *See, e.g.,* 1 *Goldstein Trial Techniques* §§ 10.16-10.22, at 10-16 to 10-21 (Callaghan & Co. 3d ed. 1984) (urging extensive introductory remarks and providing examples); *see generally* Tanford, *supra* note 1, at 277 nn. 52, 54 (citing authorities).

[16] *Accord,* A. Julien, *Opening Statements* §§ 1.12, 1.13, at 1-16, 1-18 (Callaghan & Co. 1980) (calling the advocate who uses self-effacing statements "Mr. Fairness" and noting that such an advocate "is fair to everybody except his own client"). *Contra, e.g.,* J. Appleman, *Preparation and Trial* 190 (Coiner Pub., Ltd. 1967) ("It must be explained to the jury that you were not present at the scene, and your understanding of some of the facts may prove to be in error...."); *id.* at 792 ("It is often well ... to admit candidly to the jury that your views are probably biased."); *id.* (urging that the jury be told that the advocate, "through [his] intense study of the case, may have gotten too close to it and may be mistaken").

[17] *See, e.g.,* Y. Kamisar, W. LaFave & J. Israel, *Modern Criminal Procedure* 1346 (West 6th ed. 1986); 1 Goldstein, *supra* note 15, § 10.10, at 10-13.

The Importance of Enthusiasm

Opening statement is no time for modesty or understatement.[18] The advocate's delivery must be enthusiastic and confident.[19] Although the jury will not fully credit the advocate's characterization of his evidence, that characterization is nonetheless the starting point for the jury's discounting process. Thus, the jury's skepticism should not lead the advocate to abandon his efforts to persuade: if he ranks his case as a ten out of ten, the jury may decide that it is a seven, but if, in a deliberate effort to understate his case (as some commentators urge),[20] he describes it as a seven, the jury will surely rank it a four or less.[21] For this reason, we find no merit in the advice of some authorities that jurors should be told to "keep their minds open" and "not to reach a decision until the court has instructed them on the law."[22] Of course, we do not recommend or suggest that an advocate should misrepresent the strength of his case. Deliberately inflating the strength of a case may constitute unethical conduct.[23]

---

[18] *Contra,* Schweitzer, *supra* note 11, § 176, at 483, 506 ("[U]nderstate your case. It is proof of your sincerity and integrity."); Sonsteng, Haydock & Boyd, *supra* note 11, at 195 ("Understatement can be a useful credibility-building device for an opening statement presentation.").

[19] *Cf.* I *Corinthians* 14:8 ("If the trumpet give an uncertain sound, who shall prepare himself to the battle?"); G. Kennedy, *The Art of Persuasion in Greece* 144 (Princeton Univ. Press 1963) (stating that a speaker's "intense earnestness ... is the most effective way to carry off sophistic arguments").

[20] *See* note 18, *supra.*

[21] *See, e.g.,* Carlson & Imwinkelried, *supra* note 6, § 3.3(D), at 32 (noting that "jurors tend to discount what the attorneys say during trial").

[22] Schweitzer, *supra* note 11, § 187, at 506.

[23] *See* Model Code of Professional Responsibility, DR 7-102(A)(5) (an attorney may not "[k]nowingly make a false statement of law or fact"); Tanford, *supra* note 1, at 289. *See also* Chapter Twelve, *infra,* pages 273-274 (noting arguments an attorney can make when his opponent has not fulfilled his promises in opening statement). Furthermore, gross inflation or overstatement can result in increased costs of introduction (namely, significantly increased jury discounting of the advocate's claims).

The Beginning and the Ending of the Opening Statement

It is critical for the advocate to begin and end his opening statement on a strong note. He should start by immediately summarizing, in a sentence or two, what his evidence will show. For instance, in a medical malpractice case, plaintiff's attorney may begin his opening statement as follows:

> The evidence in this case will show that on January 10, 1987, Mr. Jones suffered permanent brain damage as a result of the defendant's carelessness and negligence in failing to detect Mr. Jones's brain tumor.

At the end of the opening statement, after summarizing the evidence, the advocate should return to this theme in a manner similar to the following:

> After you have heard all the evidence, you will see that it points to only one conclusion: that the defendant is liable for his negligence in failing to detect my client's brain tumor.

In sum, the advocate must portray for the jury throughout his opening statement — and particularly at the beginning and the end — an aura of complete confidence in the strength of his case. As we have noted,[24] the advocate is viewed as a "hired gun" who is expected to present his case in its best light. If he appears ambivalent or troubled about his position, he cannot expect the jury to be enthusiastic about it in the jury room.

Timing of the Defense Opening Statement

A threshold issue for a defense attorney is whether to make an opening statement or to waive it altogether. We agree with those commentators who note that there is

[24] *See* Chapter Two, page 19, *supra.*

virtually never any reason for a defense counsel to waive his opening statement.[25] At a minimum, an opening statement enables the defense to emphasize that the evidence warrants a verdict in its favor. This opportunity should not be forfeited unless there are compelling reasons to do so in a particular case.

The more difficult issue — in jurisdictions that give attorneys the choice — involves the *timing* of the defense opening statement. In a number of jurisdictions, a defense counsel must present his opening statement (if he intends to make one) directly after the prosecutor's or plaintiff's opening statement, unless the court, in its discretion, permits defense counsel to reserve his opening statement until after his opponent has rested.[26] Other jurisdictions, however, leave the decision to the advocate. Some trial manuals, citing the "primacy" and "recency" theory — namely, that individuals remember best what they hear first and what they hear last — advise the defense attorney to give his opening statement immediately after the government's (or plaintiff's) opening statement.[27] Most defense lawyers in fact follow this advice.[28]

---

[25] *See, e.g.*, 1 Goldstein, *supra* note 15, § 10.09, at 10-12; Mauet, *supra* note 4, § 3.3 at 51; Tanford, *supra* note 1, at 286.

[26] *See, e.g.*, W. LaFave & J. Israel, *Criminal Procedure* § 23.3, at 875 (West 1985); 1 Goldstein, *supra* note 15, § 10.09, at 10-12 to 10-13.

[27] *See, e.g.*, K. Hegland, *Trial and Practice Skills* 109 (West 1978) ("[T]here is real pressure on the defense to say something early on. He who gets to tell his side first has a great advantage. Psychologists call it 'primacy' or 'preemption'. . . ."); P. Bergman, *Trial Advocacy* 250 (West 1979) (urging such a strategy); F. Bailey & H. Rothblatt, *Successful Techniques for Criminal Trials* § 9:2, at 242 (Lawyers Co-op. Pub. Co. 1985) ("In some jurisdictions, defense counsel is permitted to reserve his opening statement until the conclusion of the prosecution's case. This is not usually the best policy. As a general rule you will do best to take the sting out of the prosecutor's opening at once.") (citations omitted). *Cf.* Tanford, *supra* note 1, at 286 (noting that in most cases, the defense opening should immediately follow the opponent's opening, but giving arguments for deferring the defense opening); Mauet, *supra* note 4, § 3.3, at 51-52 (noting occasions where deferring opening statement benefits the defense).

[28] *See, e.g.*, Mauet, *supra* note 4, § 3.3, at 51 (noting common practice of defense attorneys).

Whatever the merit in the primacy/recency theory, there are several advantages to giving an opening statement immediately after the plaintiff's or prosecutor's statement. To begin with, the defense avoids giving the jury the impression that he waited to hear his opponent's evidence before deciding on his defense. Although we have found that the risk of this is not substantial,[29] it is clearly a factor to consider. Moreover, this approach allows the jury to think about the defense as it listens critically to the prosecutor's or plaintiff's presentation.

There are, however, strong reasons for deferring the opening statement until after the opponent has rested. Only then will the defense fully know what the plaintiff's (or government's) case is about and what the best defense strategy will be. At the same time, such an approach avoids giving the opponent insight into the defense theory, thus preventing him from organizing his presentation and selecting evidence with that information in mind. Of course, if defense counsel is sure that he is not going to present a defense, then he must give his opening statement immediately after his opponent's statement, or else he will lose the opportunity altogether.

The worst strategy, in our view, is for a defense counsel who plans to put on a case to stand up, right after the prosecutor's or plaintiff's opening statement, and say basically nothing of substance. We have heard the following type of argument made by numerous criminal defense lawyers who are uncertain at the outset of the trial as to what evidence they will be introducing:

> Although the defendant is not required to present a defense, we plan to do so. We will show you that the

[29] At least in the case of a criminal defendant, any suggestion to this effect by the prosecutor would almost certainly be improper. *Cf. Brooks v. Tennessee,* 406 U.S. 605 (1972) (striking down statute requiring that if a defendant wanted to testify, he had to do so first; court rejected arguments that statute was necessary to ensure a defendant's honesty); *Sherrod v. United States,* 478 A.2d 644, 647 (D.C. 1984) (improper for prosecutor to comment on defendant's decision to testify as last defense witness).

> government's case has numerous gaps and does not establish proof beyond a reasonable doubt. We therefore ask you to keep an open mind during the government's presentation. Thank you.

This type of opening statement accomplishes nothing. Even assuming that the primacy/recency theory is valid, the only point that the jury will remember is that the defense plans to put on a case. Had defense counsel waited, he would have been able to fill in the details and show just how he planned to attack the government's case.

In sum, defense counsel's decision whether to postpone his opening statement until after his opponent has rested entails a variety of considerations. While the common practice is *not* to reserve the opening statement, there may sometimes be compelling reasons to do so.

8

Direct Examination

It is difficult to overstate the importance of direct examination. Most commentators view it as the most consequential part of the trial.[1] This chapter demonstrates how sponsorship theory can bolster the effectiveness of direct examination. Specifically, it provides guidance on seven topics: (1) the importance of anticipating the cross-examination of the witness; (2) planning the content of the direct examination; (3) the manner of conducting direct examination; (4) preparing witnesses for direct examination and cross-examination; (5) tactical considerations faced by an advocate who has more than one witness with testimony on a given point; (6) deciding whether — and how — to conduct redirect examination; and (7) examination of witnesses by the court.

---

[1] *See, e.g.,* J. Tanford, *The Trial Process: Law, Tactics and Ethics* 329 (The Michie Co. 1983) ("Direct examination is the most important part of the trial."); T. Mauet, *Fundamentals of Trial Techniques* § 4.1, at 75 (Little, Brown & Co. 2d ed. 1988) ("Experienced trial lawyers recognize that most trials are won on the strengths of their case in chief . . . ."); R. Keeton, *Trial Tactics and Methods* § 2.1, at 10 (Little, Brown & Co. 2d ed. 1973) ("[M]ore cases are won by evidence on direct than by that on cross-examination.").

The Need to Anticipate Cross-Examination

The rule of using only strong evidence dictates that an advocate should not call a witness unless he has determined that the value of the witness's favorable testimony outweighs the sponsorship costs of calling him. In assessing the probative value of a witness, the advocate must anticipate the degree to which his opponent's cross-examination may ultimately reduce that probative value. Only if the witness can be viewed as strong *after* taking into account the likely cross-examination will the advocate be justified in calling him.[2]

Content of the Direct Examination

Planning the content of direct examination involves the application of the same considerations that are implicated by any other evidence selection decision. Here, however, instead of selecting among various witnesses and items of tangible evidence, the advocate will be selecting among subject-matter areas. Ultimately, his task is to decide which questions to ask and which to leave unasked.

This section provides guidance on the content of the direct examination. It begins by discussing what favorable evidence should be elicited. It then discusses whether — and when — to elicit neutral and harmful testimony.

Elicit Only Favorable Points Qualifying as Strong

The advocate who has decided to call a witness and is considering what questions to ask should apply essentially the same rule that applies to evidence selection generally: elicit only strong points. Given the sponsorship costs associated with introducing evidence or asking questions of witnesses, sponsorship theory counsels brevity as the guid-

[2] One method for anticipating an opponent's cross-examination is set forth on page 188, *infra.*

ing principle.[3] Accordingly, a witness should not be taken through a laborious analysis of every detail relating to the events in question.

For example, assume that a witness to an automobile accident testifies that the defendant hit the plaintiff's car after running a red light. If, upon being asked to describe his opportunity to view the incident, he responds, "Excellent; I was very close and my vision was unimpeded," there is no need to inquire much further, if at all. If the cross-examiner chooses not to inquire, then the answer will stand unchallenged. Frequently, however, the cross-examiner will be uncertain of the witness's answers, and will therefore probe, hoping to uncover something helpful. If he does, each answer that bolsters the plaintiff's case will have far more impact than if the plaintiff himself had elicited it.[4]

Consider, for example, in the above-mentioned automobile accident suit the costs a cross-examiner would incur by making the following effort to discredit an eyewitness:

Q: Your vision is rather poor, isn't it?
A: Not with my glasses on, and I was definitely wearing my glasses at the time of the accident.

---

[3] A number of commentators agree that brevity should be a guiding rule. *See, e.g.*, K. Hegland, *Trial and Practice Skills* 19-20 (West 1978); F. Wellman, *Day In Court* 146 (MacMillan Co. 1926) ("I am inclined to put clearness, simplicity, and brevity before everything else in the conduct of a case in court, including the examinations of witnesses and the attempt to keep salient facts ever prominent before the jury."); H. Spellman, *Direct Examination of Witnesses* § 5:5, at 85 (Prentice Hall 1968) (noting that "the introduction [of a lay witness] should be very brief" and that questions relating to his general background should be "few").

[4] *Accord, e.g.*, F. Bailey & H. Rothblatt, *Successful Techniques for Criminal Trials* § 11:20, at 308 (Lawyers Co-op. Pub. Co. 1985) ("It is far more effective from [the prosecutor's] standpoint for [the cross-examining defense counsel] to get hit with unfavorable testimony than for him to introduce it on direct."); J. Appleman, *Successful Jury Trials* 181 (Coiner Pub., Ltd. 1952) (noting benefit of holding back favorable facts on direct examination so that they will be brought out on cross-examination, "thus having a much more dramatic effect than if elicited upon direct testimony").

Q: But you weren't really concentrating on the intersection, were you?
A: In fact, I was. I was looking at the plaintiff's Cadillac and thinking to myself how beautiful the car looked. That's when your client's car crashed into it.

These answers are far more powerful for the plaintiff when elicited during cross-examination because the cross-examiner has raised the stakes by asking the questions.

The technique of brevity creates a dilemma for the cross-examiner. If he decides not to cross-examine on a point made on direct examination, the jury may treat that testimony as uncontested. On the other hand, if the cross-examiner elicits testimony that does not substantially undercut the direct testimony, he will bear the costs of having gone to the effort of conducting an unproductive examination.

Consider, for instance, the foregoing automobile accident example in which the plaintiff's eyewitness, on direct examination, gives only a skeletal description of his opportunity to observe. Assume further that the cross-examiner is equipped with information on the constituent facts, such as the precise distance of the witness from the accident. In this circumstance, the cross-examiner must make the difficult decision whether to elicit such details.

If the cross-examiner asks no questions, the direct examiner can argue in summation that the excellence of the witness's opportunity to observe is established as an uncontested, unrebutted fact. If the defense attorney decides to ask questions, each fact elicited that favors the plaintiff will be given greater weight than if plaintiff's attorney had elicited it.[5] Similarly, where the points elicited on cross-examination are neutral, such cross-examination will appear unproductive. Thus, if the cross-examiner elicits that the eyewitness was a distance of 20 feet from the accident, such evidence will have the jury

[5] *See* note 4, *supra.*

thinking: "How does that help the defense?" The plaintiff enjoys the benefit of having the jury's skepticism about the significance of that fact directed at his opponent's case rather than at his own.

This tactical dilemma facing the cross-examiner is even greater when he is equipped with little or no information about the constituent facts. This is often the case in the criminal context, where discovery is very limited.[6] By adroit use of brevity and an appreciation of sponsorship theory, the direct examiner can box his opponent into a no-win situation.

In planning the content of his direct examination, the direct examiner should be careful to avoid costs of overtrying. Each additional question that he asks risks sending a message to the jury that the additional point was needed to make the witness credible or to bolster the direct examiner's case. If the additional point is not very probative, the point should be eliminated from the examination. By definition, limiting the examination to "strong" points entails a careful consideration of these possibilities.

The direct examiner should also avoid the appearance of any unusual efforts to elicit a point, such as where the point requires a lengthy process to refresh the witness's recollection by showing him a series of documents or transcript pages. If such an undertaking is required, the direct examiner must ensure that the jury will conclude, based on the strength of the point elicited, that it was truly "worth the effort." Moreover, because the jury normally assumes that the direct examination was preceded by extensive pre-trial preparation, it may conclude that the need to refresh the witness's recollection only serves to reflect that *no* amount of preparation could ensure that the witness would testify as the direct examiner wanted.

In sum, the direct examiner must apply all three costs of sponsorship in considering the use of favorable testimony. This process will ensure that his presentation is

---

[6] *See* Chapter Four, page 77, *supra.*

limited to favorable testimony that outweighs the sponsorship costs of its use.

The rule of eliciting only strong testimony applies to all witnesses — occurrence witnesses (including those that are hostile), records witnesses, other custodial witnesses, character witnesses, and expert witnesses. The case of the expert witness illustrates the point.

When the decision is made to present expert testimony, the advocate must confront the initial question of how much of the expert's qualifications to bring out.[7] Under sponsorship theory, only the highlights should be emphasized. For instance, where an expert witness is a member of more than 20 professional organizations, there is nothing to be gained by having the witness recite a long list of organizations that will be unfamiliar to the jury. It is more powerful for the witness simply to state that he belongs to more than 20 organizations, listing perhaps two or three of them. If the other side asks the witness to identify some of the other organizations, the credibility of the witness will be enhanced more than it would have been had the direct examiner brought out that same information.

As to the length of the expert's testimony, the testimony should be kept as brief as possible. Assuming, as is usually the case, that the expert is more knowledgeable in the subject matter than opposing counsel, cross-examination in the areas that the direct examiner has chosen not to cover will generally work to the direct examiner's benefit. More often than not, the expert will be able to show that the cross-examiner's labored efforts stem not from a flaw in the witness's testimony but from the lawyer's inadequate understanding of the expert's field.

Of course, before calling an expert witness, the advocate must have addressed the more fundamental question of whether his case is enhanced by calling the witness at all. As with other witnesses, the decision to call an expert

[7] Evidentiary rules typically require the expertise of such a witness to be established. *See, e.g.,* Fed. R. Evid. 702; *see generally* Tanford, *supra* note 1, at 431-432.

should be made only after a careful determination that his testimony as a whole is strong. The aura established for an expert witness when his list of impressive credentials is paraded before the jury is wholly undercut when the substance of his testimony is not compelling.

Omit Neutral Points

Because of the sponsorship rule limiting the direct examination to strong points, it follows that neutral details should not be elicited during direct examination.[8] For instance, there is generally little reason to go into a lengthy inquiry concerning a lay witness's educational background, employment history, or other biographical facts. Such neutral evidence generally adds little or nothing to the presentation.

The use of neutral evidence has been rationalized on the ground that such questioning gives the witness a chance to "relax and get used to testifying in the courtroom environment."[9] In fact, however, this device of asking "warm-up" questions may be hazardous.

To begin with, such questions may open the door for damaging cross-examination that the direct examiner has not thoroughly anticipated. Moreover, a seemingly innocuous question may provide the opponent with just the ammunition that he needs to make an effective argument in summation.[10] Accordingly, the time to get the witness ready for the rigors of trial is *not* in front of the jury but in

[8] *Cf.* Spellman, *supra* note 3, § 4:7, at 76 ("As a general rule, ... defendant's counsel should develop uncontroverted facts only when it is necessary to reaffirm these facts as a framework for the full understanding of the testimony of a defendant's witness."); *id.* § 5:8, at 94 ("Counsel ... should avoid the injection of details that may ... divert the attention of the fact-finder from the question to be decided.").

[9] Mauet, *supra* note 1, at 90.

[10] *See* Chapter Twelve, pages 267-268, *infra* (techniques for criticizing the opponent for eliciting neutral evidence).

pre-trial practice examinations, preferably in an actual courtroom setting.

The General Rule Against Impeaching One's Own Witness

Under the common law, an attorney was generally *prohibited* from impeaching his own witness.[11] Although this prohibition has been abandoned in most jurisdictions,[12] this trend does not mean that impeaching one's own witness is sound trial strategy. To the contrary, the earlier approach is largely consistent with what sponsorship theory counsels as tactically sound. Specifically, an advocate should normally not elicit testimony on direct examination that is harmful to his case. Instead, he should generally leave that task to his opponent. Thus, unless the cost of apparent efforts to omit the evidence are so enormous as to warrant the tactic,[13] an advocate should not impeach his own witness.[14]

Evidentiary rules often set forth specific categories of permissible impeachment of a witness. The Federal Rules of Evidence, for example, permit impeachment by use of

---

[11] *See, e.g.,* Thomas, *The Rule Against Impeaching One's Own Witness: A Reconsideration,* 31 Mo. L. Rev. 364 (1966).

[12] *See, e.g.,* Fed. R. Evid. 607 & Adv. Comm. Notes.

[13] *See* Chapter Four, pages 88-94, *supra.*

[14] The commentators are virtually unanimous in urging just the opposite. *See, e.g., Dombroff on Direct and Cross Examination* § 2.2, at 7 (Wiley Law Pub. 1985) ("The obvious advantage ... is that new matters are not raised out of the mouths of your witnesses under questioning by your opponent."); Keeton, *supra* note 1, § 2.20, at 54-55 ("Ordinarily if the harmful evidence is directly related to the issues in the case and is a matter that in all probability your opponent will inquire about on cross-examination, it is preferable to produce it on direct examination."); *but cf.* J. Sonsteng, R. Haydock & J. Boyd, *The Trial Book — A Total System for the Preparation and Presentation of a Case* § 6.3, at 219 (West 1984) (noting that a weakness that will come out on cross-examination should generally be elicited on direct examination, although "[i]t may be left for re-direct if the witness has an effective response for cross-examination inquiries").

prior convictions[15] and by use of a witness's prior inconsistent statements.[16] The commentators are nearly unanimous in urging that these matters should be elicited in the direct examination.[17] We can recall no trial, however, in which a direct examiner was (or would have been) better off eliciting prior convictions or prior inconsistent statements himself instead of letting his opponent do so. Thus, in our view, the advocate will be safe in assuming, absent extraordinary circumstances, that he should *never* elicit such matters in direct examination. For such matters, sponsorship theory counsels that the same fact, when elicited on cross-examination, is ordinarily much less damaging than when it is brought out on direct examination. For example, under sponsorship theory, where the advocate impeaches his own witness, the weight given to that impeachment will be maximized, while the weight given to the substantive testimony will be at a minimum. Moreover, by not eliciting the matter himself, the advocate preserves his ability to argue with credibility in summation that the matter has no significant bearing on the assessment of the witness's testimony.

One explanation for eliciting weaknesses is that the attorney doing so will gain credibility with the jury.[18] As previously demonstrated,[19] however, this rationale does not withstand analysis. The jury will tend to view the direct examiner's acknowledgment of the harmful matter as, on balance, self-serving, and therefore not worthy of credit. Moreover, an attorney who elicits harmful items on direct examination in an effort to enhance his own credi-

---

[15] *See* Fed. R. Evid. 609(a) (impeachment permissible based on prior felony convictions and other convictions involving crimes of dishonesty).

[16] *See* Fed. R. Evid. 613(b).

[17] *See, e.g.,* Spellman, *supra* note 3, § 5:5, at 85 (noting the advantage in eliciting unfavorable facts, such as the witness's prior criminal record, on direct examination because such a strategy "deprive[s] the opposition of the opportunity to bring out [such] unfavorable facts on cross-examination").

[18] *See* Chapter Four, page 97 & note 47, *supra.*

[19] *See* pages 97-102, *supra.*

bility with the jury does so at the expense of the *witness's* credibility. The direct examiner cannot make much use of the witness's honest answer, since the jury will assume that the attorney would not have asked the question without assuring himself that an honest reply would be forthcoming.

It should be emphasized, however, that while sponsorship theory generally counsels against bringing out weaknesses on direct examination, such matters should be disclosed by the witness *without hesitation* if he is asked about them during cross-examination. As indicated below, it is critical for an advocate to instruct his witness to be forthcoming and truthful at all times. Evasive answers, and those brought out only after repeated prodding, serve to undermine the witness's credibility.

Manner of Conducting Direct Examination

This section discusses the bearing of sponsorship theory on the manner of direct examination. As will be seen, the theory confirms the value of a number of well-accepted techniques.

The most fundamental technique for direct examination is that an attorney should normally avoid asking leading questions on direct examination. Indeed, evidentiary rules generally prohibit an attorney from doing so.[20] A tactical rationale frequently advanced for not using leading questions is that the weight given to the testimony will

[20] *See, e.g.*, Fed. R. Evid. 611(c) (barring leading questions on direct examination "except as may be necessary to develop the witness' testimony"); S. Goldberg, *The First Trial: Where Do I Sit? What Do I Say?* 213-225 (West 1982); Sonsteng, Haydock & Boyd, *supra* note 14, § 6.3, at 218 (noting general prohibition but listing numerous exceptions, such as the use of leading questions on preliminary matters, to identify a topic, to refresh the recollection of a witness, and to lay the foundation for exhibits). *See* page 185 & note 23, *infra* (discussing use of leading questions in examining hostile witnesses).

be reduced if the jury views the direct examiner rather than the witness as the source of the testimony.[21]

This reasoning comports with sponsorship analysis, which also predicts a reduction in the weight given to direct testimony elicited through leading questions. The amount of the reduction will depend on the degree to which the witness is associated with the party conducting the direct examination. Thus, the reduction will be small when the witness is the advocate's own client, because the advocate is viewed essentially as the client's *alter ego.*[22] It will also be small when the witness, although not the client, is party-associated. The reduction will be greater when a neutral witness is involved. It will be at its maximum when a hostile or adverse witness is being examined. This last point reveals that, unless the direct examiner is forced to ask leading questions of a hostile witness in order to control the witness,[23] he should avoid doing so whenever possible.[24]

To illustrate the difference in impact between leading and nonleading questions, assume that a government investigator, who had been dispatched to an oil tanker after a spill, is called to testify concerning his encounter with the tanker's allegedly intoxicated captain. The use of leading questions, if permitted, might proceed as follows:

Q: When you reached the bridge of the ship and found the captain, there was an odor of alcohol, wasn't there?

A: Yes.

---

[21] *See, e.g.,* Goldberg, *supra* note 20, at 213-215. The rule against leading questions is also supported by policy considerations. By using leading questions, the direct examiner is suggesting the answers to the witness. *See, e.g.,* Fed. R. Evid. 611(c), Adv. Comm. Note; Tanford, *supra* note 1, at 296.

[22] *See* Chapter Two, *supra,* page 21.

[23] The law permits a direct examiner to ask leading questions of a hostile witness. *See, e.g.,* Sonsteng, Haydock & Boyd, *supra* note 14, § 6.3, at 218.

[24] A similar analysis applies for cross-examination. *See* Chapter Eleven, *infra,* page 242.

Q: And the odor was overpowering, wasn't it?
A: Yes.

The same information could be elicited through non-leading questions in the following manner:

Q: What happened when you reached the bridge of the ship?
A: Well, first, I have to say that when I entered the pilot house and ran into the captain, I was immediately struck by an overpowering odor of alcohol.

The latter presentation is obviously more forceful than the former one.

As a related matter, the direct examiner should strive to elicit testimony by asking as few questions as possible. The more the jury hears from the witness, the less it will be preoccupied by the notion that the witness's testimony has been packaged by the attorney.

A well-known means of avoiding leading questions is to begin as many questions as possible with one of the following five words beginning with the letter "W": who, what, when, where, and why. The simple question "What happened next?" is illustrative.

A note of caution is in order. While use of leading questions on direct examination is objectionable, questions that are plainly designed to elicit a long narrative response may also be objectionable.[25] Thus, the direct examiner who is seeking to avoid the use of leading questions must also avoid asking questions that call for a lengthy narrative.

While conducting direct examination, the advocate should use notes or a checklist. This serves to ensure that nothing important is omitted. The alternative — being forced to recall the witness to elicit a fact that the attorney

[25] *See, e.g.,* Tanford, *supra* note 1, at 300-301 (explaining that the main problem with a narrative is that it impedes an opponent's opportunity to object before the witness provides inadmissible testimony).

neglected to ask — entails considerable sponsorship costs because of the unusual efforts required. Other things being equal, the jury will be apt to view the points elicited during the second examination with greater skepticism than it viewed the points brought out during the first one.

Finally, while the direct examiner should ensure that the testimony is understandable, he should avoid unnecessary repetition. The more often a point is repeated, the more likely the jury is to view the advocate as relying on that point to win his case. Similarly, the direct examiner should maintain a "poker-face" during the examination, and should avoid nodding or providing other reactions. Any facial expressions will be interpreted as revealing his reliance on the testimony (if his expressions are approving) or his concern with it (if his gestures are disapproving).

Preparation of the Advocate's Witnesses

It is elementary that thorough witness preparation is essential to effective trial advocacy.[26] Accordingly, once the advocate has determined the content of a witness's direct examination, he should prepare a detailed outline of the questions that he intends to ask and should use the outline to conduct pre-trial practice examinations. The advocate's goal is to avoid surprises at trial, and there is nothing more damaging to the advocate's case than a harmful "surprise" out of the mouth of his own witness. Any minor loss in spontaneity as a result of pretrial rehearsals will be amply justified by the reduced risk of surprise. It goes without saying, however, that witnesses should not be rehearsed to the point of memorization.[27]

[26] Most of the leading trial manuals emphasize this point. *See, e.g.*, Mauet, *supra* note 1, § 1.5, at 11.

[27] *Cf.* I. Younger, *The Art of Cross-Examination* 26-28 (A.B.A. Monograph Series 1976) (recounting case in which cross-examination revealed that witness had memorized her direct examination).

Furthermore, no witness should be presented at trial without first undergoing one or more thorough mock cross-examinations. Such a session enables the advocate to learn the true value of the witness's testimony. It can also identify exaggeration, ill-considered misstatement, and deliberate falsehood, thus enabling the advocate to delete such testimony from his presentation. Only after completing this task will the advocate have an informed basis to decide whether a non-essential witness should even be called. The advocate may decide that the probable testimony on cross-examination would be so damaging that the witness's testimony would, on balance, be less-than-strong, neutral, or harmful.

Furthermore, only when the advocate has a clear understanding of the content of the witness's testimony can he decide which questions to pose on direct examination and which areas to leave to the cross-examiner. Of course, he cannot be certain of what questions his opponent will ask on cross-examination. Nonetheless, the process of developing and executing the mock cross-examination will facilitate the advocate's ability to predict what his opponent will ask during the actual cross-examination.

In rehearsing the cross-examination, no difficult question should be overlooked. Moreover, the witness should be exposed to any tangible, documentary, or testimonial evidence with which he is likely to be confronted at trial. Indeed, the mock examination might itself result in the identification of additional evidence with which he should be confronted.

As we have stated,[28] the witness must understand the critical need to answer *all* questions forthrightly and without hesitation, even those dealing with the most difficult matters. The witness should also be informed, however, that he should *not* gratuitously offer any information. Such conduct might underscore whatever interest he has in the outcome of the case. Moreover, the witness might

[28] *See* page 184, *supra.*

be bringing up harmful evidence that the cross-examiner had not even considered eliciting.

The witness should further be advised that the cross-examiner need not be permitted to control the witness's answer — for example, by cutting off the witness in the middle of a sentence — so as to present it out of context. Under sponsorship theory, the direct examiner is better off when the cross-examiner is forced to elicit any explanation that may exist for a harmful point.

For instance, if an eyewitness was not wearing his glasses at the time of the incident in question but was wearing contact lenses, the witness need not simply answer "No" to the question of whether he was wearing glasses. He can say, "No, but I was wearing contact lenses."[29] If the cross-examiner tries to cut the witness off after the word "No," the advocate can consider objecting and asking the court to let him finish the answer. If the court does not grant that request, the advocate can still elicit the fact during his redirect examination.[30]

One rough gauge of the adequacy of witness preparation will be the extent of redirect examination that is required. Ideally, the witness's answers on cross-examination will be so responsive and well-considered that no redirect examination will be necessary.[31] Perhaps an even more important gauge, however, is whether the cross-examiner goes into matters that the advocate and his witness had not explored during the mock sessions. In the best of all worlds, the cross-examiner will touch upon only those areas that had been covered prior to trial. A witness is much more apt to make inadvertent errors when he is confronted unexpectedly with a matter and has not had time to think through his answer.

[29] As noted above, however, the witness should be cautioned against appearing overly eager to supply information gratuitously.

[30] *See* pages 198-200, *infra* (discussing techniques for redirect examination).

[31] Of course, even where the witness has provided careful testimony on cross-examination, some redirect examination may be necessary where the cross-examiner has successfully restricted the witness's ability to explain an answer.

Multiple Witnesses

When multiple witnesses are available to testify regarding the same area, some commentators urge a mandatory rule that all of them should be called to testify.[32] Sponsorship analysis reveals the dangers of such an approach. The following sections address such dangers in a variety of contexts.

Multiple Favorable Witnesses on the Same Point

Where the testimony of each of several witnesses on the same disputed point, if introduced alone, could be characterized as strong, an attorney might be tempted to call all of them. Under sponsorship theory, such a strategy would not necessarily be sound. At some point, the calling of additional witnesses would become counterproductive. For example, calling three (or perhaps even two) favorable witnesses to prove a simple point, such as whether a traffic light was green or red, is apt to strike the jury as a concession that the advocate deems each witness's testimony as essential. The cost of overtrying in calling an additional witness may at some point exceed the witness's incremental probative value. Once this threshold of diminishing returns is reached, the overall presentation will, on balance, be harmed by the sponsorship of the additional witness.[33]

[32] *See, e.g.*, A.E. Morrill, *Anatomy of a Trial* 108 (C.P.I. 1968). *Cf.* Appleman, *supra* note 4, at 211 ("All occupants of an automobile always must be called or accounted for, irrespective of the fact that they may know nothing relating to the events.").

[33] A note of caution is in order. In some jurisdictions, certain advocates will have no choice in the matter. For instance, some jurisdictions require a prosecutor to call all available eyewitnesses to a crime. *See generally* W. LaFave & J. Israel, *Criminal Procedure* § 23.3, at 876 (West 1985). In these jurisdictions, an advocate subject to such a rule may wish to tell the jury that he is required by law to produce all occurrence witnesses. He can then identify for the jury those witnesses who are sufficient for a verdict in his favor.

One Strong Witness and One or More Less-Than-Strong Witnesses on the Same Point

Some manuals advise calling multiple witnesses to testify on the same factual area, irrespective of the strength of each witness.[34] Sponsorship theory rejects this advice. Regardless of how much the opponent may criticize the advocate for presenting a "one witness case," the problem is magnified when the advocate presents a second less-than-strong witness, since the jury may view the weak witness as a concession that the strong one is insufficient. Because of this cost of overtrying, where the advocate has one strong witness and one or more less-than-strong witnesses on the same issue, sponsorship theory unequivocally counsels use of only the strong witness.

A case that we recall illustrates the importance of not calling less-than-strong witnesses. The defendant was charged with a late-night burglary of a record store. Two eyewitnesses had viewed the burglary from their apartment windows. Based on descriptions given by the witnesses, the police stopped a suspect and later brought the witnesses to look at him. One witness positively identified the suspect. The other said that, while it "looked like" him, there were differences in clothing and appearance, although the similarities probably outweighed the differences.

The prosecutor opted to introduce both witnesses, a strategy he soon regretted when defense counsel, during closing argument, focused most of his attention on the less-than-strong witness. The jury ultimately acquitted the defendant. The error in the prosecutor's strategy was that, by introducing a less-than-strong witness, he was implicitly conceding that the strong witness was not sufficient to convict. The jury was thereby encouraged to concentrate on whether the additional witness was enough to put the government's case "over the top," a shift in focus

[34] *See* authorities cited in note 32, *supra*.

that was enhanced by defense counsel's focus in summation on the less-than-strong witness. By introducing both witnesses, the prosecutor undermined his ability to make a credible argument that the first witness was sufficient to convict.

Notably, defense counsel had advised the court that if the prosecutor did not put on the second witness, he intended to do so. This would have been a far better situation for the prosecutor. He could then have attacked the strength of this "defense" evidence — a witness testifying that the defendant resembled the suspect and that the similarities probably outweighed the differences. The prosecutor could have noted that the defendant's own witness "ruled him in, not out." In any event, even if the defense had not presented the witness, the government's case still would have been more compelling with just the strong eyewitness.

Multiple Witnesses Who Agree on Collateral Details

The basic rule advising brevity in direct examination — including not bringing out unnecessary detail — has been discussed earlier in this chapter. Even if an advocate who has decided to call multiple witnesses generally embraces this rule, however, he may be tempted to stray from it when those witnesses agree on matters of collateral detail. The reasoning would be that this agreement on collateral detail will bolster the witnesses' credibility concerning the more important matters.[35] As noted in Chapter Four,[36] however, this strategy is generally unsound because corroborative detail evidence is normally less-than-strong. Moreover, no amount of pretrial preparation can ensure against some shade of inconsistency resulting from such a direct examination. Thus, the decision to undertake this

[35] *See, e.g.*, A. Amsterdam, B. Segal & M. Miller, *Trial Manual for the Defense of Criminal Cases* § 395, at 1-537 (Amer. Law Inst. 1984).

[36] *See* pages 69-70, *supra*.

type of bolstering should be approached with great caution.

Even assuming that the advocate is justified in believing that the witnesses' consistency on collateral detail is strong evidence, he might still be better off not eliciting the detail himself. This would be true if he has reason to believe that the cross-examiner will elicit such detail in an uninformed attempt to develop an inconsistency between the witnesses. In these circumstances, the direct examiner may want to consider the strategy, described in Chapter Four,[37] of refraining from using strong evidence in the expectation that his opponent will elicit it.

In the civil context, an opponent is most likely to fall into that trap when there has been insufficient discovery. In the criminal context, in which discovery is limited, it will be quite common because there is no general requirement that an advocate disclose the names of witnesses or the substance of their testimony.[38]

For example, in a case in which the defendant is charged with negligently striking the plaintiff-pedestrian with his vehicle, and where the disputed issue is whether plaintiff ran into the street against the traffic signal, the observations of plaintiff's eyewitnesses will be critical. If all of them noticed that the defendant's rear license plate was missing, plaintiff's lawyer might be tempted to elicit this fact from each of them in the belief that this attention to detail, even if collateral, could enhance their credibility.

Nonetheless, even if plaintiff's attorney determines that this factual detail is strong, he may be better off not eliciting it himself. If defense counsel does not know about the witnesses' agreement concerning that detail and is the type of attorney who is likely to "fish" for inconsis-

---

[37] *See* pages 71-76, *supra.*

[38] *See generally* 33 F.R.D. 53, 53-128 (1963) (comprehensive discussion concerning discovery in criminal cases); LaFave & Israel, *supra* note 33, § 19.3, at 725-741. *Cf.* Chapter Four, page 75, note 20, *supra* (discussing prosecutor's duty to disclose exculpatory evidence).

tencies, plaintiff's lawyer might be advised to let defense counsel do so. As previously noted, the impact on the jury is greatly enhanced when the cross-examiner, whom the jury assumes is striving to put on his best case, raises the stakes by attempting to demonstrate *inconsistencies* between the witnesses, and succeeds only in eliciting the consistencies on even the most collateral details. By contrast, the jury is considerably less impressed when those details are brought out on direct examination. The advocate is implicitly telling the jury that it is important to his case that these details match. The jury then expects them to match and is apt to be highly critical if they do not.

Multiple Witnesses Who Disagree on Matters of Detail

Earlier in this chapter we touched upon the problems that arise when witnesses disagree on various details and the advocate, unaware of such disagreement, unwittingly elicits the discrepancies during direct examination.[39] When an advocate is *aware* of such discrepancies prior to trial, however, he is in a position to decide on the best strategy for dealing with the problem. This section addresses that issue.

The threshold question, of course, is whether to call witnesses who will offer conflicting testimony. For example, assume that an advocate has two witnesses, each of whom, if called alone, could be characterized as strong. Assume further that the two witnesses disagree on a particular detail. In these circumstances, the direct examiner must decide whether the benefit from calling both witnesses would outweigh any costs incurred by the revelation of the inconsistency. To make this calculation, he must consider whether *he* would be the one to elicit the discrepancy. Sponsorship theory counsels that, as a general rule, he should not do so. Eliciting the discrepancy himself would be tantamount to conceding that it is mate-

[39] *See* page 192, *supra.*

rial to the case. Instead, if he decides to call both witnesses, he should let his opponent bring out the discrepancy.

A case tried by a former colleague illustrates why eliciting discrepancies can be harmful. The case involved an armed robbery in which both the victim and an eyewitness identified the perpetrator. The only discrepancy between the witnesses — which the prosecutor himself elicited — was that one witness recalled the gun being in the suspect's right hand while the other recalled that it was in his left hand. The jury ultimately acquitted the defendant. In later discussions with the prosecutor, the jury revealed that, in its view, the discrepancy alone had created a reasonable doubt.

The prosecutor might have been better off calling only the victim. He would then have had one solid identification and no contradictions. If the *defense* had taken the unusual step of calling the eyewitness, the discrepancy would have appeared trivial to the jury, since the defense would have been sponsoring the witness. Moreover, the prosecutor could have emphasized in summation the odd defense strategy of calling a witness who positively identified the defendant as the armed robber. Defense counsel's pathetic reliance on the discrepancy to make his case would be hard for him to dispel.

Assuming that the prosecutor had a valid reason to use both witnesses, such as a concern that the victim was not entirely convincing, he should nonetheless have let the *defense* elicit the inconsistency. That way, the prosecutor would have been able to argue with credibility that the discrepancy was totally irrelevant. As a practical matter, the burden would have been on defense counsel to show why this disagreement on a small detail during a terrifying incident should negate two strong, positive identifications of the defendant.

Redirect Examination

Deciding Whether to Conduct Redirect Examination

After cross-examination is completed, the advocate will be afforded an opportunity to conduct redirect examination. As an initial matter, it should be noted that the scope of redirect examination is normally limited by law to matters raised in the cross-examination.[40] Although it is usually within the discretion of the trial court to allow redirect examination on new topics,[41] courts generally do not allow such examination.[42] Thus, if an advocate neglected to elicit an important matter on direct examination, he may not be permitted to raise it on redirect examination. For that reason, he should not consciously withhold truly essential testimony during direct examination on the assumption that he will be able to inquire about it later.

From the standpoint of sponsorship, there is an important distinction between direct and redirect examination. With respect to the former, the jury tends to assume that the advocate is relying on the information elicited in order to win his case, since he took the effort to call the witness in the first place. By contrast, the advocate conducting redirect examination is merely trying to undo his opponent's gains on cross-examination. Furthermore, there is little additional effort expended in conducting redirect examination because the advocate is merely asking additional questions of a witness who is already on the stand. Thus, the costs incurred in asking a question on redirect examination are apt to be less than those incurred by asking the same question on direct.

---

[40] *See, e.g., United States v. Lopez,* 575 F.2d 681, 686 (9th Cir. 1978). *See generally McCormick on Evidence* § 32, at 69-70 (West 3d ed. 1984).

[41] *See, e.g., United States v. Taylor,* 599 F.2d 832, 838-839 (8th Cir. 1979); *cf.* Fed. R. Evid. 611(a) (giving trial court "reasonable control over the mode and order of interrogating witnesses").

[42] *See, e.g.,* J. Nolan, *Trial Practice: Cases and Materials* 81-82 (West 1981).

The decision whether to conduct redirect examination depends upon the purpose of the opponent's cross-examination and the extent to which that purpose was accomplished. If the cross-examiner exceeded the scope of the direct examination and used the witness to establish points favorable to the cross-examiner's case, the mirror-image rule for selection of discrediting evidence should be used. Specifically, the direct examiner should conduct redirect examination only if the reduction in the benefit to the cross-examiner's case outweighs the sponsorship costs of the redirect examination. On the other hand, if the cross-examination was aimed at discrediting the witness, the advocate should employ the rule of using only strong evidence. In particular, redirect examination in this case should be conducted only if the recoupment in benefit to the direct examiner's case outweighs the costs of conducting the redirect.

In both situations, sponsorship theory comports with the common sense conclusion that if an advocate has not been harmed by cross-examination, he should not undertake redirect examination.[43] By rising to conduct redirect, the advocate is communicating a concern about the significance of the points elicited on cross-examination. This concern is heightened with each additional question he asks.

For instance, assume that a plaintiff driver is suing an automobile manufacturer for injuries resulting from "sudden acceleration" (acceleration without depression of the gas pedal). Assume further that during the cross-examination of the plaintiff, defense counsel elicits the inconsequential fact that the plaintiff had never had the wheels of his one-year-old vehicle aligned. At most, the fact that plaintiff's maintenance of his vehicle was not perfect is only slightly harmful to his case. In considering whether to rehabilitate the plaintiff by eliciting testimony

[43] *See, e.g.*, Tanford, *supra* note 1, at 370 ("If cross-examination has not weakened the direct, then you would be wise to forgo redirect examination.").

regarding his otherwise impeccable maintenance record, plaintiff's attorney should probably decide against doing so. He certainly should avoid redirect examination requiring, for instance, refreshing plaintiff's recollection through the use of multiple service records. The jury may view such unusual effort as reflecting a serious concern on the part of plaintiff's attorney, thus suggesting that the points scored by defense counsel were significant. On the other hand, if the advocate can show that the plaintiff *had* aligned the wheels by means of an easily obtainable document, he might be warranted in doing so, assuming that the document could be authenticated by the plaintiff himself during the redirect examination.

Manner of Redirect Examination

Evidentiary rules normally require the advocate conducting redirect examination to employ non-leading questions.[44] An exception applies where leading questions are necessary to focus the attention of the witness to the specific area of inquiry.[45] The privilege of using leading questions on redirect for this limited purpose will often afford the redirect examiner with an important tactical opportunity.

Many trial manuals stress the cross-examination technique of cutting off the witness when he seeks to provide an explanation for a damaging fact.[46] The privilege of using leading questions on redirect examination permits

---

[44] *See, e.g.,* 3 F.X. Busch, *Law and Tactics in Jury Trials* § 445, at 951 & n. 50 (Bobbs-Merrill Co., Inc. 1959) (citing authorities).

[45] *See, e.g., McCormick on Evidence, supra* note 40, § 6, at 13 ("[Leading questions] may be employed to suggest a subject or topic, as distinguished from an answer."); M. Graham, *Federal Rules of Evidence* § 611.8, at 524 (West 1986) (noting that the use of leading questions is permissible on redirect examination to focus the witness's attention to the subject matter).

[46] *See, e.g.,* Younger, *supra* note 27, at 28 ("A trial lawyer must *never* permit the witness to explain anything on cross-examination.") (emphasis added). *See* Chapter Eleven, *infra,* pages 241-242 (rejecting such unqualified advice).

the redirect examiner who decides to elicit the explanation himself to enhance the cost of apparent efforts to omit that the cross-examiner incurred by cutting off the witness. To illustrate this point, assume that a cross-examiner in a murder case has elicited the following testimony:

Q: Officer, isn't it a fact that you waited an hour before transporting the gun to the property office of the police station?
A: Yes, but ...
Q: Thank you. And isn't that a violation of police department procedures that require officers to turn in seized weapons *immediately?*
A: Well, technically, but ...
Q: Just a yes or no answer is fine, Officer. Now let me ask you this [the defense attorney then moves onto another subject].

On redirect examination, the prosecutor can proceed as follows:

Q: My opponent asked whether you took the gun directly to the property office. What were you trying to say when he cut you off?
A: I wanted to say that I was on my way to the property office when I saw a severely injured pedestrian on the side of the road. I stopped to administer first aid and call an ambulance. Once the ambulance arrived, I drove directly to the property office and turned the gun over to the property clerk.

The use of leading questions for this purpose on redirect examination, if successful, will tax the cross-examiner with substantial costs of apparent efforts to omit the rehabilitative testimony. The advocate should keep in mind, however, that he should not use leading questions for the purpose of suggesting an answer to the witness. As explained above,[47] such a technique is not only impermissi-

[47] *See* pages 184-187, *supra.*

ble but is tactically unwise as well, since the witness's testimony will be given less weight if the jury feels that the testimony was suggested by the direct examiner.

Examination by the Court

Once a witness has been examined by all parties, the judge may be inclined to ask questions of his own, as he is permitted to do in most jurisdictions.[48] Examination of witnesses by the court raises various sponsorship-related issues.

As an initial matter, it should be clear that an item of favorable evidence is given more weight when it is introduced by the judge rather than by the advocate who stands to benefit from it.[49] The judge, as a disinterested participant, is not apt to be viewed with suspicion except in the unusual case where he has shown himself to be biased in favor of one side. Accordingly, the jury will not suspect that he "packaged" the witness's testimony. Moreover, his implicit statement that the matter is material will not tend to be discounted as it is when the interested advocate sponsors a matter favoring his case. To the contrary, because it represents the view of a jurist, it will be received as an indication of the materiality of the matter.[50]

---

[48] *See, e.g.,* Fed. R. Evid. 614(a), (b); 3 D. Louisell & C. Mueller, *Federal Evidence,* § 363, at 578-579 n.64 (Lawyer's Co-op. Pub. Co. 1979) (citing numerous state statutes).

[49] Most authorities are in accord. *See, e.g.,* Louisell & Mueller, *supra* note 48, § 365, at 585; *cf. United States v. Karnes,* 531 F.2d 214, 217 (4th Cir. 1976) (noting that the jury in the case may have afforded witnesses called by the court "greater credibility" than if they had been called by the party who benefited by the testimony).

[50] As the example of the judge makes clear, the rhetoric of the *disinterested* speaker, under sponsorship theory, will involve certain *benefits* of sponsorship rather than costs. Moreover, these benefits generally increase with the prestige and credibility of the speaker. The fundamental flaw of the conventional wisdom, which implicitly posits such benefits from the introduction of favorable evidence, is its failure to take into account the jury's view of the advocate as an *interested* speaker.

An advocate can reap practical benefits by being aware of the foregoing point. To begin with, an advocate, after getting permission to approach the bench, should consider objecting when a judge pursues a line of questioning that favors his opponent. One argument in support of such an objection would be that the questions jeopardize the judge's aura of impartiality,[51] and that his opponent is free to pursue the inquiry.

In addition, he should be alert to that rare opportunity when he may legitimately request that the court call a witness favoring his case. One category of witnesses for which courts have occasionally granted such a request is where the witness is considered unsavory, and the party seeking his testimony does not want to vouch for him.[52] By the same token, the advocate should be equally alert to object when his opponent attempts to have the court call a witness to support the opponent's case.[53]

Finally, whenever the judge elicits a fact favoring the advocate's case, the advocate should emphasize to the jury that *the judge* was the one who asked the question and elicited the favorable matter. This will enable the advocate to reap the benefit from the fact that the judge, rather than an interested advocate, introduced the evidence.

****

This chapter has addressed issues involving the direct examination of witnesses. It has emphasized the importance of following the rule of eliciting only strong points.

---

[51] *Cf.* Chapter Two, page 18, note 3.

[52] *See, e.g., United States v. Leslie,* 542 F.2d 285, 288-289 (5th Cir. 1976); Louisell & Mueller, *supra* note 48, § 364, at 580.

[53] *See, e.g., Estrella-Ortega v. United States,* 423 F.2d 509, 510 (9th Cir. 1970) (upholding trial court's refusal of a criminal defendant's request that court call as witness a government informer that the government chose not to call; court rejected defendant's claim that such a step was necessary "[to] prevent [the informer's] unattractive gloss from reflecting on [the defense] case").

The advocate must frequently confront not only whether to call certain witnesses or elicit certain testimony but also whether to use documents or other exhibits. Moreover, he will often be presented with the opportunity of stipulating to certain facts as a substitute for presenting evidence. The next chapter addresses the principles that should guide his consideration of such matters.

9

Non-Testimonial Evidence

This chapter addresses the topics of tangible evidence and evidence in the form of stipulations. As will be seen, sponsorship theory provides important guidance on the use of such evidence. As with testimonial evidence, the advocate cannot make an intelligent decision on whether — or how — to use such evidence until he has balanced the benefits of the evidence against the sponsorship costs.

Tangible Evidence

The Probative Value and Sponsorship Costs of Exhibits

As many commentators have recognized, exhibits can be very powerful. Exhibits can dramatize concepts or establish points where testimony alone may be inadequate.[1] For example, where a defendant is charged with posses-

[1] *See, e.g.*, J. Tanford, *The Trial Process: Law, Tactics and Ethics* 321 (The Michie Co. 1983) (asserting that exhibits "can convey information that may be impossible to communicate in words"). *Cf.* S. Schweitzer, *Cyclopedia of Trial Practice* § 204, at 542-543 (Lawyers Co-op. Pub. Co. 2d ed. 1970); T. Mauet, *Fundamentals of Trial Techniques* § 5.1, at 155 (Little, Brown & Co. 1988) (noting that exhibits have more impact than testimony because they are "more interesting" and "more reliable").

sion of a large quantity of drugs for distribution and claims that the drugs were for personal use, the prosecutor is better off introducing the actual drugs seized from the defendant rather than simply offering testimony concerning the amount.

Another legitimate rationale for introducing an item of real or demonstrative evidence is that it serves as a substantial aid in the presentation of the case. For example, a diagram of a scene at issue — such as the scene of an automobile accident — may be necessary for the jury to follow the testimony. Likewise, a photograph or X-ray may be necessary or useful to enable the jury to understand complicated medical testimony of the eyewitnesses. Similarly, in a case involving large numbers of documents or numerical compilations, a diagram summarizing these materials may be important to enable the jury to follow the testimony.

A case tried by one of the authors illustrates the probative value of an exhibit. The defendant was charged with shooting the victim in the mouth. The victim's version of the event was that the shot was fired from a distance of about ten feet. Defense counsel opted to give his opening statement immediately after the prosecutor's statement. In his statement, defense counsel represented that the evidence would show that the victim was the one with the gun, and that the gun went off accidentally during a struggle, with the barrel of the gun only about an inch from the victim's face.

In his case-in-chief, the prosecutor called the physician who had treated the victim. The physician testified that the hole in the victim's face where the bullet had entered was approximately the diameter of a pencil. He also testified that there were no burn marks or visible gunpowder residue on the victim's face. The prosecutor also called a firearms expert, who had fired the weapon used in the incident (which had been seized by the police) into a cardboard diagram from various distances. The cardboard diagram was displayed to the jury. The bullet hole caused by a shot fired at a range of ten feet was about the size of a pencil, and there were no burn marks or gunpowder residue. The bullet hole caused by a shot fired at the one-inch range, however, was about three inches in diameter, and the boundary of the hole showed visible burn marks and gunpowder residue. The defense had no answer to this compelling exhibit, and the jury ultimately convicted the defendant.

Notwithstanding the immense probative value of some exhibits, there can also be great danger in using exhibits, as commentators have correctly recognized.[2] These dangers correspond with the three costs of sponsorship.

First, the advocate's use of virtually any exhibit will entail costs of introduction. To begin with, the jury is apt to view an advocate's use of an exhibit as a statement that it is material and probative, and it will tend to discount that implicit claim. Moreover, the jury is likely to view the exhibit as being packaged in its best possible light. Accordingly, the jury will be apt to study the exhibit carefully to see if it contains some latent support for the opponent's case. Similarly, opposing counsel will likely scrutinize the exhibit for features that corroborate his case, and he will almost certainly bring such features to the jury's attention.

Thus, before an advocate decides to introduce an exhibit, such as a photograph of the scene at issue, he must scrutinize it for harmful features.[3] For example, in a malpractice action in which the principal issue involves damages, the plaintiff should introduce photographs of the victim where they are gruesome or powerful, and the defense should consider introducing the photographs where the injuries are difficult to observe or appear trivial. In a landlord-tenant dispute involving claims of poor living

[2] *See, e.g.,* Tanford, *supra* note 1, at 321; Mauet, *supra* note 1, § 5.4, at 200.

[3] *Accord, e.g.,* Mauet, *supra* note 1, § 5.4, at 200 ("review the exhibit[] to determine if there is anything, directly or inferentially, that your opponent can use to support his positions").

conditions, the tenant should introduce photographs of the apartment only if such photographs reveal terrible conditions. If the jury's likely reaction to the photographs is, "this place isn't so bad," then the tenant should not introduce such pictures.[4]

Second, the advocate using an exhibit may incur costs of overtrying. For example, exhibits designed as aids to the presentation must be carefully scrutinized. To assess the costs of overtrying incurred by the use of such an exhibit, the advocate should ask himself whether, in response to his opponent's claim in summation that the exhibit did not advance the advocate's case, he can credibly respond that it facilitated the jury's understanding of the case.[5]

Third, the advocate must consider whether the use of an exhibit would result in costs of unusual efforts. The more elaborate the exhibit, the greater the opponent's ability to attack and criticize it. These costs of efforts must be assessed in deciding whether (and in what form) to introduce an exhibit and whether to conduct a view or demonstration.

For example, an advocate should not take a jury to view the scene of a crime or accident — a step the jury is likely to view as quite unusual — unless something substantial can be accomplished. Similarly, a normal 3-inch by 5-inch photograph will incur less costs of efforts than a blown-up version. If enlarging the photograph fails to serve any legitimate purpose, the enhanced size will, in the jury's eyes, serve only to emphasize the advocate's reliance on that photograph.[6]

---

[4] While this point may seem obvious, it runs counter to the suggestion that photographs depicting the scene at issue should virtually *always* be introduced. *See, e.g.,* D. McCarty, *Psychology and the Law* 411 (Prentice-Hall 1960).

[5] *Cf.* K. Hegland, *Trial and Practice Skills* 7 (West 1978) ("[u]se diagrams and demonstrations" to make "the testimony clear and understandable").

[6] *Contra, e.g.,* M. Dombroff, *Unfair Tactics* § 14.12, at 482 (Wiley Law Pub. 2d ed. 1988) ("A rule of thumb whenever you deal with demonstrative evidence is that you should make the particular piece of evidence, whether a chart, graph, diagram, model, or any other technique available to you, as large as possible. Indeed, the limiting factor should not be what you think is too large, but rather

An advocate should also exercise caution regarding the manner in which he establishes a foundation for an exhibit — that is, how the advocate demonstrates that the exhibit is "what its proponent claims."[7] The more lengthy and involved the process is,[8] the more the advocate is apt to incur sponsorship costs. In some circumstances, the advocate must also establish a proper chain of custody in order to demonstrate that the item has not been tampered with. The advocate must recognize that where the custodial chain is a lengthy and elaborate one, he may incur considerable sponsorship costs. For this reason, the advocate should attempt, wherever possible, to obtain a stipulation from his opponent that the exhibit is authentic.[9] By the same token, the advocate should recognize that if he agrees to stipulate to the authenticity of one of his opponent's exhibits, he enables his opponent to *save* sponsorship costs.

Even if the advocate cannot obtain such a stipulation, there are other techniques that can be used to streamline the process of authenticating an exhibit. For instance, the advocate should have the foundational questions for his exhibits thought out — and perhaps written out — well in advance, and he should rehearse the questions with the authenticating witness prior to trial.

Moreover, the advocate should reflect at length before requesting that an exhibit be "published" to the jury during trial. Typically, the trial must stop for several moments as each juror looks at the exhibit, one juror at a time. The advocate's apparent reliance on the exhibit will be at its maximum in such a circumstance.

---

how large an exhibit the courthouse doors and elevators permit you to bring into the courtroom.").

[7] Fed. R. Evid. 901(a).

[8] *See generally* E. Imwinkelried, *Evidentiary Foundations* 35-81 (The Michie Co. 2d ed. 1989) (sample foundations for authenticating evidence); Mauet, *supra* note 1, § 5.3, at 162-200 (same).

[9] The topic of stipulations is treated more fully in a later section of this chapter.

Furthermore, an advocate should avoid the costs incurred by over-emphasizing his reliance on exhibits in argument. Devoting substantial time in summation to parading exhibits before the jury may well be counterproductive.

In contrast to the approach dictated by sponsorship theory, many advocates feel compelled to buttress their cases with less-than-strong physical evidence.[10] For instance, advocates frequently introduce photographs or diagrams that merely depict the scene at issue but do nothing to advance the advocate's relative position vis-a-vis his opponent. Advocates must avoid any inclination that they may have to adorn their cases with irrelevant exhibits. This approach not only fails to *advance* the advocate's case, it actually *harms* it.

One final point merits emphasis. The advocate deciding whether to introduce a party-associated exhibit must, as we explained in Chapter Five, consider its use on disputed issues even if it is less-than-strong, and must consider its use on undisputed issues even if it is not necessary to establish his legal burden of proof. To illustrate the latter, the prosecutor should normally introduce or account for the murder weapon in a murder case. Similarly, the plaintiff's attorney in a products liability case should normally produce or account for the defective product. Because of its preconceptions about custody of such exhibits, the jury will normally be unpersuaded by the argument that the opposing counsel could have introduced them. The advocate who introduces such basic evidence incurs no substantial costs of overtrying.

Substitutes for Exhibits

In certain circumstances, the advocate may wish to consider using a substitute for an exhibit instead of introduc-

[10] *Cf.* McCarty, *supra* note 4, at 411 ("Photographs of the scenes and persons are a 'must' in most cases ...."); P. Bergman, *Trial Advocacy* 119 (West 1979) ("[A]dvocates should search for potential uses of real evidence during trials.").

ing the item *in specie*. The reason is that occasionally, because of an irrelevant flaw in the actual exhibit, a substitute is more effective in making the advocate's point. An armed robbery case tried by one of the authors after a prior trial had produced a hung jury illustrates the point. In that case, the weapon used to commit the crime was a toy pistol.[11] The first prosecutor who tried the case had introduced the gun *in specie*, and the jury was unable to reach a verdict after four days of deliberations. Although the precise reasons why the first jury could not reach a verdict were not known to the second prosecutor, he was nonetheless concerned about the potentially adverse influence of the toy pistol. At the first trial, the victim had described her terror upon seeing the weapon, which glistened under a streetlight that was located near the crime scene. The toy pistol, however, looked harmless under ordinary lighting conditions, such as those in the jury room.

Upon his review of the physical evidence, the second prosecutor located a photograph of the toy pistol that the first prosecutor had opted not to use. That photograph depicted the pistol on the street where the defendant had dropped it after the crime. In that photograph, the pistol appeared more like the victim had described it: glistening under the streetlight. Opting to present the government's case in its "best light," the second prosecutor introduced only the photograph.[12] The jury returned a guilty verdict

[11] A toy pistol is legally sufficient to establish the "while armed" element of armed robbery. *See, e.g., Boyles v. State*, 46 Wis.2d 473, 175 N.W.2d 277 (1970) (unnecessary for prosecution to show that gun used to commit attempted armed robbery was a lethal weapon); *People v. Schofield*, 124 Mich. App. 134, 333 N.W.2d 607 (noting that a toy gun, when brandished as if it were a real gun, may support armed robbery conviction), *rev'd on other grounds*, 417 Mich. 988, 334 N.W.2d 376 (1983). *But cf., e.g., Cooper v. State*, 201 Tenn. 149, 297 S.W.2d 75 (1956) (holding that a toy pistol is not a "deadly weapon").

[12] Although the actual exhibit had been tendered to defense counsel prior to trial, he chose not to use it as part of his case. Such a decision was understandable. Since the toy was legally sufficient, see note 11, *supra*, defense counsel's

in less than 30 minutes. As this example illustrates, notwithstanding the jury's preference to see the best evidence of a tangible item, namely, the item itself,[13] using a substitute (or relying solely on testimony concerning the item) will occasionally be to the advocate's advantage.

Stipulations

Because an opponent's admission on a given point is normally *at least* as probative as evidence on that point from an impartial source, such as the judge,[14] it follows that an advocate should normally prefer a stipulation on a point favorable to his case over the alternative of having to prove the point himself.[15] A formal stipulation serves to highlight the opponent's concession, and it enables an advocate to capitalize on that concession by emphasizing that the fact was so clear that his opponent did not even put him to his proof. These advantages are lost if the advocate must introduce testimony to prove the fact. Use of the

---

reliance on the appearance of the gun — and his indirect concession that his client was the assailant — would have struck the jury as a weak defense.

[13] The jury's expectation to see the *best* evidence reflects suppositions about the fact finder's preferences similar to those underlying the best evidence and hearsay rules. Under the former rule, the original of a writing must be produced if its terms are material, unless the writing is unavailable through no fault of the proponent. *See generally McCormick on Evidence,* §§ 229-243, at 702-723 (West 3d ed. 1984). *Cf. Freeman v. Commercial Union Assurance Co.,* 317 S.W.2d 563, 568 (Tex. Civ. App. 1958) (requiring under the "best evidence rule" for writings that the document "relat[e] to a matter which ... form[s] the foundation of a cause, or the defense thereto"); *Doman v. Baltimore & O.R. Co.,* 22 S.E.2d 703 (W.Va. 1942) (same). *See also* Fed. R. Evid. 801-806 *et seq.* (rules governing hearsay which, absent circumstances of reliability, restrict evidence of out-of-court declarations offered for the truth of the matter asserted and require the testimony of the declarant himself).

[14] *Cf. Bruton v. United States,* 391 U.S. 123, 139-140 (1968) (White, J., dissenting) ("Even the testimony of an eyewitness may be less reliable than the defendant's own confession.").

[15] *Cf.* 2 F.X. Busch, *Law and Tactics in Jury Trials* § 219, at 443 (Bobbs-Merrill Co., Inc. 1959) ("The party having the burden of proof usually gains more by a formal stipulation than his opponent....").

testimony is apt to be discounted by the jury, as predicted by the cost of introduction.

The approach of many trial lawyers is to *refuse* to stipulate to facts favorable to their cases. The reasoning is that the advocate shortchanges his case unless the favorable evidence comes in through the testimony of live witnesses and tangible exhibits. We have found from our experience, however, that the value of the opponent's stipulated concession usually exceeds the power of the witness's live testimony, as adjusted by sponsorship costs.

In our view, the only disadvantage in obtaining a stipulation of an advocate's favorable facts is when such facts are not fully communicated to the jury in the stipulation. Consider, for example, the decision of whether an advocate should seek to obtain a stipulation from his opponent concerning the qualifications of the advocate's expert witness. Such a stipulation is often preferable to the introduction of evidence concerning the expert's credentials. This is particularly true when the expert's qualifications, while substantial, are not likely to impress the jury. Where that is so, a stipulation enables the advocate to argue that his expert's qualifications are so strong that his opponent consented to relieve him from proving them.[16] On the other hand, if the expert's credentials are unusually impressive and the opponent, in agreeing to stipulate, will not allow mention of specific accomplishments, then the advocate may be better off not stipulating and instead putting on evidence relating to the expert's credentials.

For the same reasons, an advocate should be reluctant to stipulate to evidence that is favorable to his opponent's case. His opponent can use the stipulation to bolster the strength of that evidence in the jury's eyes. Moreover, the opponent avoids the sponsorship costs incurred by putting on the evidence himself. Of course, countervailing

---

[16] *Contra, e.g.,* J. Frederick, *The Psychology of the American Jury,* § 6-202, at 225 (The Michie Co. 1988) ("Do not stipulate to the credentials of your witness. Let the jury be impressed with the witness's qualifications.").

considerations, such as pressures from the court, may cause an advocate to temper this strategy. Although, strictly speaking, a court cannot *force* an advocate to accept a stipulation,[17] it may be unwise for an attorney to be stubborn on minor matters if the court is likely to become irritated. If the advocate has no choice as a practical matter but to agree to a stipulation favorable to his opponent, he should attempt to keep the terms of such a stipulation to a bare minimum.

*****

Having discussed the advocate's own case, we now turn to a discussion of what the advocate should be doing during his opponent's presentation.

[17] *See, e.g., People v. McClellan,* 80 Cal. Rptr. 31, 37, 457 P.2d 871, 877 (Cal. 1969).

10

The Opponent's Presentation

This chapter addresses the tasks that an advocate must undertake during his opponent's opening statement, examination of witnesses, and closing argument. The tasks are divided into two areas: the need to monitor the opponent's conduct at trial and the need to voice appropriate objections.

Monitoring the Opponent's Presentation

The advocate takes his seat at counsel table after completing the direct examination of his star witness. He pulls out a fresh note pad and listens with rapt attention as his opponent's cross-examination begins. His main concern is in identifying any damaging points that his opponent will succeed in eliciting during the cross-examination. He resolves to note these points on his pad so that his redirect examination can neutralize them. With pen in hand, he listens intently to avoid missing any such point.

As the cross-examination proceeds, however, it begins to meander. Many of the cross-examiner's questions simply enable the witness to reiterate his testimony on direct examination in even stronger terms. Other questions appear to reflect shifting points of attack and inconsistent theories of his case, none of which makes any headway. After a few minutes of this, the advocate drops his pen altogether, having made only a few notes of instances in which his witness was caught in a seeming inconsistency.

The advocate, by taking this familiar approach, has performed only half of his job and has missed a golden opportunity to gather concessions from his opponent. Although noting damaging points is a critical task, sponsorship theory reveals that it is also critical for the advocate to note the unproductive questions that the cross-examiner poses and the answers to those questions that the cross-examiner receives.

One of the key teachings of sponsorship theory is that everything an opponent says or does can potentially be used against him. It is surprising how often a remark by opposing counsel, especially when it is ill-conceived or careless, can provide the advocate with ammunition to resolve a disputed point in the advocate's favor. For that reason, an advocate must make note of every assertion the opponent makes, every question he asks, and every piece of evidence that he introduces. Each represents a potential concession that something is material to the advocate's case, and this record will enable the advocate to evaluate, at the end of each day of trial, how these actions of opposing counsel can be used against him.

The importance of focusing on the opponent's own words cannot be overstated. An argument that would otherwise appear to be setting up a straw man can be very powerful when the opponent has, by his own remarks, conceded the materiality of a point. The Vice-Presidential debate in the 1988 Presidential election provides an illustration. The following remarks were made in response to the moderator's question concerning Senator Dan Quayle's qualifications to assume the Vice Presidency:

> Quayle: I have far more experience than many others that have sought the office of Vice President [of] the country. I have as much experience in the Congress as Jack Kennedy did when he sought the Presidency.
>
> ***
>
> Senator Lloyd Bentsen: Senator, I served with Jack Kennedy. I knew Jack Kennedy. Jack Kennedy was a friend of mine. Senator, you're no Jack Kennedy.
>
> ***
>
> Quayle: That was really uncalled for, Senator.
>
> Bentsen: You're the one that was making the comparison, Senator....[1]

Had Senator Quayle not brought up the comparison with President Kennedy, Senator Bentsen's remarks would have appeared unfair and desperate. Because Senator Quayle did so, however, Senator Bentsen's remarks were viewed as very powerful and were considered decisive in the general public impression that Senator Bentsen had won the debate.

For some unknown reason, the trial tactics literature virtually ignores the importance of monitoring the opponent's conduct. Indeed, when the subject is alluded to at all, it is often for the purpose of advising the attorney *not* to do so. For example, one commentator[2] advises defense attorneys to do the following during the prosecutor's opening statement:

> With every faculty you have, you listen and watch the effect the prosecutor's opening is having on the jury, and as an experienced trial counsel, you will not

[1] N.Y. Times, Oct. 6, 1988, at B22 (transcript of debate).

[2] L. Stryker, *The Art of Advocacy* 45-46 (Zenger Pub. Co., Inc. 1979).

> spend much time in taking notes; a date, a fact, a name, a phrase perhaps, but little more.
>
> Sir Charles Russell, one of England's greatest advocates, one day glanced around at his junior and said, "What are you doing?" "Taking a note," was the answer. Russell looked at him and said: "What the devil do you mean by saying you are taking a note? Why don't you watch the case?" Watch the case! I agree with Judge Parry who, in recounting Russell's observation, declared it to be "the golden rule."

Sponsorship theory unequivocally endorses the approach of the young English lawyer, not that of his distinguished mentor, Sir Charles Russell. The benefits of carefully recording the opposing counsel's remarks for possible use as concessions far outweigh the missed opportunity to stare at the jury. In our experience, an advocate has no reason to be concerned that he will miss a chance to assess the jurors' expressions as they listen to his opponent. Little, if any, relevant information can be gleaned thereby; the jurors are normally expressionless during opening statements. It is far more important for the advocate to ensure that *he* has fully comprehended — and recorded — his opponent's remarks.

In sum, the advocate should endeavor to record the substance of virtually anything his opponent says — be it in opening statement, closing argument, or in questions posed to witnesses. The advocate should also record the substance of the witnesses' responses to the opponent's questions. What may seem innocuous or irrelevant at the time may turn out to be critical in light of later events at trial. Furthermore, the advocate cannot simply rely on expedited transcripts to preserve his opposing counsel's remarks and questions. Aside from the considerable expense of such transcripts, even an overnight service temporarily deprives him of the information at a time when he may need it most to facilitate his preparation of the case.

It should be apparent that monitoring the opponent's conduct is important not only for defense lawyers but also for plaintiffs' attorneys and prosecutors. This is because, as we have previously noted,[3] *any* advocate who has met his applicable legal burdens (if any) will derive an equal benefit from exposing the weaknesses of his opponent's case as he will from advancing the strengths of his own case.

At first blush, this tactic would seem to be available to prosecutors and plaintiffs' attorneys only when the defense has opted to present a case and put on evidence. In fact, however, it can also be used when the defense has put on *no* evidence. Even in this circumstance, defense counsel will almost invariably be advancing a theory of the case that supports a verdict in his client's favor. The defendant's position will be reflected either explicitly in defense counsel's opening statement or closing argument or implicitly in the questions he poses during his cross-examination.

The plaintiff's attorney or prosecutor must pay careful attention to defense counsel's remarks and questions to identify his opponent's theory of the case. In his own closing argument, the plaintiff's attorney or prosecutor must identify the defendant's theory and demonstrate, based on the evidence, the lack of merit in that theory.[4]

The principle that an advocate should strive to demonstrate the lack of merit in his opponent's position applies *a fortiori* to defense lawyers, who often find themselves without much defense evidence. For reasons that we have previously explained,[5] a defense attorney will score as many points by identifying the flaws in the plaintiff's or prose-

[3] *See* Chapter Two, pages 35-36, *supra.*

[4] In a criminal case, the prosecutor must be careful not to suggest that the defense has any duty to support his contentions by presenting evidence. Any such suggestion may constitute grounds for reversal. *See* Chapter Six, page 142, note 7, *supra.*

[5] *See* Chapter Two pages 34-36, *supra.*

cutor's case as he will from persuading the jury that he has a valid defense. Thus, the defense attorney should adopt an aggressive trial strategy in which his opponent's case is thoroughly dissected and criticized.

Objections

One of the most over-utilized devices at trial is the objection. This is certainly not the fault of the trial literature. The leading commentators leave no ambiguity about the need to exercise great caution in voicing objections, stressing that, as a general rule, an advocate should object only where he is likely to be harmed by the evidence.[6] However, some law school and continuing legal education courses on trial advocacy are so preoccupied with teaching advocates how to *identify* an objectionable question that they devote insufficient attention to the difficult issue of whether an objection would be tactically wise.

Recognizing an improper question or an objectionable piece of evidence, while important, is only the first step in deciding whether to voice an objection. An advocate must understand the considerable costs involved in objecting in front of a jury. This portion of the chapter sets forth the bearing of sponsorship theory on the decision whether to object. As will be seen, the conclusions dictated by spon-

---

[6] *See, e.g.*, T. Mauet, *Fundamentals of Trial Techniques* § 8.2, at 332 (Little, Brown & Co. 2d ed. 1988) ("Unless you are reasonably sure that the answer to a question will hurt your case, it is usually better not to object."); J. Tanford, *The Trial Process: Law, Tactics and Ethics* 302 (The Michie Co. 1983) (listing factors that must be considered before objecting); R. Keeton, *Trial Tactics and Methods* § 4.2, at 167 (Little, Brown & Co. 2d ed. 1973) (noting that an objection can serve to emphasize the evidence objected to); J. Nolan, *Trial Practice: Cases and Materials* 129 (West 1981) (noting that frequent objections may lead the jury to sympathize with the opposing attorney and his client); 5 F.X. Busch, *Law and Tactics in Jury Trials* § 604, at 298-299 (Bobbs-Merrill Co., Inc. 1959) (noting that jurors become angry at an attorney's frequent objections).

sorship theory are similar to those urged by the trial tactics literature.[7]

The Decision Whether to Object

The sections that follow set forth the considerations pertinent to the decision whether to object. The first section sets forth the applicable rule for the advocate who can object outside the jury's presence. The second section provides the rule when the advocate must object in the jury's presence. As will be seen, when the advocate must voice his objection before the jury, the task of analyzing the merits of objecting is more complicated. Invariably, the advocate who must object in the jury's presence suffers in ways that are avoided when he is able to object when the jury is not present.

Objections Outside the Presence of the Jury

There is an easily stated rule for an advocate who is deciding whether to object outside the jury's presence to his opponent's introduction of evidence: he should do so if and only if the evidence is strong evidence from the opponent's perspective. The first implication of this rule — counseling the advocate to object when the evidence is strong — should be obvious. The objection, if sustained, will prevent the jury from hearing evidence that is sufficiently favorable to the opponent's case to outweigh his sponsorship costs of using it.

The second implication of the rule — advising the advocate *not* to object when the evidence is less-than-strong —

[7] This discussion assumes that an objection is not required to preserve an error for appeal. Depending on the likelihood of reversal on appeal as a result of preserving an error, an objection that is otherwise not tactically warranted may be sound. *See generally* Keeton, *supra* note 6, § 4.12, at 190-195 (discussing objections to preserve errors for purposes of appeal).

is less obvious. Here, the advocate should refrain from objecting not only to evidence that is favorable to the *advocate* but also to certain evidence that, if introduced by a neutral source, would be considered by the jury to favor his *opponent's* case. Because the sponsorship cost of using any less-than-strong evidence will by definition outweigh its probative value, allowing the jury to consider such evidence, *as introduced by the opponent,* would serve to *reduce* the persuasiveness of the opponent's case. Accordingly, the advocate should *welcome* his opponent's use of such less-than-strong evidence.

An advocate who must object in front of the jury incurs risks that are not incurred by an advocate who can object outside the jury's presence. For this reason, the advocate who has decided to object should do so outside the jury's presence whenever possible. Thus, where an advocate is aware of objectionable evidence prior to trial, he should consider filing a motion *in limine* in order to obtain a ruling in advance of trial.[8] The advantage of this approach, of course, is that the advocate avoids the risk of adverse speculation incurred by objecting in front of the jury.

Frequently, however, the advocate will have no warning prior to trial that his opponent plans to ask a particular objectionable question. In that situation, he might consider voicing his objection at the bench. In that way, he can argue against the admission of the evidence without the jury hearing his presentation. Of course, even when this device is used, the jury will soon figure out that the advocate's repeated requests for bench conferences are an effort to keep out evidence. Thus, this approach will not necessarily eliminate the risks of objecting before the jury. It should also be noted that the advocate cannot apply this approach too frequently, since the trial judge, who wants

[8] *See, e.g.,* Tanford, *supra* note 6, at 313 (discussing use of motions *in limine* to keep out inadmissible evidence); R. Carlson & E. Imwinkelried, *Dynamics of Trial Practice* § 6.2, at 83 (West 1989) (same).

to move the proceeding along quickly, is apt to become irritated. If the advocate finds that he cannot object outside the jury's presence, then he must consider the factors described below.

Objections in the Presence of the Jury

In deciding whether to voice an objection that can only be made before the jury, the advocate must assess the harm to his case from the admission of the evidence against the risk of adverse jury speculation if his objection is sustained. If the objection is overruled, the jury will hear the evidence in the context of the advocate's having taken pains to keep it out. When this is so, the advocate making the unsuccessful objection will incur costs of perceived efforts to omit. Specifically, the jury will be apt to interpret the advocate's efforts as a sign that he is concerned about the negative effect that such evidence will have on his case. For that reason, the jury will tend to give it greater weight. The advocate is thus worse off when evidence is admitted over his objection than he is when it comes in without objection.[9]

On the other hand, if the objection is sustained and the evidence never comes in, the jury will be apt to speculate that the evidence would have materially advanced his opponent's case. This follows from the jury's assumption that opposing counsel will seek to present only evidence that materially favors his case. Although the jury is typically admonished not to speculate what the witness would have said had an objection not been sustained,[10] human nature suggests that jurors will have great difficulty con-

[9]*Accord,* Keeton, *supra* note 6, § 4.2, at 167-168 (noting that "the added emphasis given to [an opponent's item of evidence] by your unsuccessful effort to keep [the jurors] from considering it may cause it to be more damaging than if you had permitted it to come in without objection").

[10]*See, e.g.,* 1 E. Devitt & C. Blackmar, *Federal Jury Practice and Instructions* § 10.13, at 273 (West 3d ed. 1977).

trolling their urge to engage in such speculation. Where the evidence is less-than-strong for the opponent, the advocate, by successfully objecting, will achieve only a Pyrrhic victory. His opponent, in addition to not suffering the consequences of offering less-than-strong evidence, may actually *benefit* from the jury's speculation that the excluded evidence would have materially advanced his case.

Accordingly, as with objections made outside the presence of the jury, the advocate should not even consider objecting to the evidence unless it is strong for his opponent. Assuming for purposes of this analysis that the opponent's evidence is strong for his case, the rule on whether to object in the presence of the jury will depend on the advocate's degree of certainty that the objection will be sustained.

Where the Objection is Virtually Certain to be Sustained

If the objection is virtually certain to be sustained, the advocate should object only where the harm from the item coming into evidence, as adjusted for the opponent's sponsorship costs, would outweigh the risk of adverse speculation if the jury is prevented from considering the evidence. As noted above, where the jury is not permitted to consider evidence because an objection is sustained, it will be apt to assume that the omitted evidence would have materially favored the opponent's case. Unless the actual evidence would be even more damaging to the advocate's case than the risk of this possible adverse speculation, the advocate is better off allowing the jury to hear the evidence.

Where the Advocate Is Uncertain Whether the Objection Would Be Sustained

Where the advocate's grounds for objecting are of questionable legal merit, he obviously cannot be certain that his objection will be sustained. As noted above, if he objects in these circumstances and his objection is overruled, that objection will increase the weight given by the jury to the evidence once it is admitted. Specifically, the objecting advocate will incur costs of apparent efforts to omit by trying to keep evidence from the jury.

Thus, even where the opponent's evidence is strong for his case, if the advocate must take the chance that he will be overruled in the presence of the jury, he may not be justified in objecting. Put another way, the less certain that the advocate is regarding the merit of his potential objection, the more powerful his opponent's evidence must be before he should consider objecting.

One additional problem bears discussion. On occasion, the advocate required to make the foregoing cost/benefit calculations will not have information concerning the substance — and thus the strength — of his opponent's objectionable evidence. For instance, his opponent might ask a witness, "And what did you hear that individual say to the neighbor?" In such a case, the question appears to call for inadmissible hearsay but the advocate may have no idea what the witness's answer would be. In that circumstance, the advocate may wish to request permission to approach the bench in order to get a proffer from his opponent concerning the expected response from the witness. If that approach does not work, then the advocate must attempt to ascertain from the context of the question and the other evidence being elicited from the witness whether the testimony would likely be strong for his opponent. Ultimately, before deciding whether to object, the advocate must make his best guess concerning the strength of the potentially inadmissible evidence that his opponent is attempting to elicit.

Assuming that the advocate has decided to object in front of the jury, it is important for him to use the proper technique. Most significantly, regardless of the importance of the evidence that he is trying to keep from the jury, he must remain calm and unexcited. Costs of perceived efforts to omit or, alternatively, risks of adverse jury speculation regarding excluded evidence, are increased considerably when an advocate jumps to his feet suddenly and shouts "objection" in a loud and nervous voice as if something devastating is about to happen.[11]

Considerations Involving Specific Objections

This section addresses the merits of making various specific types of objections. After first discussing a number of generic categories of objections, it focuses in detail on one specific objection: cross-examination that exceeds the scope of the direct examination.

As a preliminary matter, we note that it is not possible to draw any sweeping conclusions with respect to the types of objections that should always be made or that should never be made. Nonetheless, there are certain types of objections that, if meritorious, should often be made because of the potential harm to the advocate's case from the admission of the evidence. Examples include objections to evidence of subsequent remedial measures, compromise and offers to compromise, payment of medical expenses or other similar expenses, pleas and plea discussions, liability insurance, and a rape victim's past behavior.[12] Of course, if the witness's answer in any of these circum-

[11] *Cf.* Carlson & Imwinkelried, *supra* note 8, § 6.3(E), at 88 ("In almost all cases, you should remain low-key and business-like when you object.").

[12] *See, e.g.,* Fed. R. Evid. 407-412.

stances would not harm the advocate's case, then the advocate should not object.

For example, a prosecutor should ordinarily object if a defense attorney in a rape case seeks to question the victim about her active sexual past. The prosecutor, however, would obviously be unwise to object if the victim had been a virgin prior to the incident. By allowing the evidence to come in, he could capitalize in summation upon defense counsel's unproductive cross-examination.[13] By keeping the evidence out, the prosecutor may cause the jury to speculate — erroneously — that the victim was sexually active.

The foregoing sections have assumed that the objections, if successful, would keep out evidence. There are, however, certain types of objections that are largely formal in nature in the sense that they generally do not result in the exclusion of evidence. Examples include objections to questions that are leading; were previously asked and answered; call for a narrative response; are ambiguous, compound, or indefinite as to place or time; call for speculation; misstate or comment upon the evidence; and are argumentative or assume a fact not in evidence.[14] The value of making such objections may be minimal, and the attorney risks appearing overly concerned with trivial matters. Thus, an attorney might well decide not to voice objections to such questions or to do so only after a series of similar improper questions.

One objection that warrants special treatment because of its unique relationship to sponsorship is the objection challenging cross-examination that exceeds the scope of direct examination.[15] An advocate who is not attuned to

[13] Techniques for capitalizing on an opponent's unproductive cross-examination are contained in Chapter Twelve, *infra,* pages 258-259.

[14] *See generally* R. Carlson, *Successful Techniques for Civil Trials* §§ 2:1-2:22, at 77-103 (Lawyers Co-op. Pub. Co. 1983).

[15] The permissibility of conducting cross-examination outside the scope of direct examination depends upon the rules of evidence in the particular juris-

sponsorship considerations might conclude that this is a futile objection, even when the cross-examiner is eliciting strong evidence for his case, since the cross-examiner can simply recall the witness himself. In fact, however, sponsorship theory counsels that it is to the opponent's advantage to present his case through the advocate's witnesses if he can do so.[16] Moreover, if the opponent is forced to recall the witness, *he* will incur all of those costs. For that reason, other considerations aside, the advocate should seek to limit the scope of such cross-examination when evidence harmful to his case is being elicited.[17]

To illustrate the point, assume that a witness can testify to facts A, B, and C, all of which are favorable to the direct examiner, but that he can also testify to fact D, which involves a different subject and a fact *unfavorable* to the direct examiner. A seasoned cross-examiner will try to bring out fact D on cross-examination if it was not brought out on direct. This can be quite harmful, since

---

diction. Although many jurisdictions limit cross-examination to matters covered on direct, others permit essentially unlimited cross-examination. *Cf.* Fed. R. Evid. 611(b) (cross-examination limited to scope of direct except where court in its discretion rules otherwise); *see generally McCormick on Evidence* § 24-27, at 56-61 (West 3d ed. 1989) (discussing alternative approaches). Of course, regardless of the rule, some cross-examiners will either purposefully or unknowingly exceed the scope of direct examination.

[16] *Cf.* F. Bailey & H. Rothblatt, *Successful Techniques for Criminal Trials* § 22.3, at 498 (Lawyers Co-op. Pub. Co. 1985) ("Favorable evidence obtained on cross-examination is probably more valuable than the testimony of your own witnesses .... Anything that [an opponent's] witness says for your side can be argued as beyond question."). *See generally* Chapter Eleven, pages 233-234, *infra* (encouraging technique where permissible).

[17] In those jurisdictions that limit cross-examination to the scope of the direct examination (*see* note 15, *supra*), an advocate who insists that the cross-examiner must recall the witness to inquire beyond the scope of the direct is within his legal rights. *See, e.g.,* 4 *Jones on Evidence* § 25:2, at 111 (Lawyers Co-Op. Pub. Co. 6th ed. 1972) ("[I]f a party wishes to examine a witness as to matters other than those covered by direct examination, he must do so by calling the witness in his own behalf, and not by cross-examining him."); *cf. Resurrection Gold Mining Co. v. Fortune Gold Mining Co.,* 129 F. 668, 675 (8th Cir. 1904) ("If the cross-examiner would investigate [subjects beyond the scope of direct examination] ... he may and he must make him his own witness, and *stand sponsor* for the truth of [the] testimony.") (emphasis added).

the cross-examiner is making his case through the direct examiner's witness, and the jury is apt to credit fact D more heavily than facts A, B, and C.[18]

Furthermore, if the objection is sustained, the advocate is better off regardless of what strategy the cross-examiner adopts in the face of such a ruling. To begin with, unless fact D is critical to the cross-examiner, he will probably be reluctant to take the step of recalling the witness, a step that juries normally view as rather extraordinary.[19] Indeed, unless fact D constitutes strong evidence for the cross-examiner's case, the whole strategy of recalling a witness in his own case would be counterproductive. If fact D is less-than-strong for the cross-examiner, the direct examiner can comment in summation along the following lines:

> You must have thought, when my opponent went to the effort of recalling [the witness], that you were going to hear something extraordinary, perhaps even a recantation of his earlier testimony. You must have been surprised when [the witness] merely testified to [fact D].

In any event, even if the cross-examiner finds it beneficial to recall the witness, the direct examiner is still better off than if the cross-examiner had elicited the information on cross-examination. Since the cross-examiner is now unquestionably burdening his case by offering the witness with respect to fact D, the jury will most likely give it less weight than it would have given that same fact had it been brought out through cross-examination.

---

[18] Under sponsorship theory, fact D would be credited even more fully if it had been elicited during direct examination. Thus, the direct examiner does not solve the problem by eliciting fact D himself.

[19] *Cf.* H. Wouk, *The Caine Mutiny* 389 (Doubleday 1952) (eyebrows of fictional foreman of jury "signaled astonishment" when defense counsel announced his intention to have a witness whom he had just finished cross-examining recalled as his own witness).

In short, the "beyond the scope" objection is not a purely formal one. It may result in evidence *never* being introduced because the cross-examiner may decide not to recall the witness. Even if the cross-examiner does recall the witness, his sponsorship of that witness will reduce the harmful impact of the testimony.[20]

[20] Similar reasoning applies to the objection that the opponent has unfairly introduced only part of a writing or recorded statement and should be required to introduce additional portions as well. *See, e.g.,* Fed. R. Evid. 106. Although such an objection would seem trivial, since the advocate can simply introduce the remainder of the item himself, sponsorship theory reveals that the advocate is better off when his opponent is forced to introduce the portions damaging to his case.

11

Cross-Examination of the Opponent's Witnesses

Experienced trial lawyers know that, unlike on television, witnesses almost never "crack" under cross-examination. Indeed, cross-examination normally fails to achieve major inroads. Nonetheless, many attorneys feel that, regardless of what they will accomplish, they will be harmed more by refraining from asking questions than by asking them. For some, cross-examination is a time to take a stand before the jury by communicating, through questioning, a lack of belief in the witness's testimony. For others, it is a time for "fishing" in the hope that something favorable to the cross-examiner will be elicited. Still others conduct cross-examination out of a fear that the client will not believe that his cause is being effectively advanced without at least an attempt to discredit the opponent's witnesses.

If the advocate consults the trial literature for guidance, he will find conflicting advice. Many commentators urge a restrictive approach and advise that cross-examination to discredit a witness should not be undertaken unless the direct examiner's case has been significantly harmed.[1] Others, however, suggest that it is rarely wise to forgo cross-examination.[2] As we shall show, cross-examination is appropriate in only two circumstances: (1) where the cross-examiner can elicit a strong point for his own case or (2) where he can elicit a point sufficiently harmful to his opponent's case to outweigh the sponsorship costs of asking the question.

The first section discusses general issues relating to cross-examination and explains why sponsorship costs are generally lower on cross-examination than on direct examination. The second section addresses the considerations that are relevant when a cross-examiner is inquiring for the purpose of building up his own case. The third section focuses on considerations pertinent to cross-examining for the purpose of discrediting a witness. Finally, the fourth section discusses a number of techniques for conducting cross-examination.

---

[1] *See, e.g.,* J. Nolan, *Trial Practice: Cases and Materials* 104 (West 1981); J. Tanford, *The Trial Process: Law, Tactics and Ethics* 394 (The Michie Co. 1983); R. Carlson & E. Imwinkelried, *Dynamics of Trial Practice* § 10.2(D), at 162-164 (West 1989); C. Fricke, *Planning and Trying Cases* 373 (West rev. ed. 1957). *Cf.* T. Mauet, *Fundamentals of Trial Techniques* § 6.2, at 212 (Little, Brown & Co. 2d ed. 1988) (noting that cross-examination is not "essential" where you have not been harmed); J. Clark, *Preparation of Cross-Examination* 3 (P.L.I. 1946) (noting that cross-examination of a "witness who testifies as to a purely formal matter or as to incidental facts which are not in dispute or as to matters which are not damaging" is "purposeless," can be "harmful," and "creates an atmosphere of needless contentiousness").

[2] *See, e.g.,* A.E. Morrill, *Trial Diplomacy* 59 (C.P.I. 1971); L.W. Lake, *How to Cross-Examine Witnesses Successfully* 93 (Prentice-Hall 10th ed. 1970) (section entitled "Only Lawyers Without Trial Experience Fail to Find Sensible Questions to Ask [on Cross-Examination]"). *Cf.* R. Keeton, *Trial Tactics and Methods* § 3.3, at 98 (Little, Brown & Co. 2d ed. 1973) (an attorney should generally conduct some cross-examination unless he is "willing to adopt the witness' testimony"); Mauet, *supra* note 1, § 6.8, at 263 (suggesting that in some instances cross-examination is "obligatory," even though "you have nothing that has a chance of succeeding, [because] the jury will expect some kind of cross-examination").

The Lower Sponsorship Costs of Cross-Examination

The sponsorship costs incurred by cross-examination are generally lower than those incurred by direct examination. To begin with, the costs of introduction are normally reduced. As noted in Chapter Two,[3] when an advocate calls a witness, the jury tends to assume that he took pains to package the witness's testimony, organizing and perhaps even sculpting it to reflect his best case. This attitude is one of the two major sources for the discounting phenomenon reflected by the cost of introduction. By contrast, little, if any, of this skepticism is directed towards the cross-examiner. To a great extent, the jury's skepticism is still directed toward the direct examiner. Accordingly, an advocate will generally incur lower costs of introduction by eliciting a point on cross-examination than he would have incurred had *he* called the witness and elicited the same point on direct.[4]

There is a second reason why the cost of introduction is generally lower on cross-examination. As we have explained,[5] when an advocate asks a question on direct examination, he is implicitly conceding the materiality of the testimony. Specifically, the jury assumes that the direct examiner deems the questions posed on direct examination to have justified calling the witness at trial. By contrast, the jury assumes that the cross-examiner deems the questions posed on cross-examination to have justified merely inquiring of a witness already called to court by his opponent. Thus, the concession of materiality resulting from eliciting a given point in a direct examination will, other things being equal, be greater than that involved in eliciting the same point during cross-examination.

---

[3] *See* Chapter Two, pages 27-28, 37-38, *supra.*

[4] To the extent that the cross-examiner strays beyond the scope of the "packaged" direct examination, the difference in the cost of introduction incurred by direct examination and cross-examination will diminish.

[5] *See* Chapter Two, pages 36-37, *supra.*

The cross-examiner will also normally incur lower costs of overtrying. Specifically, the jury is far less apt to conclude that the cross-examiner is relying on a given response to win the case than it is with respect to the lawyer who took the greater step of calling the witness himself. Thus, the cross-examiner's implicit concessions regarding the strength of his evidence and of his opponent's evidence are not apt to be as great.

The foregoing discussion should not be read to suggest that the cross-examiner suffers *no* costs of introduction and overtrying. Whenever a cross-examiner asks a question, he is signaling to the jury that the subject matter of the question is material and that the witness's answer is important to the cross-examiner's case. For instance, when the cross-examiner attempts to discredit a witness and fails, he may suffer considerable harm. Each question posed by the cross-examiner raises the stakes for his case with respect to what the answer will be, since the cross-examiner is suggesting to the jury, with virtually every question he asks, that he expects to expose a flaw or weakness. When the witness simply reaffirms or bolsters his testimony on direct, the cross-examiner looks worse than if the question had not been asked at all.

Unlike the costs of introduction and overtrying, the cost of unusual efforts will not depend on whether such efforts were undertaken by the direct examiner or the cross-examiner. A cross-examiner who takes unusual steps to prove a point — such as impeaching a witness through the use of a large number of documents — will incur substantial costs of efforts even though he did not call the witness.

In sum, while the cost of unusual efforts does not depend on the distinction between direct and cross-examination, the costs of introduction and overtrying *do* depend on that distinction. These two costs are apt to be considerably lower on cross-examination than on direct. Even with respect to these two costs, however, an attorney errs in believing that he suffers no costs by conducting unproductive cross-examination. The cross-examiner must recognize that in cross-examination, as in direct and redirect examination, there is no such thing as a "free" question.

Cross-Examining for Purposes of Advancing One's Case

We have already remarked on the tactical advantages that an advocate reaps by presenting his own case through his opponent's witnesses.[6] Even though the advocate's questions raise the stakes of the witness's response and result in some sponsorship costs, such costs are greatly reduced by the fact that the witness was called by the opponent.

Thus, where local practice permits,[7] one worthwhile goal of cross-examination is to establish one's case through the opponent's witnesses if the opportunity arises. Each witness whom the advocate is relieved from calling, and each question that he is no longer required to ask in his own presentation, benefits him by minimizing his sponsorship costs.

Here, as with direct examination, the advocate should not elicit a point unless it qualifies as strong. Eliciting less-than-strong evidence is, by definition, an unproductive strategy that results in a net harm to the cross-examiner's overall presentation. In evaluating whether a given point qualifies as strong, the advocate should keep in mind, as explained above, that the sponsorship costs incurred by cross-examination are apt to be lower than those incurred by direct examination. He should also recognize, however, that the extent of the difference is not as great when the cross-examination exceeds the scope of direct examination. This is because the jury will be less apt to assume that the witness's cross-examination testimony was packaged

---

[6] *See* Chapter Ten, pages 225-226, *supra*.

[7] *See* Chapter Ten, pages 225-226, note 15, *supra*.

by the direct examiner when such testimony pertains to topics that were not covered during the direct examination.

A cross-examiner who is considering the use of his opponent's witness to advance his own case must recognize that he may face the difficult tactical posture of asking the jury to credit the witness's testimony on some matters yet reject it on others. For instance, if an eyewitness to an armed bank robbery identifies the defendant as the robber but states on cross-examination, contrary to the government's theory, that the assailant did not brandish a weapon, defense counsel will have great difficulty relying on the latter testimony while at the same time challenging the identification. Although this is not impossible to achieve in the proper case,[8] it complicates the cross-examiner's presentation and may make the tactic ill-advised.

Undercutting the Testimony of an Opponent's Witness

The following discussion addresses the considerations pertinent to cross-examining an opponent's witness for the purpose of discrediting him. The first section focuses on identifying a theory for such cross-examination. The second section sets forth the rule for selecting questions to advance that theory.

Developing a Theory for Discrediting the Witness

Before the cross-examiner can decide whether to conduct cross-examination in order to undercut the testimony of an opponent's witness, he must first identify the possible theories for doing so. The potential theories will

[8] *Cf.* 6 J. Bentham, *Rationale of Judicial Evidence* 401 (Bowring ed. 1827) ("No man is so habitually mendacious as not to speak [falsely] a hundred times for once that he speaks [the truth]").

normally fall into one or more of the following: (1) the witness fabricated the testimony or shaded it in the opponent's favor; (2) the witness, while attempting to be truthful, was mistaken; and (3) even if the testimony is correct, it does not materially advance the opponent's case.

Evidence supporting the first theory will often include, for example, prior convictions or bad acts, indications of bias or interest in the outcome, opinion and reputation evidence showing lack of veracity, and indications that the testimony was memorized. Evidence supporting the second theory would include the inadequacy of the witness's memory or his lack of ability to perceive due to such factors as poor hearing or vision. Evidence supporting either the first or second theory would include such matters as internal inconsistencies in the witness's testimony, the inconsistency of the testimony with that of other witnesses, and the fact that the testimony is illogical or does not comport with human experience.

The third theory — that the witness's testimony does not materially favor the opponent's case — can be advanced by questions that define and limit the witness's testimony. Here, a successful cross-examination will serve to demonstrate that the testimony, even if true, is essentially irrelevant. For example, in a drug distribution case tried by one of the authors, three men testified that they were in the same area as the defendant on the day in question and did not see him selling any narcotics. Each witness conceded under questioning, however, that he was paying no particular attention to the defendant and was definitely not watching the defendant's every move. The prosecutor was able to argue with credibility that the witnesses' testimony proved nothing.

In selecting a theory for discrediting the witness, the cross-examiner must recognize the potential dangers of advancing more than one theory simultaneously.[9] Most

---

[9] *See* Chapter Three, pages 50-52, *supra* (discussing risks in advancing alternative theories).

significantly, he should understand that he may incur costs of overtrying by advancing alternative theories. For example, if the cross-examiner expends unusual efforts in attempting to show that the witness's testimony was fabricated, he will have difficulty arguing that the testimony, even if true, does not materially bear on the verdict.

The Rule for Selecting Questions to Undercut the Testimony of an Opponent's Witness

As should be clear from the discussion in Chapter Four,[10] the rule for selecting questions to undercut the testimony of an opponent's witness mirrors the rule of using only strong evidence in the advocate's own case. That rule is that *an advocate should cross-examine to discredit only where the amount by which he can reduce the probative value of the testimony outweighs the sponsorship costs incurred by him in doing so.* In applying this rule, the cross-examiner should take into account the fact that by reducing the probative value of the evidence introduced by his opponent, he will have increased his opponent's costs of overtrying.[11]

In applying this rule, the advocate should recognize that as long as he can elicit testimony sufficiently harmful to his opponent's case to outweigh the sponsorship costs, he should do so. He should not set any artificial limit on how long he spends on his cross-examination or on how many questions he asks.

In contrast to this view, at least one commentator advises an inflexible rule of *never* eliciting more than three points on cross-examination.[12] In our experience, such a rule can result in the loss of valuable cross-examination. There are often more than three points available that qualify as sufficiently harmful to the opponent, and in

[10] *See* pages 106-107, *supra.*

[11] *See* Chapter Four, page 106, *supra* (describing this phenomenon).

[12] *Trial Techniques with Irving Younger* 51 (R. Oliphant ed. 1978).

such circumstances, all of the points should be elicited. One needs only to picture an inexperienced trial lawyer following the commentator's advice who has four powerful ways to undercut the witness, hopelessly unable to decide which of the four to omit. Sponsorship analysis suggests that so long as sponsorship costs are outweighed, the more points that an advocate can make, the better off he is. Of course, as should be clear,[13] at some point the sponsorship costs of eliciting an additional harmful point may outweigh its value. This will occur, for instance, when the jury begins to conclude that the advocate feels the need to elicit the additional point in order to discredit the witness and that the prior points are insufficient to accomplish that purpose.

Just as the advocate should not feel compelled to limit his cross-examination to three points, he should not ask a single question to discredit unless he determines that the harm to his opponent's case will outweigh his own sponsorship costs. For instance, where the advocate must make substantial efforts to elicit only a minor point, he is far better off not asking any questions. In this circumstance, the advocate should state confidently: "I have no questions of the witness."[14]

In short, an advocate should not conduct cross-examination without a careful cost/benefit analysis. This is so even though the sponsorship costs of cross-examination are lower than those on direct. Indeed, notwithstanding the lower sponsorship costs of cross-examination, we believe that the main problem in cross-examination — for inexperienced and experienced lawyers alike — is conducting too *much* cross-examination, not too little. We have seen case after case in which the points elicited are minor or trivial and thus harmful to the cross-examiner's case, once his sponsorship costs are considered. Accord-

[13] *Cf.* Chapter Eight, page 190, *supra.*

[14] Followers of the television series "Perry Mason" will recall that this fictional giant of the law regularly employed this tactic.

ingly, as with any other evidence selection decision, the cross-examiner should proceed with caution in deciding whether to ask a particular question on cross-examination. His general approach should be one of reluctance to ask additional questions rather than one of reluctance to stop.

Notwithstanding the foregoing, there is one situation in which the advocate should be extremely hesitant simply to announce "no questions." That is where the witness at issue is the opponent's central witness. In the jury's eyes, cross-examination of the opponent's central witness is a critical point in the trial. A complete failure to cross-examine might be viewed as an admission by silence.[15] Because of the great harm in letting a crucial witness leave the stand without any cross-examination, the advocate should make a thorough search of all potential avenues of impeachment to find something to use against the witness. If the cross-examiner has conducted such a search, he will usually find at least one or two points that he can make to cast doubt on some aspect of the witness's testimony or otherwise render it less probative.

It is extremely rare that the testimony of a central witness cannot be undermined by some cross-examination. In the first place, because of the lower sponsorship costs incurred by cross-examination generally, the advocate has somewhat more flexibility in eliciting matters on cross than he does on direct. Moreover, if the witness's testimony was strong for the opponent's case, as the testimony of the central witness is likely to be, the costs of overtrying incurred by cross-examination are generally even lower than otherwise. The damage from the implicit concession that the witness's direct examination was strong enough to warrant cross-examination will be at a minimum, since the jury will most likely see that damage regardless of whether the advocate decides to cross-examine.

Finally, the opponent's central witness will often be heavily interested in the outcome of the case. This will

[15] *Qui tacet consentire videtur* (he who is silent appears to consent).

obviously be true in the case of the defendant and the plaintiff (or complainant). The jury assumes, for example, that such a witness would have declined to cooperate with the opposing lawyer prior to trial and that the witness's testimony thus could not have been packaged by that lawyer. With such witnesses, cross-examination emphasizing bias will normally be appropriate.

In the many trials in which we were personally involved as trial counsel, we can recall only one trial where the attorney might have been better off conducting no cross-examination of his opponent's central witness. This was an assault case where a neutral and attentive eyewitness, just a few feet from the assault, gave testimony that totally precluded the defendant's claim of self-defense. Defense counsel conducted some cross-examination but only made matters worse for his case, since the witness merely reiterated his testimony on direct. In that case, as damaging as it would have been, the defense might have been better off asking no questions. Even here, however, defense counsel might have benefited by showing that the witness was thoroughly prepared by the prosecutor. For example, the defense could have elicited that the witness had attended several witness conferences with the prosecutor and had carefully reviewed his prior statements and grand jury testimony.[16]

Cross-Examination Techniques

This section collects some basic techniques for conducting effective cross-examination once the threshold decision to cross-examine has been made. Sponsorship theory sheds light on why these techniques are important.

First, a cross-examiner should never ask a witness to repeat a point favoring his opponent unless the cross-examiner has a specific tactical reason for doing so. For

[16] One commentator refers to this type of cross-examination as "apparent" cross-examination. Mauet, *supra* note 1, § 6.8, at 263.

example, it is perfectly appropriate to ask a witness to repeat a seemingly damaging fact when the cross-examiner's next step is to impeach the witness with a contradictory statement. Absent such a situation, however, there is usually no reason for a cross-examiner to compound the damage from direct examination by eliciting a witness's repetition of a harmful piece of testimony. In our experience, much of the cross-examination elicited in actual trials consists of nothing more than a repetition of a witness's main points on direct. As should be clear, the answer will normally have more impact upon repetition than it did on direct examination.[17]

Second, the cross-examiner should generally not ask a question unless he knows in advance what the witness's answer will be. This point is well known and should be obvious, since the evaluation of the probative value of the expected answer is basic to deciding whether to incur the costs of asking the question. It is important to emphasize, however, that the rule is not an inflexible one.[18] There may be times — especially in criminal cases, where discovery is limited — when the cross-examiner has little choice but to probe in the dark.[19] For instance, where a witness has given harmful testimony on direct that could not get much worse, the cross-examiner may sometimes be justified in searching for weaknesses, particularly where the witness's story seems highly implausible and there is a good chance that the cross-examiner can make progress in casting doubt on that story.

---

[17] *Cf.* Wash. Post, Feb. 23, 1989, at A1, Col. 3 (noting that at the criminal trial of former White House aide Oliver North, the defense lawyer's "day long" cross-examination of a prosecution witness reportedly resulted in the witness "at times [making] points on cross-examination in even stronger language than he had on direct questioning by [the] prosecutor").

[18] *Contra,* I. Younger, *The Art of Cross-Examination* 23 (A.B.A. Monograph Series 1976) ("[Y]ou should *never* ask a question to which you do not already know the answer.") (emphasis in original).

[19] *Accord, e.g.,* F. Bailey & H. Rothblatt, *Successful Techniques for Criminal Trials* § 11.20, at 307 (Lawyers Co-op. Pub. Co. 1985).

Third, in establishing a point that damages the witness, the cross-examiner should avoid permitting the witness to offer an explanation. Instead, he should elicit only the point that disfavors his opponent's case, thereby forcing the opponent to supply the mitigating context on redirect. This tends to make the opponent, not the cross-examiner, the sponsor of the explanation.[20]

The best means of accomplishing this purpose is to use leading questions. This puts the advocate who initially called the witness in the position of being held accountable for any imperfections in the explanation. Even if the explanation is a plausible one, the cross-examiner is better off letting his opponent elicit it, since the jury is likely to give it less weight.

Some commentators suggest strict rules of *never* using non-leading questions on cross-examination and *never* permitting a witness to explain an answer.[21] While these rules are generally sound, we believe that there are times when both of them must be violated.

For instance, it will frequently be counterproductive for an advocate to attempt to cut off a witness's answer. An advocate who makes substantial efforts to do so may suggest to the jury that he has something to hide. As a result, the jury may give the testimony heightened weight when the witness ultimately gives his complete explanation.[22]

---

[20] *But see* Chapter Eight, pages 198-200, *supra* (discussing methods of redirect examination for making the cross-examiner largely responsible for the witness's explanation).

[21] *See, e.g.*, Younger, *supra* note 18, at 23 ("[Y]ou should *never* ask anything but leading questions on cross-examination.") (emphasis added); *id.* at 28 ("A trial lawyer must *never* permit the witness to explain anything on cross-examination.") (emphasis added); *cf.* K. Hegland, *Trial and Practice Skills* 72-73 (West 1978) (reciting benefits of leading questions); R. Carlson, *Successful Techniques for Civil Trials* § 4:8, at 200 (Lawyers Co-op. Pub. Co. 1983) (stating that the use of leading questions is a "principle[]" of cross-examination); Mauet, *supra* note 1, § 6.4, at 216 (noting that "[o]pen-ended questions are disastrous on cross-examinations" and that "[q]uestions that ask 'how' or 'why' or elicit explanations of any kind invite disaster ... [and] are best avoided altogether").

[22] *See* Chapter Eight, page 199, *supra.*

Thus, a cross-examiner will only harm his case by taking pains to hide a witness's explanation, such as by interrupting the witness and shouting, "I just asked for a 'yes' or 'no' answer."

The rule of using only leading questions on cross-examination is likewise not an inflexible one. To begin with, where the cross-examiner concludes that he must probe even though he does not know the precise answer,[23] he obviously cannot ask leading questions. More fundamentally, the technique of using leading questions is generally beneficial only when the cross-examiner knows or suspects that a complete explanation will put the witness's answer in a perspective that is more favorable to the opponent's case. When the cross-examiner is virtually certain that the witness's answer *and* his explanation will benefit the cross-examiner's case, it will normally be in his interest to ask *nonleading* questions. As we explained in Chapter Eight with reference to direct examination,[24] an advocate can reduce his sponsorship costs by using nonleading questions. This applies *a fortiori* to cross-examination of an opponent's witnesses, since the jury has no reason to suspect that the witness's responses were verified in advance in a pre-trial witness conference.

Fourth, as in most trial situations, the cross-examiner must maintain a "poker face," regardless of how harmful he views the witness's response. The cross-examiner does not want to signal to the jury that his case was harmed by testimony that he has elicited.[25]

Fifth, the manner in which cross-examination is conducted bears critically on the sponsorship costs that are incurred. To minimize the cost of efforts, the cross-examiner must not appear to be expecting to accomplish very much, if anything, as a result of his questioning. The only

---

[23] *See* page 240, *supra.*

[24] *See* pages 184-187, *supra.*

[25] *Accord, e.g.*, J. Kestler, *Questioning Techniques and Tactics* § 1.23, at 23 (Shepard's/McGraw Hill, Inc. 1982).

message communicated by a lengthy and acrimonious cross-examination is that he *needs* to make inroads to win the case.

For example, in impeaching a witness with a prior conviction, the cross-examiner should not advance towards the witness waving a certified copy of the conviction, booming loudly, "Isn't it a fact, sir, that you were convicted of second degree burglary in 1985?", and then return to counsel table with a triumphant smirk after receiving the witness's affirmative response. The jury will only conclude that the advocate deemed it significant to his case to establish the point. Instead, the advocate should casually ask the witness during the course of his examination: "Are you the same John Jones who was convicted of second-degree burglary in 1985?" After receiving an affirmative response, he should then move immediately to his next point.

In short, the cross-examination should appear effortless. If great efforts — such as a lengthy impeachment involving numerous documents — are necessary to elicit a point, then cross-examination may not be appropriate.[26]

Finally, the cross-examiner should keep in mind, in crafting his cross-examination, that an alert opponent will be monitoring his every move. The cross-examiner should thus avoid asking questions that supply his opponent with ammunition for closing argument. Most importantly, as Chapter Twelve demonstrates,[27] the questions should not suggest alternative or inconsistent theories.

To summarize, an advocate faces difficult issues in deciding whether to cross-examine and, if so, what questions to ask. While the sponsorship costs are low, thus permit-

---

[26] An effort-minimizing "best case" advocate will use that evidence which gives him the greatest value for the quantum of effort expended. Thus, labored efforts on cross-examination to elicit minor points will underscore the limited amount of superior evidence available to the advocate. *See* Chapter Two, note 39, *supra* (noting applicability of constrained optimization techniques).

[27] *See* pages 277-281, *infra.*

ting more leeway in examination, a labored examination dwelling on minor points will be counterproductive. The cross-examiner must keep in mind that even one ill-considered question can seriously damage his case.

12

Closing Argument

When the time has come for closing argument, the jurors will have heard all of the evidence and perhaps will have arrived at some initial conclusions. Because of their inexperience, however, they will understandably lack confidence in these initial assessments and will have many questions on their minds. They will be waiting anxiously for the lawyers' remarks.

In a rape case, for example, they will look to the lawyers for guidance in assessing the victim's testimony. Have they been too gullible regarding certain aspects of her testimony? They will be waiting to see if defense counsel raises that issue. Did defense counsel go "too far" — that is, was he too abusive — in cross-examining the victim on her previous intimacies? The jurors will be looking to see if the prosecutor makes an issue out of this. They will be relying on each trained advocate to explain the defects and inadequacies of his opponent's presentation, as well as the merits of his own case. Each advocate's view of the evidence will come to represent the best-case scenario for his side and the worst-case scenario for his opponent's side. Criticisms not made — as well as strengths not identified — may be lost forever.

This chapter provides guidance on how to craft a persuasive closing argument. The first section discusses various general considerations. The second section offers a detailed framework for structuring the argument. In particular, it emphasizes the critical need for the advocate to present his own evidence in its best light and his opponent's evidence in its worst light. It also stresses the value of highlighting the opponent's concessions. The third section focuses on arguments to rebut the opponent's remarks.

General Considerations

Comment on the Advocate's and Opponent's Respective Strengths and Weaknesses

If the advocate has adhered to the guidance set forth in this book, his case will be concise and easily analyzed for the jury. If the opponent has failed to adhere to sponsorship theory, then his presentation will be overloaded with extraneous evidence, comments, and questions that do not advance his theory of the case. Moreover, there will normally be many concessions by opposing counsel that an advocate can emphasize. For these reasons, the advocate's discussion of the flaws in his opponent's case may consume even more time than his discussion of his own evidence.

The techniques that an advocate should employ in discussing the strengths and weaknesses of his own case and that of his opponent can be easily derived from the principles outlined in Chapters Two and Four. As explained in Chapter Two, no juror during deliberations will be apt to espouse a favorable argument or perception concerning the advocate's case that the advocate himself fails to make.[1] This means that arguments not made in summation will probably not be made for the advocate in the jury

[1] *See* Chapter Two, pages 20-21, *supra.*

room. To be sure, a juror will occasionally make such an argument. For instance, in a criminal case, there will sometimes be a member of the jury who delights in making himself appear astute by espousing theories of innocence not even urged by defense counsel. The advocate is obviously unwise, however, in deliberately omitting a favorable argument and relying on such an argument to be made for him by a juror. For this reason, when the advocate has put on evidence, he must discuss that evidence in its best light. He likewise must discuss his opponent's evidence and contentions in their worst light.

Sponsorship theory counsels that arguments by an advocate designed to accomplish this task must never be delivered half-heartedly.[2] As with opening statements, this is no time for understatement,[3] since anything the advocate says that favors his case or criticizes his opponent's case will be heavily discounted by the jury.[4] Although an advocate is not permitted to state his personal belief or opinion on disputed matters of fact,[5] he plainly wants to avoid communicating a *lack* of belief in matters

[2] *Cf.* A. Kruger, *Modern Debate: Its Logic and Strategy* 193 (McGraw-Hill 1960) ("Since most people are disturbed when they experience feelings of doubt, [the] appeal [by the confident manner] attempts to allay their doubts and help make up their minds. Debaters often use this technique by introducing such terms as 'certainly,' 'obviously,' 'perfectly clear' and 'surely.'").

[3] *Contra, e.g.,* T. Mauet, *Fundamentals of Trial Techniques* § 7.2, at 276 (Little, Brown & Co. 2d ed. 1988) (describing understatement as a potentially "powerful argumentative tool").

[4] President Bush's practice of describing his administration's proposals in glowing terms is consistent with this approach. *See, e.g.,* N.Y. Times, May 30, 1989, at A-1, col. 6 (noting that President Bush characterized as "revolutionary" his United States/Soviet conventional troop reduction proposals for Western Europe, which he unveiled at the Spring 1989 NATO summit). *Cf.* L. Pearson, *The Art of Demosthenes* 9 (Scholars Press 1981) ("Demosthenes ... often overstate[d] his case ... [with the] object ... [of] forc[ing] his opponents to suggest to the jury the kind of judgment that they will be willing to pass.").

[5] *See, e.g.,* Model Code of Professional Responsibility, DR 7-106(C)(4) (forbidding attorneys from expressing personal opinion); 1 *American Bar Association, Standards for Criminal Justice* (2d ed. 1980), Standard 3-5.8(b), at 3-87 (prosecutor); *id.,* Standard 4-7.8(b), at 4-96 (defense counsel in criminal case); *cf.* Model Code of Professional Responsibility, EC 7-24.

material to his case. The only means of ensuring against this is for him to maintain an enthusiastic demeanor regarding both the strength of his case and the weakness of his opponent's case. Where possible, his goal should be to have the jury wondering to itself why his opponent even filed the case (if the opponent is the plaintiff or prosecutor) or why, if the opponent is the defendant, he did not settle it or plead guilty.[6]

A useful way to illustrate the goal of dwelling on one's own strengths and the opponent's weaknesses is to consider two glasses of water, the first representing the advocate's theory of the case and the second his opponent's theory. No matter how much water is in the two glasses, the advocate's strategy for summation must be to emphasize the full part his glass and the empty part of his opponent's glass.[7]

As set forth more fully below, an important technique is for an advocate to compare his case with a hypothetically weak case in the same subject area. This technique facilitates the jury's appreciation of the evidence that the advocate presented to support his case. Similarly, it is useful for him to compare his opponent's case with a hypothetically strong case in the same subject area, thus facilitating the jury's appreciation of how much better his opponent's

---

[6] Of course, the advocate must avoid stating that his opponent should have given up his right to a trial.

[7] As to the latter, consider an example from the oratory of Demosthenes' teacher, Isaeus:

> [My opponent] ought to have given us figures and brought witnesses: he ought to have gone through each ... item in the account.... He ought to have examined the decrees, the amounts imposed, the amounts paid, the persons who collected them, and then, if all was satisfactory, he ought to have accepted my statement; or, if it was not, he ought *now* to have brought witnesses regarding any false item in the outlay which I charged....

II R. Jebb, *The Attic Orators from Antiphon to Isaeus* 305 (Russell and Russell, Inc. 1962) (quoting from an oration of Isaeus). *Cf.* Aristotle, *Rhetoric,* 1392a1, *translated in* II *The Complete Works of Aristotle* 2217 (Princeton Univ. Press, Barnes ed. 1984) ("[T]he topic of size is common to all oratory; all of us have to argue that things are bigger or smaller than they seem....").

case could have been. By the same token, the advocate should avoid discussing the degree to which his glass is empty and his opponent's glass is full. That is his opponent's job.

The Advocate's Goal of Minimizing His Burden of Proof

An overriding goal of any trial attorney should be to minimize the degree to which the jury views him as having the burden of persuasion. For the plaintiff's attorney or prosecutor, there is, of course, an initial burden of proof that he must satisfy as a matter of law. The first task of such an advocate will be to impress upon the jury that the evidence that he has presented satisfies this burden. If the defense has opted to put on a case, the advocate should frame the issue for the jury as one of determining whether his opponent's evidence is sufficient to overcome the advocate's otherwise sufficient case.[8]

If the defense has not put on a case, then the plaintiff's attorney or prosecutor should frame the issue as one of whether the defense *contentions* are sufficient to overcome the advocate's otherwise sufficient case. As suggested in Chapter Ten,[9] in this latter case, the advocate must define the defendant's version of the facts using defense counsel's opening statement and the questions that defense counsel asked on cross-examination. In his closing argument, the prosecutor or plaintiff's lawyer should identify for the jury the defendant's competing version of the facts and expose the weaknesses in that version, just as he would have done had the defense chosen to support its competing theory by presenting a case.

The perspective of the defense lawyer is different from that of the plaintiff's lawyer or prosecutor. Since the de-

---

[8] A prosecutor, of course, must be careful not to suggest that the defense has any burden or was required to put on a case.

[9] *See* pages 213-218, *supra*.

fense has no burden of proof except with respect to affirmative defenses, any talk of the merits of the "defense case" plays into the hands of his opponent. It tends to shift the burden — and thus the jury's tendencies to discount and scrutinize — to the defense.

The best of all worlds for defense counsel is where he is not forced into the position of having to discuss his evidence at length. This will be true when his opponent has called all available witnesses and introduced all pertinent exhibits, including those favoring the defense theory of the case. In such a case, all of the jury's tendencies to discount and scrutinize will be directed at his opponent. This will be even more true where defense counsel's opponent took the additional step of volunteering all matters favorable to the defense as part of the direct examination of those witnesses.

Even where defense counsel has opted to put on his own case or conduct extensive cross-examination of his opponent's witnesses, he should attempt to focus his primary attention on scrutinizing and attacking his opponent's case. He should suggest, where appropriate, that the evidence that he introduced is really part and parcel of evidence that his opponent introduced and is best viewed that way.[10] Of course, defense counsel should recognize that it is essential for him to stress the probative value of evidence that he does choose to introduce. He does not want to open himself to attack for abandoning his own evidence.[11]

---

[10] *Cf.* Chapter Eight, pages 198-200, *supra* (discussing analogous technique for redirect examination).

[11] An example illustrating many of the foregoing points can be found in the oratory of Antiphon, an ancient Athenian orator sometimes called the "father" of Sophist rhetoric. In *On the Murder of Herodes,* a speech (generally deemed his most important) that was written for delivery by a defendant charged with murder, Antiphon had the defendant pointedly avoid suggesting explanations of how some other individual could have committed the crime, it not being the defendant's business to show who was or might have been the murderer. The greatest stress in the argument was placed on the unreliability of a central prosecution witness. The defendant did not dwell upon his alibi, or attempt to

The Rule of Using Only Strong Contentions

In crafting a closing argument, the advocate must recognize that any comment or contention that an advocate considers making must be subjected to the same cost/benefit analysis that applies to evidence. A comment about an item of evidence, for example, may be discounted by the jury because of the costs of introduction. Specifically, the jury may assume that the advocate carefully chose (or packaged) his words and phrasing to make the point in the most persuasive manner possible. This cost of packaging can be countered, at least in part, by using the technique of deprecating one's own oratorical skills while complimenting those of the opponent. This technique may also serve to undermine the jury's assumption that it has seen the advocate's best case while fortifying its assumption that it has seen the *opponent's* best case.

In recognition of the jury's suspicion that the summation is packaged, the advocate should carefully prepare his remarks to achieve at least the corresponding benefit of packaging.[12] At the same time, he should avoid the impression that he carefully prepared and packaged every phrase.

In addition to the packaging component, there is the concession of materiality component: the advocate will be viewed as conceding the materiality of any point that he makes.[13] And, because of the cost of overtrying, the com-

---

prove it, but mentioned it only incidentally. Finally, there was little or no bid for sympathy. *See* R. Jebb, *The Attic Orators from Antiphon to Isaeus* 55-61 (MacMillan and Co. 1893) (containing foregoing analysis).

[12] *Cf.* Jebb, *supra* note 11, at lxxi (noting that "Demosthenes would never speak [without preparing his remarks] when he could help it").

[13] Superior advocates will be alert to capitalize on an opponent's concessions of materiality. *See, e.g.,* W. Wyse, *The Speeches of Isaeus* 217 (Cambridge Univ. Press 1904) (containing following excerpt: "You will learn best the justice of our cause from our opponents .... [T]hey rest their claim to inherit [the decedent's] estate [on the contentions] that they are somehow related to him and that for a time he was friendly with them. Will not this answer be in favor of us rather

ment might cause the jury to give less weight to the advocate's other comments.

In addition, there are costs of unusual efforts to assess. Consider, for example, defense counsel's decision whether to raise his voice and denounce as an "outrage" the government's prosecution in the face of such flimsy evidence. The situation is similar to the decision of whether to introduce an enlargement of a photograph. In both situations, the advocate must decide whether the benefits are worth the costs of unusual efforts. Just as he should not introduce an enormous blow-up of a photograph that does not advance his case, he obviously should not scream at the top of his lungs, "What I say is *not* evidence!" By the same token, if an advocate spends excessive time making a given comment or contention, he will incur costs of unusual efforts. Those efforts must be justified by the favorable value of the comment or contention.

Finally, as should be apparent from the foregoing chapters, juries view concessions of counsel as very significant and place heavy reliance on them. Thus, closing argument should be used not just to summarize the evidence in the case but also to summarize and exploit any concessions — explicit as well as implicit — made by opposing counsel during the trial. If the opponent's conduct at trial strayed from principles of sponsorship, the advocate will have collected many concessions to stress to the jury. At the same time, the advocate who has adhered to sponsorship theory in his conduct of the trial will have minimized his risk of exposure to such criticism during his opponent's summation. The advocate, of course, should not reflexively highlight every concession made by his opponent. As with any other comment, the value of the opponent's concessions must outweigh the sponsorship costs of bringing them to the jury's attention.

than of them? We are nearer relations, we, as all the world knows, were on more friendly terms with him.").

In sum, in crafting his closing argument, the advocate must adhere to the general rule of using only strong contentions and comments. Less compelling arguments should be omitted.[14]

Framework for Argument

In our experience, the optimum organization for a closing argument — for plaintiffs' attorneys, prosecutors, and defense attorneys alike — consists of five parts: initial remarks; comment on the evidence introduced by the advocate carrying the initial burden of proof; transitional remarks; comments on the evidence and contentions of the advocate not carrying the initial burden; and concluding remarks. The following sections give guidance on crafting each of these portions of the summation.

The sections are set forth in the order that they should be delivered by the plaintiff's attorney or prosecutor. The defense attorney should transpose the section entitled "Comment on the Opponent's Case" with the section entitled "Comment on the Advocate's Case." In this way, he can dwell first on how the opponent's evidence fails to sustain the burden of proof before turning to how his own evidence confirms that the defense should prevail.[15]

Initial Remarks

The advocate's initial remarks should focus solely on the issues in dispute and how the evidence requires a

---

[14] This sponsorship rule is consistent with the practice of the orator Antiphon, who is said to have "tend[ed] to pick out one argument and ... not systematically exhaust all possible arguments." G. Kennedy, *The Art of Persuasion in Greece* 131 (Princeton Univ. Press 1963).

[15] *Accord,* Aristotle, *supra* note 7, at 1418b1 (translated in *Complete Works of Aristotle,* at 2266) ("Both in political speaking and when pleading in court, if you are the first speaker you should put your own arguments forward first, and then meet the arguments on the other side by refuting them and pulling them to pieces beforehand.... If you speak later, you must first, by means of refutation and counter-deduction, attempt some answer to your opponent's speech ... [by] attack[ing] that first....").

verdict in the advocate's favor. For example, in a negligence case involving a defense of unavoidable accident, defense counsel should begin his argument along the following lines:

> Ladies and gentlemen of the jury: At the beginning of the trial, I told you that the evidence would show that the accident in this case was unavoidable. You have now heard all of the evidence and I submit to you that it clearly leads to only one conclusion: the defendant is not liable for plaintiff's injuries.

The advocate should then proceed directly into a discussion of the evidence.

In contrast to this approach, many trial attorneys believe that a closing argument should begin with a discussion of neutral legal principles, such as noting that what the lawyers say is not evidence. In our view, there is nothing to be gained by such remarks.[16] The advocate is not advancing his case in the least by highlighting points of law that do not lead the jury to rule in his favor. In addition, while there may be times that the advocate will want to deprecate his own skills,[17] it is not wise for him to tell the jury that his memory is not as good as the jury's and that the jury's recollection should control.

One leading commentator[18] provides the following passages as the ideal way to begin a closing argument:

> This is my final opportunity to talk to you about this case. At the outset let me say that if my recollection of any of the facts or testimony given in this trial

---

[16] Some commentators recognize this point. *See, e.g.,* S. Goldberg, *The First Trial: Where Do I Sit? What Do I Say?* 206 (West 1982); J. Jeans, *Trial Advocacy* § 8.11, at 205-206 (West 1975). Others, however, believe that such discussion is useful. *See, e.g.,* T. Mauet, *Fundamentals of Trial Techniques,* § 7.5, at 297, 311 (Little, Brown & Co. 1988).

[17] *See* page 251, *supra.*

[18] 1 S. Schweitzer, *Cyclopedia of Trial Practice* § 273, at 701-702 (Lawyers Co-op. Pub. Co. 2d ed. 1970).

> is at variance with your own, accept your own recollection. It is as good or better than my own.
>
> I have lived with this case for some time, and there is always the possibility that during the excitement of a trial, I will not have had the full opportunity to observe all the facts in their true light. If my recollection of any matter is erroneous, I assure you it is not intentional.
>
> It is my purpose in this final argument to sum up the facts and the facts alone. I will try to add up the testimony and evidence presented in this trial, and see if we can arrive at a total that will do justice to the plaintiff, to the defendant, and to your own consciences as jurors.
>
> It is also my purpose to state the facts fairly and frankly, and to make my comment as honest and sincere as it is in my power to make. Please bear in mind that my comment, like that of my opponent, is naturally biased.
>
> Remember further that neither my opponent nor myself saw this accident, [and] our powers of deduction and inference are no better than your own. You know now as much about this case as the lawyers or the judge. And I ask that you remember that fact when you begin your deliberations upon the issues.

In our view, this presentation serves no useful purpose. The advocate will probably have lost the jury's attention before he even begins to discuss the evidence. Moreover, such a presentation might actually damage the advocate's case.

First, the advocate has given the jury reason to doubt the accuracy of his recollection, and the jury may therefore be less inclined to focus on what he says during the rest of his argument. Second, the advocate has underscored that his view of the case is biased. While the jury no doubt assumes this, there is no reason to underscore the point. Third, the advocate has undermined the force of his presentation by pointing out that an attorney's power of deduction and inference is no better than that of the jury. A jury looks to the advocate, a trained professional, for guidance in identifying the merits of his case and the weaknesses of his opponent's case. If the jury concludes that the advocate has no special skills in assessing the evidence, then it will be less inclined to credit his arguments.

In short, the above-quoted introduction to a closing argument accomplishes nothing with respect to the advocate's goal of obtaining a verdict in his favor. At best, such remarks are neutral principles that will benefit both sides equally. At worst, such statements will cause the jury to lack confidence in the advocate when he begins to focus on the evidence. Accordingly, we believe that the above-quoted passage should be viewed as a model of how *not* to begin a closing argument.

On a related matter, while it is important to be courteous and well-mannered, we caution against the use of kind words for the jury, such as praise for its patience and attention. Remarks of this type have no realistic chance of swaying the jury to render a verdict in the advocate's favor and may be interpreted as patronizing or insincere.[19]

Comment on the Advocate's Case

Highlighting Strengths

The first task for an advocate in summarizing the merits of his case is to highlight the strengths of the case. If the advocate has followed the principles of sponsorship in the presentation of his case, this task will involve a brief recounting of the testimony of each witness that he has called, each major point elicited therefrom, and each exhibit introduced. If any of his witnesses or exhibits do not

[19] *Cf.* G.W. Keeton, *Harris's Hints on Advocacy* 35 (Stevens & Sons, Ltd. 18th ed. 1943) ("Nothing makes a jury more keenly sensitive of your contempt for their mental capacity than flattering them.").

bear mention at this point, he probably should not have introduced such evidence in the first place.

With regard to the structure of the argument, we believe that a presentation in a story or chronological form is more effective than a straight witness-by-witness approach. The latter approach tends to bore and confuse the jury.

Minimizing Reliance on Any One Item of Evidence

When the advocate has introduced multiple items of strong evidence, he will often be in a position to argue that certain items, standing alone, warrant a verdict in his favor. The approach when he has introduced such evidence is to isolate and identify for the jury each such item. This approach will minimize his cost of overtrying by communicating that he is not relying on any particular piece of evidence to win.[20]

An example will illustrate the point. Assume that the defendant in a civil automobile accident case is alleged to have been negligently driving while intoxicated. Assume further that the arresting police officer can testify that the defendant's breath had a strong odor of alcohol, that the defendant could not maintain his balance, and that his speech was slurred. Finally, assume that the breathalyzer test revealed a blood alcohol level consistent with intoxication. Plaintiff's attorney could argue along the following lines:

> The testimony of the arresting officer concerning the defendant's intoxicated state at the scene of the accident is, by itself, easily sufficient to hold the defendant liable by a preponderance of the evidence. Without any other evidence, that testimony is far more than the plaintiff needs. However, we also have scien-

[20] *Cf.* Jebb, *supra* note 11, at 51 (citing example of Antiphon stressing in argument the independent sufficiency of two separate grounds for a verdict in his favor).

tific evidence showing the defendant's high blood-alcohol level. That scientific evidence, without more, also easily proves defendant's intoxication. Taken together, the evidence is overwhelming and establishes negligence beyond all doubt.

This argument is important in keeping the jury from concluding that the advocate felt that he needed *all* of his evidence to win.

Comparison of the Advocate's Case to a Hypothetically Weak Case

Where appropriate, the advocate should compare the degree of evidence supporting his case to a hypothetically weak case of a similar type. This directs the jury's attention to the "full part of the glass," as it were, and maximizes its appreciation of the advocate's evidence. It further serves to bolster a contention, in cases where it is warranted, that the advocate's evidence is "strong" or "overwhelming."

For example, assume a negligence case involving an automobile accident where the plaintiff's case is supported by two strong eyewitnesses and by a sobriety test revealing the defendant's intoxication. In such a case, the plaintiff should point out that the jury is not being asked to find liability based on a single witness of doubtful strength. Rather, the plaintiff has offered *two strong* witnesses, as well as strong scientific evidence.

Highlighting the Opponent's Unproductive Cross-Examination

Juries invariably perceive cross-examination as a time for testing. They tend to believe that the major reason for asking questions on cross-examination is to challenge the witness's version of the facts. If the advocate's witness gives satisfactory answers to his opponent's questions, the advocate should note for the jury that cross-examination is the greatest engine ever developed for determining truth and that his opponent's efforts to test the witness only serve to underscore the accuracy of the testimony. The opponent will have no credible means of disputing the advocate's characterization of his reason for examining the advocate's witness. The jury will be apt to conclude that the witness's answers were verified.

Even if the matters elicited are slightly harmful to his case, the advocate can belittle them by characterizing them as "awful revelation[s]."[21] Furthermore, the greater the effort expended by the opponent in his failed attempt, the more powerful the argument will be. Where appropriate, a compliment regarding the opponent's skills and high proficiency as an attorney will emphasize the meagerness of the results of his cross-examination.

Finally, where opposing counsel asked no questions of one of the advocate's witnesses, the advocate should argue that the witness's testimony was undisputed and conceded by the opponent. The opponent will have great difficulty countering such an argument.

Highlighting Jury Instructions That Support the Advocate's Case

As we explained in Chapter Eight,[22] because of the costs involved when an advocate introduces any item of evidence, regardless of its strength, he is better off if his evidence is introduced by his opponent or by the court. This phenomenon of reduced sponsorship costs applies as well to statements concerning the law. If the advocate summarizes the applicable law in his closing argument, the jury will tend to view that discussion with skepticism. The advocate can reduce that skepticism, however, by

[21] R. Traver, *Anatomy of a Murder* 464 (Dell 1958) (phrase used in fictional summation).

[22] *See* pages 71, 200-201, *supra*.

prefacing his discussion of legal points, where applicable, with the phrase, "As the Judge will tell you ...."[23] The jury will be impressed when the judge later confirms what the advocate has said.

Thus, for example, if the advocate represents a defendant in a case in which the government's chief witness was a paid informant, the advocate should emphasize that the judge will instruct the jury that the testimony of the witness "must be examined and weighed ... with greater care than the testimony of an ordinary witness."[24]

Discussing the Purpose of the Advocate's Introduction of Evidence Bearing on Undisputed Issues

As explained in Chapter Three, the advocate with the burden of proof must introduce evidence to satisfy his legal burden even on elements of his claim that are not disputed by his opponent. In summation, such an advocate should, of course, stress his opponent's failure to dispute the element. In addition, however, he will want to refer to the evidence that he introduced to satisfy the undisputed elements and tell the jury that his introduction was merely designed to meet technical legal requirements. This will serve to ensure that he suffers no costs of overtrying from the use of such evidence.

Techniques for Arguing Alternative Theories

As we explained in Chapter Three,[25] although an advocate should never advance inconsistent theories, there are apt to be occasions in which it is useful for him to advance

---

[23] Numerous commentators have recognized the value of this technique. *See, e.g.*, F. Bailey & H. Rothblatt, *Successful Techniques for Criminal Trials* § 21:10, at 482 (Lawyers Co-op. Pub. Co. 1985) (counseling defense reference to the court's instruction regarding high burden of proof in a criminal prosecution).

[24] 1 E. Devitt & C. Blackmar, *Federal Jury Practice and Instructions* § 17.02, at 524 (West 3d ed. 1977) (sample jury instructions).

[25] *See* pages 50-52, *supra*.

alternative consistent theories. In Chapter Three, we gave the example of a defendant charged with heroin distribution who had an alibi defense but who could also cast doubt on the accuracy of tests showing that the substance was heroin.[26] As we indicated, the defense attorney might find it beneficial to argue that his client was not the one who sold the substance and that, in any event, the substance was not heroin.

The important point for an advocate to keep in mind in arguing alternative theories is that he must not suggest that he is conceding the inadequacy of evidence supporting either theory. In the heroin case, for example, the advocate should *not* argue: "Even if you believe that my client was the one selling the substance, there is insufficient evidence to show that it was heroin." Such an argument might be read by the jury as an implicit concession that the evidence linking his client to the sales activity was compelling and that the advocate felt that, in order to win, he needed to convince the jury that the substance sold was not heroin.

Instead, the advocate should underscore that each theory is independently strong. In the above heroin case, for example, the advocate may wish to suggest that the case before the jury is one of those rare cases where the government's evidence is so weak that the jury can in essence return two not guilty verdicts rather than just one: one for the defendant and one for the real seller, who got away but who was also innocent of any criminal activity (except taking money under false pretenses). The advocate making such an argument must, however, avoid imparting the impression that he is relying on the inadequacy of the chemical tests to win. In that regard, he must be careful to focus his indignation on the insufficiency of the evidence bearing on identification.

---

[26] *See* pages 51-52, *supra*.

Transitional Remarks

After completing his discussion of the burdened party's evidence,[27] the advocate should make some transitional remarks before addressing the evidence and contentions of the non-burdened party. For the plaintiff's attorney or prosecutor, the transition should set forth a brief recapitulation — no more than several sentences — of his own evidence, along with the submission that his burden of proof is easily met by that evidence. He should then turn the jury's attention to the defense presentation. Thus, immediately after his recapitulation, the advocate should make remarks consistent with the following:

> That, ladies and gentlemen, is the plaintiff's case — a strong case for liability. Now, what is the defense theory of the case?

The advocate should then proceed directly into a discussion of the defense evidence and contentions, employing the guidance contained in the following section.

In substance, the defense attorney will want to do precisely the mirror image of what we recommend for his burdened opponent. Thus, after discussing his opponent's evidence at length in accordance with the guidance set forth in the following section, he should briefly recapitulate the failings in his opponent's case and evidence, and conclude that his opponent's evidence totally fails to meet his burden of proof. Assuming that he has put on evidence of his own beyond evidence designed merely to rebut, he should then turn the jury's attention to his own proof. The following provides an illustration of defense counsel's transition:

[27] As we noted above, both sides will discuss this evidence first. For plaintiffs' lawyers and prosecutors, this will be a discussion showing the strength of the evidence. For defense counsel, this will mean attacking the evidence using the techniques in the section entitled "Comment on the Opponent's Case."

> That, ladies and gentlemen, is the plaintiff's evidence. Standing alone, it fails utterly to make his case. But it is even worse for the plaintiff, since the *defense* has compelling evidence that affirmatively shows the defendant's lack of liability. Now, what is the defense evidence?

The defense attorney would then discuss his own evidence in accordance with the principles contained in the foregoing section.

Comment on the Opponent's Case

As we have noted throughout this book, the jury expects the advocate to expose the shortcomings of his opponent's case. In mounting his attack, however, the advocate must avoid the appearance of creating a "straw man." To accomplish this, the advocate must limit his criticism of the opponent's case to matters that the opponent has put into issue.

This book has demonstrated that virtually any action of opposing counsel — even a solitary question posed on cross-examination — may qualify as a subject matter for attack. Thus, before developing a plan for criticizing his opponent's case, the advocate should carefully review his notes containing his record of opposing counsel's statements, questions to witnesses, and evidence introduced. So long as opposing counsel put a matter in issue by one of these three means, the advocate should consider that matter a candidate for use in his attack, regardless of — indeed, often because of — how little the matter bears on the dispute.

The rule here, which mirrors the rule of using only strong evidence, is to inflict all rhetorical blows that outweigh the sponsorship costs of doing so. In this regard, the advocate need not be concerned that his rhetorical attack on his opponent's case will alienate the jury. As we have stated, the jury expects it of him.[28]

One final preliminary point should be made. As previously noted,[29] the advocate should strive to minimize his reliance on any one item of his own evidence. By contrast, he will want to emphasize that his opponent *needed* each item of evidence to have any chance of winning.

Before making *any* argument suggested below, the advocate must assure himself that the argument is permissible in his jurisdiction. Courts differ widely in the extent to which they circumscribe arguments of counsel. Moreover, the propriety of an argument may depend on whether the case is civil or criminal.

The advocate should be especially mindful not to attribute the opponent's actions to his *beliefs*.[30] Thus, if the opponent has called a strong witness and a weak one, the advocate cannot state:

> Mr. Smith called that second witness [the weak one] because he obviously believed that the first one was not sufficient.[31]

Rather, assuming no governing authorities to the contrary, the advocate should argue:

---

[28] As previously noted, such advocacy has ancient and honored antecedents in the oratorical tradition of ancient Greece. For example, scholars have suggested that Demosthenes' speech *On the Crown* is "the masterpiece ... of the spoken word" notwithstanding his devastating charges against his opponent. *See* Kennedy [*Greece*], *supra* note 14, at 229. *See also* II Jebb, *supra* note 7, at 304 (describing Demosthenes' approach of not arguing in a "stately manner" but rather "at close quarters, with the grip as of wrestlers").

[29] *See* pages 257-258, *supra*.

[30] *Cf.* Model Code of Professional Responsibility, DR 7-106(C)(4) (providing that an attorney must not "[a]ssert his personal opinion as to the justness of a cause, as to the credibility of a witness, ... or as to the guilt or innocence of an accused; but he may argue, on his analysis of the evidence, for any position or conclusion with respect to the matters stated herein.").

[31] The ancient Greek orators were apparently not subject to such restrictions. *See, e.g.*, Wyse, *supra* note 13, at 661 (containing following excerpt from speech of Isaeus: "My opponents ... [n]ot content with arguing [their first contention] ... shelter themselves behind a second plea ....").

My opponent called that second witness for an obvious reason: because the first was not sufficient.

The Opponent's Evidence

Minimizing the Significance of the Opponent's Strong Evidence

The advocate must at some point in his argument address the question of what weight the jury should give to his opponent's strong evidence. He cannot simply ignore that evidence, since the jury will be waiting to hear his views on the matter. If he is silent on the issue, they will be apt, in the worst case scenario, to take his silence as a concession that he has no explanation and that the evidence can properly be given great weight.[32]

Thus, the advocate must state his client's best case position regarding his opponent's strong evidence. Above all, he must exploit whatever shortcomings there are in the evidence. Specifically, he should emphasize any concession or admission suggested by the evidence.[33]

If the evidence is testimonial in nature, he must initially identify his theory for undercutting the witness.[34] In particular, whatever theory that the advocate developed on cross-examination for showing that the witness has not harmed his case, he must exploit and emphasize that theory during summation. After showing that the witness does not warrant a verdict in his opponent's favor, the advocate should, where appropriate, emphasize his opponent's heavy reliance on the witness. Where that witness is the only witness that the opponent called to establish the

[32] *See* page 238, note 15 *supra.*

[33] Capitalizing on admissions of the opponent was a technique of Isaeus. *See, e.g.,* Wyse, *supra* note 13, at 229 (speech of Isaeus in which the jury was asked rhetorically: "How ... can you grant [the adversaries] more than they have claimed for themselves, and refuse to us even what is conceded by [them]?").

[34] The method for determining the theory for undercutting a witness was described in Chapter Eleven, *supra,* pages 234-236.

point on which he testified, the advocate should emphasize the absence of corroboration and the fact that the opponent's proof boils down to a "one-witness" case. And where the opponent has introduced multiple items of evidence, the advocate should point out that the opponent needs every single item to win, and that even the totality of that evidence falls far short.

Although the advocate must address his opponent's strongest evidence and contentions, he should minimize his efforts in refuting them. Specifically, too much effort expended in discussing the opponent's strongest evidence can result in a harmful concession of the materiality of the advocate's weak counterpoints. Similarly, the advocate should not overly emphasize his opponent's strongest points. This means that he should avoid dealing with them at either the outset of his address or at the end of the argument. The jury typically assumes that the advocate devotes his greatest attention to preparing his first and last remarks on any topic. It is also normally at its most attentive at the beginning of the advocate's address. Thus, the optimal point to mention the opponent's strong evidence or contentions is somewhere in the middle of the argument.[35]

---

[35] The foregoing points are reflected in the oratory of the Greek orator Demosthenes. On the occasion of his most celebrated speech, *On the Crown,* Demosthenes' opponent, who gave the initial speech, called on Demosthenes to deal first with the opponent's strongest contentions — two technical points about the legality of the motion to award Demosthenes a golden crown for his service to the state. *See Orations of Demosthenes* 373-375 (Colonial Press 1900). At the outset of his speech Demosthenes refused, calling it "but just, that [he] first speak a few words" about other of his opponent's allegations, "most of them the grossest falsehoods, ... [so] that none of [the audience] be influenced by matters foreign to the cause." *Id.* at 405. Demosthenes then dealt with these weaker contentions of his opponent at length, returning later to dispute only briefly the opponent's stronger contentions, after which he turned immediately to other matters. *See generally Demosthenes' Public Orations* 314-316 (Everyman's Library 1966) (providing paragraph-by-paragraph synopsis of *On the Crown*).

Criticizing the Opponent's Introduction of Less-than-Strong Evidence

One of the most important portions of an advocate's closing argument will be his discussion of his opponent's less-than-strong evidence. If the opponent is unacquainted with sponsorship considerations, he probably will have marshaled less-than-strong exhibits and elicited less-than-strong testimony.[36] As the next several sections reveal, the advocate can benefit enormously by highlighting this less-than-strong evidence.[37]

Less-than-Strong Favorable Evidence

If the opponent has introduced any favorable evidence that is less-than-strong, the advocate should challenge him in summation to explain how such evidence materially advances his case and, if it fails to do so, why he introduced it at all. The advocate should suggest to the jury the "obvious reason" why the opponent was forced to introduce such meager evidence: because his other evidence was so weak. The advocate can then note that the additional evidence obviously does not "shore up" the opponent's case.

Less-than-Strong Elaborate Exhibits

Where opposing counsel has introduced an elaborate exhibit, the advocate should first determine whether the

---

[36] *Cf. Silkwood v. Kerr-McGee Corp.*, Civ. No. 76-0888 (W.D. Okla. May 14, 1979), *reprinted in* R. Cover, O. Fiss & J. Resnik, *Procedure* 990 (Foundation Press, Inc. 1988) (closing argument by plaintiff's attorney Gerald Spence emphasizing that his opponent "kept calling witnesses and calling witnesses, [and] I sort of got the impression that he's fallen in love with us over here and just didn't want to quit calling witnesses").

[37] *Cf.* II Jebb, *supra* note 7, at 286 (noting that Isaeus customarily placed "the stress of the assault precisely on the enemy's weakest point and assail[ed] it with blow upon blow").

effort undertaken to prepare the exhibit was warranted by some legitimate need, such as to aid in the jury's understanding of the case. If so, the advocate should not criticize it merely because it is elaborate. If, however, no such justification for the exhibit exists, the advocate should emphasize opposing counsel's efforts in having prepared it and should point out that it did nothing to advance the opponent's case. He should consider asking opposing counsel to explain to the jury precisely what the exhibit proves.

Less-than-Strong Scientific Evidence or Expert Testimony

Where the opponent has introduced less-than-strong scientific evidence or expert testimony, the advocate should stress to the jury that the opponent's other evidence alone proves nothing and that the opponent therefore needed corroborative scientific evidence or expert testimony. The advocate should consider challenging his opponent to demonstrate how the opponent's scientific evidence or expert testimony provides the necessary corroboration.

The Witness Who Fails to Deliver

The opportunity to attack an opponent for having called a witness who fails to perform on direct examination as anticipated will not arise frequently, since the opponent and his witness will have presumably taken great care to rehearse the examination prior to trial. Occasionally, however, a witness is put on the stand without having been properly prepared. Moreover, even the most well-rehearsed witness can occasionally disappoint the attorney who called him. This is particularly likely on cross-examination, where the witness may not have anticipated or thought about a particular line of questioning. Whenever an opponent's witness does not perform well, the advocate can profit by highlighting that fact in summation.

For instance, assume that an accomplice agrees to provide testimony favorable to the government as part of a plea bargain. If he is called by the prosecutor in the expectation — perhaps announced to the jury — that he will "finger" the defendant, and if he fails to do so in whole or in part, defense counsel should stress to the jury that the evidence the prosecutor needed for a verdict was not forthcoming. He should also point out that, however distasteful the use of the accomplice might have been to the prosecutor, the government had no choice but to rely on him in light of the weakness of its other evidence. The defense can further note that such reliance was ultimately misplaced, since the accomplice did not salvage what was otherwise a hopeless case.

Whenever an opponent's witness fails to deliver, the advocate should emphasize, where appropriate, that his testimony is consistent with the advocate's case. In these circumstances, if the advocate was able to elicit anything favorable in his cross-examination of the witness, he should consider stating that had the jurors not known otherwise, they would have concluded that the witness had been called to testify for the advocate's case.

If the damaged witness was central to the opponent's case, the tactic of dramatizing the witness's failure to perform will be even more powerful. Perhaps because of the television drama "Perry Mason" certain colloquialisms can serve to exploit the opponent's sponsorship costs. One such example is the term "star witness." This term connotes a witness who is called to provide critical support to the case. If the opponent called such a witness and the witness was severely damaged by the advocate's cross-examination, the advocate should consider referring to him in summation as the opponent's "star witness." This term not only emphasizes the opponent's reliance on the witness but also enhances the impact of the witness's lackluster performance on cross-examination.

The advocate, of course, will want to highlight any gains he made in cross-examining the witness. This is true whether his gain was in eliciting evidence helpful to his own case or was simply in eliciting testimony that undermined the witness's direct examination.

Exploiting the Opponent's Use of Neutral Evidence

The advocate should be alert to any opportunity that his opponent gives him to make an effective argument based on his opponent's introduction of neutral evidence. As we have noted,[38] when the opponent introduces evidence that is neutral, the jury will be puzzled as to why he did so. It may view the opponent as implicitly telling it that the item of neutral evidence is important to his case. Yet, this message will confuse the jury, since the evidence will not appear to advance the advocate's case. It is critical for the advocate to use his summation to exploit the jury's bewilderment over his opponent's use of such evidence.

The trial recounted in Chapter Four[39] involving the pistol found near the defendant's feet illustrates the point. In that case, the prosecutor decided to introduce testimony regarding the arresting officer's submission of the pistol for fingerprint analysis because the test turned up no fingerprints adequate for comparison purposes. The message communicated to the jury by the prosecutor's use of the neutral fingerprint evidence was that if the pistol had turned up fingerprints matching anyone but the defendant, his other proof would have been called into doubt. Specifically, if the *absence* of the fingerprints of a third person was critical to the merits of the government's case, then the *presence* of such fingerprints might have meant that the government would not even have brought the case. The message was, in other words, that the police officer was a weak witness.

To maximize the prospects that the jury in such a case will reach this conclusion, the advocate may wish to argue along the following lines:

---

[38] *See* Chapter Four, pages 81-82, *supra.*

[39] *See* pages 82-85, *supra.*

When the prosecutor made a point out of questioning the arresting officer about his having submitted the pistol for fingerprint analysis, you must have asked yourselves: why is that fact significant? And that's a critical question, ladies and gentlemen. The answer is that, under the most charitable view of the evidence, the prosecutor's case is hanging by a thread. If the fact that no one else's fingerprints were recovered is so important to his case, isn't that because his case would have collapsed had such fingerprints been discovered? And if that is so, it can only mean that the evidence linking the defendant to the gun is extremely weak. Had the gun been in the defendant's pocket, he would not have *cared* whose prints were on it.

It is difficult to conceive of any persuasive rebuttal to the foregoing argument. The prosecutor would score no points by suggesting that the officer, in attempting to locate fingerprints, was just trying to develop more evidence against the defendant. Even the argument that he was just following police procedures is problematic. Logically, this could only mean that the importance of dispositive fingerprints has been institutionally recognized by the government. The only means of foreclosing this kind of criticism is by carefully avoiding any endorsement of the significance of neutral evidence.

One technique for enhancing the damage suffered by the opponent from introducing neutral evidence is to highlight the drama and anticipation when the opponent called a witness to the stand and then to note the surprise the jury must have felt when it actually heard the neutral testimony. Assume, for example, that a defendant charged with causing an accident by running a stop sign calls as a witness a hitchhiker who was a passenger at the time of the accident. Assume further that the hitchhiker testifies that he fell asleep in the car and therefore could not comment on whether the defendant ran the stop sign. Plaintiff's lawyer could argue as follows:

> When the hitchhiker took the stand, you must have thought, "Here it comes, the bombshell, the witness who will corroborate the defendant's claim that he came to a full stop at the stop sign." You must have been shocked when the hitchhiker said that he was asleep and therefore didn't see anything.

Even if defense counsel warned the jury in opening statement that the hitchhiker would not provide anything useful, plaintiff's lawyer can still employ a variant of the above argument:

> You must have thought, when you heard the defense attorney say in opening statement that one of his witnesses was asleep at the time, that you had to have misunderstood what the attorney had said. And when the hitchhiker took the stand, you must have thought, "Now I'll be able to see if I heard correctly." And you must have been relieved but puzzled to learn that there was nothing wrong with your hearing, only with the defendant's case.

Under either scenario, the advocate may also wish to challenge defense counsel to explain in his summation why he called a witness who had nothing helpful to say. As we previously indicated,[40] the defense attorney will have no convincing reply.

Highlighting the Opponent's Harmful Evidence

The opponent's witness or item of evidence will sometimes constitute evidence that is unfavorable to the opponent's case. Indeed, if the opponent has adhered to the conventional wisdom of volunteering his own weaknesses,[41] his case is likely to contain a whole assortment of weaknesses that he deliberately volunteered. The oppo-

[40] *See* pages 270-271, *supra.*

[41] *See* Chapter Four, pages 95-97, *supra.*

nent's case may also contain weaknesses that he did not anticipate. In either case, the advocate should exploit such weaknesses to his full advantage in the manner recommended in earlier chapters.[42]

Highlighting the Implausibility of the Opponent's Version of the Facts

If the opponent's case is based on a series of implausible events, the advocate should point out the "amazing coincidences" that must have occurred under that version of events. This would be true, for example, where the defendant is claiming misidentification in a robbery case, even though he was apprehended near the scene of the crime and was dressed in clothing identical to that of the assailant (as described by the victim). The prosecutor can point out that, for the defendant to be the wrong man, all of the following must be true: (i) the defendant had a look-alike in town, (ii) the two men had identical clothing, (iii) the two men were on the same block at the same time dressed in that identical clothing, and (iv) the look-alike (that is, the assailant) must have left the area just before the police arrived, since the police, having thoroughly canvassed the area, saw only one man — the defendant — who matched the description.

Evidence that the Opponent Failed to Produce Unfulfilled Promises in Opening Statement

A widely used tactic to discredit an opponent is to show that he overstated his case in his opening statement.[43] Sponsorship theory endorses that tactic. By discussing specific evidence and making specific contentions in his

[42] *See, e.g.*, Chapter One, page 6, *supra*.

[43] *See, e.g.*, Mauet, *supra* note 16, § 3.2, at 47 ("[Y]our opponent during closing arguments will in all likelihood point out each representation [in your opening] that you failed to deliver on.").

opening statement, an opponent will normally have conceded the materiality of that evidence and those contentions to the verdict. For example, if he did not fulfill a promise regarding what his evidence would show, the advocate can use the opponent's own words to impress upon the jury how much stronger the opponent's case could have been.

The opponent obviously will not concede that his failure to marshal the evidence is fatal to his case. Yet, if he contends that his remaining evidence is sufficient, the jury will wonder why he made such a point of promising to produce the other evidence. And if the opponent goes further and claims that the evidence that he failed to produce is irrelevant, the jury will wonder why he bothered to mention it at all. Accordingly, where appropriate, the advocate will want to seize upon his opponent's unproven assertions and argue that the opponent's actual evidence is insufficient.

Comparing the Opponent's Case to a Hypothetically Strong One

In order to emphasize the lack of strength of the opponent's case, the advocate should compare it, if possible, with a hypothetically strong case. This will focus the jury's attention on the evidence that his opponent did *not* produce. For example, in a case involving a burglary of a store, where the defendant is apprehended by police a block away with a television set taken from the store, defense counsel should stress, among other things, the lack of fingerprints lifted from the scene and the absence of eyewitnesses to the burglary itself.

A note of caution is in order, however. Where the difference in strength between the opponent's case and a hypothetically strong case is insubstantial, the advocate's representation of the latter as strong may serve to ratify the strength of the former. Thus, this strategy will not work when the opponent has a very strong case.

Arguments Based on Missing Evidence

The foregoing section emphasized the need to discuss hypothetically how much stronger the opponent's case could have been if other evidence, such as a corroborative witness, had been available. This section, by contrast, focuses on the value of commenting on an opponent's failure to use evidence that was *in fact* available to him.

There are two fundamental ways to criticize the opponent's failure to use available evidence. The first is merely to note that the opponent's case did not include the particular item of evidence.[44] Here, the message that the advocate should drive home to the jury is that the omitted evidence would not have advanced the opponent's case.

The second type of comment is to urge the jury to infer that the omitted evidence is *adverse* to the opponent's case. This argument, as we have noted,[45] will not be persuasive where the advocate could have used the evidence himself. Indeed, missing evidence case law prohibits the advocate from urging an adverse inference from an opponent's non-production of evidence absent a demonstration that the evidence was uniquely available to the opponent.[46] Accordingly, the advocate should always consider whether he can productively — and lawfully — urge such an adverse inference when his opponent has failed to introduce certain evidence. To determine whether the argument is permissible, the advocate must consult his jurisdiction's applicable missing evidence case law.

Finally, assuming that the requirements for urging an adverse inference are met, the advocate should seek to

[44] Juries are often explicitly instructed that the absence of corroboration is a factor bearing on the assessment of credibility. *See generally* 1 Devitt & Blackmar, *supra* note 24, § 17.01, at 519-520. A sample argument of this type is set forth in Chapter Five, page 128, *supra*.

[45] *See* Chapter Four, page 64, *supra*.

[46] *See* Chapter Four, page 66 & note 6, *supra* (setting forth requirements of missing evidence doctrine).

have the court give a missing evidence instruction.[47] If the court agrees to do so, the advocate should emphasize *the court's* recognition that the jury may draw an adverse inference from the opponent's failure to call the witness in question.

The Opponent's Statements

This section describes how an advocate can use his opponent's remarks as potential concessions. Such remarks include not only opening statement and closing argument but questions of counsel as well.

Opening Statement and Closing Argument

As noted above,[48] the advocate can use his opponent's promises in opening statement wherever the evidence failed to comport with those promises. There are other benefits as well that can be obtained from a careful monitoring of the opponent's opening and closing remarks.

To begin with, any explicit concession made by the opponent about a weakness in his case — such as a problem with the credibility of one of his witnesses — should be highlighted by the advocate in summation.[49] By the same token, any admission by the opponent about the strength of the advocate's case should be stressed. Furthermore, any indications that the opponent is advancing alternative theories or has abandoned a theory should be seized upon

[47] *See* Chapter Four, page 64 & note 7, *supra.*

[48] *See* pages 273-274, *supra.*

[49] *Cf. Oscanyan v. Arms Co.,* 103 U.S. 261, 263 (1880) (noting, with reference to an admission in opening statement, that "[a]ny fact, bearing upon the issue involved, admitted by counsel, may be the ground of the Court's procedure equally as if established by the clearest proof"); *United States v. Blood,* 806 F.2d 1218 (4th Cir. 1986) (noting that defendant is bound by any clear and unambiguous admission of fact made by his attorney, whether the case is civil or criminal).

and emphasized to the jury.[50] For example, if the opponent advances a particular theory in opening statement and then advances a totally different theory in closing argument, this substitution of theories should be highlighted.

The advocate should also pay careful attention to what his opponent does *not* say in closing argument. For instance, if the opponent offered lengthy testimony from a witness and then failed to mention that witness in his summation, the advocate can point out that the opponent is apparently no longer relying on the witness. Where the advocate had previously discredited the witness during cross-examination, he can give the "obvious" reason why the opponent did not mention him: because the witness was rendered totally useless in light of the cross-examination.

Questions of Counsel

While an opponent's opening statement occasionally provides good grist for attacking his case, his questions to witnesses during direct examination and cross-examination frequently provide an even stronger basis for attack. This is because the opponent, perhaps mindful of the dangers of overstatement in opening statements, normally takes much greater care in crafting his opening statement so that he does not overextend himself. While he may also take pains in planning his direct examination, many of his questions on cross-examination are likely to be spontaneous and ill-considered. Thus, questions that the opponent asks on cross-examination often provide an even more fertile ground for criticism than those posed on direct examination.

An advocate should recognize that even one ill-considered question by his opponent can provide the advocate

---

[50] *See* Chapter Ten, page 217, *supra* (discussing how to identify and exploit the opponent's theory of the case).

with a solid basis for pointing out that his opponent is advancing inconsistent theories. For instance, in an assault case tried by one of the authors, defense counsel acknowledged in opening statement that his client had injured the complainant, but claimed that it was in self-defense. Defense counsel later cross-examined an eyewitness who was only a short distance from the incident and asked questions suggesting that the assailant was someone other than the defendant. For instance, he sought to get the witness to concede that the assailant was considerably taller than the defendant. The prosecutor highlighted these inconsistent theories in summation, asking rhetorically why defense counsel would pose such questions if his theory were really self-defense. He then suggested that perhaps the defense was forced to abandon the self-defense theory in favor of a misidentification theory because the evidence of self-defense turned out to be so weak.[51]

An attorney attempting to explain questions raising an inconsistent theory will not want to argue that he merely asked those questions without thinking or that he was wasting the jury's time on an irrelevant matter. Yet, he also will not want to concede that he is advancing inconsistent theories. Such careless questions place the examiner in a dilemma and serve only to suggest that he really has no legitimate theory.

Using questions of the opponent to demonstrate that he is espousing inconsistent or alternative theories is but one benefit of the device. In some circumstances, an opponent's questions can also be used to demonstrate that the opponent is relying on a highly improbable explanation of the evidence. For example, in a case tried by one of the authors, the police arrested several joyriding teenagers in

[51] A prosecutor who is deciding whether to make such an argument must exercise caution. If, because of unusual facts in a case, the change from one theory to another is consistent with innocence, a court may question the propriety of such an argument. *See e.g., United States v. Sblendorio,* 830 F.2d 1382, 1394-1395 (7th Cir. 1987).

a vehicle after discovering narcotics in plain view. At trial, one of the defense attorneys asked the arresting officer in an indignant tone of voice whether he was aware that the vehicle belonged to the *mother* of one of the defendants. The prosecutor used this question in summation to argue that the only theory that the defense had for how the drugs got into the car was the far-fetched one that the mother had left them there in plain view when she loaned the car to her son.

Where the opponent's questions seek to establish less-than-strong points, the advocate should remind the jury of that unproductive examination. For example, where appropriate, the advocate can point out that his opponent vigorously cross-examined the witness on minor points but carefully avoided any question going to the heart of the dispute. The advocate can assert that the witness's testimony stands as unchallenged on the crucial issues. The advocate should not allow his opponent's persistence in attempting to establish a minor point — whether successful or not — to escape the notice of the jury.

Considerations When the Defense Puts on No Evidence

As noted in Chapter Ten,[52] an advocate can criticize his opponent's theory even when the opponent has not put on any evidence.[53] The problem is in identifying that theory when the opponent does not do so in his opening statement or closing argument. One way to do so is through the opponent's questions to witnesses. A case tried by one of the authors illustrates the point.

The defendant was charged with possessing several tin foil wrapped packets of an illegal narcotic substance. According to the government's evidence — which consisted

[52] *See* page 217, *supra.*

[53] As we have noted, *see* Chapter Ten, page 217, note 4, *supra,* the prosecutor in a criminal case must not state or in any way suggest that the defense has any obligation to put on evidence.

of the observations of a single police officer on a dark night in a high-drug area — the defendant threw down the bag of tin foil objects and ran off when he saw the police. At the outset of the trial, the most probable defense theory appeared to be that the officer did not see the defendant throw down anything, and that the drugs must have already been on the ground. Defense counsel, however, had not identified any theory in his opening statement.

During his cross-examination of the police officer, defense counsel asked the officer whether he was aware that a local fast food restaurant sold small, foil-wrapped corn on the cob. The prosecutor used this question as a theme in his closing argument. He pointed out that defense counsel's question could advance only one conceivable defense theory of what happened: that the defendant threw down corn on the cob in the late night, in a high narcotics area. This theory was highly favorable to the prosecution. Assuming no police fabrication, the jury could find for the defendant only if it concluded that (i) a bag of valuable drugs just happened to be on the ground right where the tin-foil-wrapped corn was supposedly dropped; (ii) the officer saw *only* the drugs on the ground, not a bag of corn on the cob as well; (iii) the defendant was present in a high drug area late at night solely to buy corn on the cob; and (iv) the defendant felt a need to "ditch" the corn on the cob and flee when he saw the police.

Having posed such an ill-advised question, defense counsel could not challenge the prosecutor's characterization of the defense theory without admitting that he was simply "fishing" and had no firm theory. Moreover, by carelessly posing the question, defense counsel had undermined his chances for advancing a more credible theory: that the officer was mistaken or lying in asserting that the defendant had thrown down *any* object. The fact that something had been thrown down was implicitly conceded in the defense counsel's question. His careless and damaging question illustrates the principle that there is no such thing as a "free" question.

Concluding Remarks

The advocate's summation should end on a note of strength and confidence. He should not merely ask the jury to "render a fair verdict," "do justice," or "do the right thing." Rather, he should conclude by asking unequivocally for a verdict in his client's favor on each of the claims or counts of the indictment. As is true with any of the advocate's remarks,[54] concluding remarks are no place for modesty or understatement.

Moreover, an argument that does not ask for a ruling in the advocate's favor invites the following response:

> Significantly, my opponent did not ask for a verdict in his favor. He simply asked you to do what is "just" without saying which verdict would be the just one. I, on the other hand, submit unequivocally that there is only one just verdict in this case — a verdict in favor of my client.

There is no reason to invite this kind of reply when there is no benefit in doing so.

Many advocates, in preparing their concluding remarks, include comments that are designed to arouse sympathy for their client's position or antipathy towards their opponent's case. While such remarks may be considered proper if they have a foundation in the evidence,[55] the advocate must understand the sponsorship costs of arguments based on emotion. Most significantly, because of the cost of overtrying, when an advocate makes argu-

---

[54] *See* Chapter Two, page 20; Chapter Seven, page 169; Chapter Twelve, page 247, *supra*.

[55] *See, e.g.*, J. Stein, *Closing Argument*, § 22, at 1-58 (Callaghan & Co. 1989) (arguments appealing to the jury's "sympathy" are not improper if they are based on the evidence).

ments based on sympathy, the jury is apt to give less weight to the advocate's arguments based on logic.[56] In our view, comments based on emotion should be employed cautiously, if at all, only after a careful analysis of the applicable sponsorship costs. These costs are apt to be at their lowest when the advocate's case is weak on the merits. By contrast, these costs are apt to be very high when the advocate's evidence is compelling.

Rebuttal Arguments

This section provides guidance on how to rebut the opponent's closing argument. This guidance applies not only to prosecutors and plaintiffs' attorneys, who in many jurisdictions are afforded a formal opportunity to deliver a rebuttal argument, but also to defense lawyers, who must rebut their opponent's contentions in the defense summation.

General Principles

An important implication of sponsorship theory is that an advocate must rebut all of his opponent's substantial arguments if he can possibly do so. The jury will be waiting to hear his response, and his failure to give one may lead it to conclude that the contention was unanswerable and thus conceded.[57] Although this point may seem obvious, a number of commentators give just the opposite advice.[58]

---

[56] An advocate's excessive reliance on emotional appeal permits the following well-known argument by his opponent (attribution unknown):

> When you don't have the facts, you pound the law. When you don't have the law, you pound the facts. And when you don't have either, you pound the table.

[57] *See* page 238 & note 15, *supra.*

[58] *See, e.g.,* J. Sonsteng, R. Haydock, and J. Boyd, *The Trial Book* § 10.6, at 337 (West 1984) ("It is not wise to spend significant portions of the closing argument responding to the opponent's issues, positions, and argument.").

A few points bear special emphasis. First, it is extremely important for the advocate to anticipate what his opponent will argue during his summation. When an advocate fails to focus in advance on his opponent's likely argument, he may find that the best rebuttal remarks do not occur to him until after the trial is over. If the advocate has faithfully recorded his opponent's opening remarks and questions on direct and cross-examination, a careful reading of these notes will frequently enable the advocate to predict what his opponent will say in his summation.

Second, while the advocate should be reluctant to concede anything in his own argument relating to the disputed issues, he should seize upon any such concession by his opponent. In addition, he should correct any misstatements of law or fact that might affect the jury's verdict.

Finally, where appropriate, the advocate should attempt to show why his opponent's arguments do not help resolve the case in his favor. The use of the phrase, "Imagine what he'd be saying if ..." is often an effective way to preface such an attack. For instance, if his opponent suggests that, because the advocate's witnesses corroborate each other so well, the advocate's case is "too strong" or "too neat,"[59] the advocate can respond as follows: "Imagine what he'd be saying if my witnesses had contradicted each other." By the same token, if the opponent criticizes the advocate's case for inconsistencies in testimony, the advocate can respond, "Imagine what he'd be saying if they all matched perfectly. He'd say, 'It's too strong, too neat.'" It is surprising how often this technique can be employed to neutralize or even belittle the opponent's contentions. This technique works, however, only where (1) the opponent is relying on certain facts to prove a point (for instance, consistency in the testimony of several witnesses to show their lack of veracity), and (2) the absence of those same facts could plausibly be argued

[59] *See, e.g.*, Bailey & Rothblatt, *supra* note 23, § 22:4, at 498 (suggesting an "attack [of the prosecutor's case] for its perfection and strength").

to prove the same point (the *inconsistencies* in the testimony of the witnesses to show their lack of veracity). An advocate should, of course, test his own arguments before making them to see if they can survive the "imagine what he'd be saying if" test.

Countering the Opponent's Criticism for Not Introducing Harmful Evidence

It is a textbook argument to attack the opposing advocate for failing to bring out evidence unfavorable to his case. Consider, for example, an advocate's failure to bring out his client's prior murder conviction. His opponent could argue along the following lines:

> Ladies and Gentlemen of the Jury, do you recall how I had to bring out the full facts on cross-examination? The fact of the matter is: if I hadn't brought out the defendant's murder conviction, you never would have heard about it. Evidently that's how my opponent wanted it — why else would he have omitted evidence of his client's conviction in his presentation? Perhaps his strategy was a recognition that you would not render a favorable verdict if you heard all of the evidence. Plainly, consideration of the *full* story — *all* of the evidence — requires a verdict in my client's favor.

This can be a powerful argument. Many would use such an argument to make the opposing counsel look unfair.[60] Sponsorship analysis, however, suggests a different rationale for the tactic: maximizing the opponent's costs of apparent efforts in omitting the evidence. The argument

[60] *See, e.g.*, Bailey & Rothblatt, *supra* note 23, § 22.3, at 498 ("[A] reason for highlighting favorable cross-examination is to show the unfairness of the case against the defendant. Argue that it was up to the prosecution to present the entire picture. Instead you had to coax the prosecution witness to reveal the whole truth....").

suggests to the jury that it would have been easier for the opponent simply to have introduced such evidence instead of going to such lengths to omit it from his presentation. Whatever its rationale, this criticism for omitting harmful evidence is presumably a major reason why the conventional wisdom advises an advocate to introduce evidence harmful to his case.

If the advocate has adhered to sponsorship principles in *omitting* a harmful item, he will have concluded that the decision was warranted notwithstanding the cost of apparent efforts that he incurred by doing so. His task in responding to criticism for omitting the harmful matter will be to *minimize* any costs of apparent efforts stemming from his omission of the item. Put another way, he should stress to the jury that the omission of the fact was justified and that the alternative of introducing it would have also been seized upon by his opponent.

For example, in the case of a defense lawyer who did not bring out his client's prior criminal conviction, that lawyer could argue as follows:

> Ladies and Gentlemen of the Jury, my opponent has suggested that the fact that I did not bring out my client's prior criminal conviction somehow suggests that I didn't think you'd render a verdict in my favor if you heard it. That is simply wrong. I wasn't trying to *hide* something from you. I obviously knew that my opponent could bring it out if I didn't. I didn't bring it out because it has *nothing* to do with this case. The fact of the matter is: the prosecutor has such a weak case that he's desperately trying to convict my client by relying on a crime he committed ten years ago for which he has already paid his dues.

The defense lawyer should also add the "imagine what he'd be saying if" argument, noting that if he *had* brought out the conviction, the prosecutor would have accused him of conceding its importance.

As the above discussion reveals, the defense attorney who does not volunteer a harmful matter in his client's case can argue with credibility that the matter is not important to the verdict. By contrast, the conventional wisdom's approach of volunteering weaknesses would leave the defense in a troublesome situation. The prosecutor could argue:

> Even the defense lawyer concedes that his client's prior conviction is important to his credibility. That's why he took the step of bringing it out himself instead of waiting for me to do so.

Since the jury assumes that an advocate puts on only his best case, it will be apt to agree with the prosecutor's implicit suggestion that defense counsel's tactic was unusual. And if the jury does agree, it will be apt to give the weakness heightened weight. The best the defense lawyer could say in response would be:

> That conviction has nothing to do with this case. I just wanted you to hear *all* of the evidence so you would see that, even with the prior conviction, the only reasonable verdict in this case is "not guilty."

This type of argument, which essentially attempts to derive a "benefit" from overtrying, is not apt to help the defense. The jury will most likely see two messages contained in such an argument: that defense counsel is conceding the harmfulness of the conviction and that he is urging that his evidence is nonetheless sufficient to support a verdict of not guilty. As predicted by sponsorship theory, the jury will be apt to credit the former and heavily discount the latter.

*****

As this chapter has revealed, closing argument is the key to capitalizing on the tenets of sponsorship theory. If the advocate's opponent has failed to follow sponsorship doctrine, he will learn the hard way — as a result of the advocate's summation — that every ill-advised question or comment and every item of less-than-strong evidence has its costs. At the same time, if the advocate has followed sponsorship principles in presenting his own case, he will minimize his exposure to damaging arguments from his opponent.

Epilogue

This book has demonstrated the importance of sponsorship in the conduct of all aspects of a jury trial. At bottom, the purpose has been to explain how an application of sponsorship theory can help win trials. As we have shown, sponsorship-related issues arise not only in the selection of evidence but also in arguments to the jury, objections, and even in questions posed by counsel. Indeed, sponsorship principles apply in varying degrees virtually any time an individual is seeking to persuade.

The book has also shown that the sponsorship of almost any item of evidence has a cost. Similarly, there is no such thing as a "free" argument, objection, or question. By understanding sponsorship theory, an advocate will be able to eliminate less-than-strong evidence and keep the focus of his presentation and arguments on the points that matter.

Our purpose in this book has been to present sponsorship doctrine and its application in an accessible manner. In doing so, we have made a number of simplifications. The alternative — a rigorous theoretical exposition — would have been overly dense and analytical.

The advocate may have begun to think, in reading the chapters in Part III (The Trial), that he could almost have written them himself. Such thinking reflects that the advocate understands Parts I and II well enough to apply sponsorship principles in his own trials.

It should be no secret, however, that the utility of sponsorship is not limited to that context. The same detailed principles can, in varying degrees, serve to guide the appellate attorney, the negotiator, the salesman, and the politician, to name a few. More generally, sponsorship doctrine dominates the rhetoric of *any* interested speaker, regardless of whether he faces an opponent. This is because any interested speaker is ultimately viewed as an effort-minimizing advocate striving to present his best case.

Significantly, however, sponsorship theory applies not only to the rhetoric of the *interested* advocate but also to that of the *disinterested* speaker. For instance, because of the listener's assumption of effort-minimization, the disinterested speaker stands to reap significant *benefits* of efforts by using favorable evidence. After all, a speaker who has no personal stake in the outcome is not apt to go out of his way to sponsor something unless it was "worth the effort." In short, this book's theory, which recognizes the effects of sponsorship, reaches all rhetoric.

It is important for the courtroom advocate to understand that sponsorship is not a panacea. Obviously, the most important factor in any case is the strength of the evidence. An attorney with a compelling case who is employing the conventional wisdom may well prevail over an attorney with a weak case who is employing sponsorship. Accordingly, there is no substitute for thorough investigation and factfinding to uncover all evidence that is helpful to the advocate's case.

Moreover, sponsorship doctrine does not substitute for a grasp of the basics of logical argumentation as a means of persuasion. Rather, such facility at argumentation is treated as a point of departure. Specifically, because the ultimate task of an advocate is to convince the jury that the matter being tried has (or has not) been shown to be true with a certain degree of probability,[1] he must be able to evaluate the bearing of all potential items of evidence and contentions on that ultimate probability assessment. This implicates the process of evidence evaluation described in Chapter Three.[2] Moreover, where comment based on emotion can legitimately be brought to bear, the

---

[1]*Cf.* 1 *Weinstein's Evidence,* ¶ 401[07], at 401-448 (Matthew Bender 1989) ("What is involved in a trial is assessment of the probability that the proposition 'X was the case,' or 'X was not the case' is true.").

[2]*See* pages 52-54, *supra.*

advocate must draw on his own knowledge of human nature in assessing the strength of such contentions. Both of these areas — logical and emotional proof — bear primarily on the substance rather than on the tactics of persuasion. Sponsorship theory does not purport to provide *substantive* guidance in crafting persuasive arguments based on logic or emotion.

In addition, on rare occasions juries will decide cases on wholly irrational grounds, such as the personalities of the attorneys. And juries in different parts of the country may react differently to the same type of case. Where such factors predominate, sponsorship may have reduced impact, and the advocate should search for any means by which he can legitimately neutralize them.

For many of the above areas — such as strength of the case and personalities of the lawyers — the advocate has little or no control. For example, once the advocate has completed a thorough factual investigation, he is "stuck" with his facts. Similarly, he cannot change his personality or ensure against a runaway jury. The one aspect of trial strategy that he can easily control, however, is whether to apply sponsorship principles. And we have found from our experience that the benefits to be gained from applying such principles are considerable.

Most significantly, even weak cases can be won using sponsorship principles. Similarly, such principles can serve as an insurance policy to ensure that a strong case is not needlessly lost because of an unnecessary strategy blunder, such as overtrying the case.

While the application of sponsorship theory can reap immediate benefits for the advocate, it might also have a salutary effect on our judicial system as a whole. If advocates were to apply sponsorship theory on a widespread basis, trials would be shorter and more to the point. Advocates would understand the costs of overtrying cases. Marginal and irrelevant witnesses would not be subpoenaed and called for trial. Elaborate but irrelevant exhibits would not be prepared and used. In addition, because trials would be less cluttered and the theories more easily identified, the length of jury deliberations would generally decrease. Moreover, since each advocate's purpose would be to show the jury his client's best case and his opponent's worst case, the whole goal of the adversary system — to promote the search for truth — would ultimately be advanced.

BIBLIOGRAPHY

Books

A. Amsterdam, B. Segal & M. Miller, *Trial Manual for the Defense of Criminal Cases* (Amer. Law Inst. 1984)

J. Appleman, *Preparation and Trial* (Coiner Pub., Ltd. 1967)

J. Appleman, *Successful Jury Trials* (Coiner Pub., Ltd. 1952)

R. Aron, J. Fast & R. Klein, *Trial Communication Skills* (Shephard's/McGraw-Hill, Inc. 1986)

Aristotle, *The Complete Works of Aristotle* (Princeton Univ. Press, Barnes ed. 1984)

F. Bailey & H. Rothblatt, *Successful Techniques for Criminal Trials* (Lawyers Co-op. Pub. Co. 1985)

J. Bentham, *Rationale of Judicial Evidence* (Bowring ed. 1827)

M. Berger, J. Mitchell & R. Clark, *Trial Advocacy: Planning, Analysis, & Strategy* (Little, Brown & Co. 1989)

P. Bergman, *Trial Advocacy* (West 1979)

H. Berman, ed., *Talks on American Law* (Vintage Books 1961)

F.X. Busch, *Law and Tactics in Jury Trials* (Bobbs-Merrill Co., Inc. 1959)

R. Carlson & E. Imwinkelreid, *Dynamics of Trial Practice* (West Pub. Co. 1989)

R. Carlson, *Successful Techniques for Civil Trials* (Lawyers Co-op. Pub. Co. 1983)

R. Caro, *The Years of Lyndon Johnson: The Path to Power* (Alfred A. Knopf 1983)

J. Clark, *Preparation of Cross-Examination* (P.L.I. 1946)

I *Corinthians* 14:8, The Living Bible

R. Cover, O. Fiss & J. Resnik, *Procedure* (Foundation Press, Inc. 1988)

L. Decof, *Art of Advocacy: Opening Statement* (Matthew Bender 1987)

Demosthenes, *Demosthenes' Public Orations* (Everyman's Library 1966)

Demosthenes, *Orations of Demosthenes* (Colonial Press 1900)

E. Devitt & C. Blackmar, *Federal Jury Practice and Instructions* (West 3d ed. 1977)

E. Devitt, C. Blackmar & M. Wolff, *Federal Jury Practice and Instructions (Civil)* (West 4th ed. 1987)

A.K. Dixit, *Optimization of Economic Theory* (Oxford Univ. Press 1976)

Dombroff on Direct and Cross Examination (Wiley Law Pub. 1985)

D. Drussel & J. Wade, *Plaintiff's Proof of a Prima Facie Case* (Callaghan & Co. 1982)

B. Elliott & W. Elliott, *The Law of Evidence* (Bobbs-Merrill Co. 1904)

J. Frederick, *The Psychology of the American Jury* (The Michie Co. 1988)

C. Fricke, *Planning and Trying Cases* (West rev. ed. 1957)

S. Gard, *Jones on Evidence* (Lawyers Co-Op. Pub. Co. 6th ed. 1972)

S. Gazan, *Encyclopedia of Trial Strategy and Tactics* (Prentice-Hall, Inc. 1962)

S. Goldberg, *The First Trial: Where Do I Sit? What Do I Say?* (West 1982)

Goldstein Trial Techniques (Callaghan & Co. 3d ed. 1984)

M. Graham, *Federal Rules of Evidence* (West 1986)

M. Graham, *Handbook of Federal Evidence* (West 1986)

S. Hamlin, *What Makes Juries Listen* (Law & Business, Inc. 1985)

K. Hegland, *Trial and Practice Skills* (West 1978)

E. Imwinkelreid, *Evidentiary Foundations* (The Michie Co. 2d ed. 1989)

T. Jackson, *The Perfect Resume* (Anchor Press Doubleday 1981)

R. Jebb, *The Attic Orators from Antiphon to Isaeus* (Russell and Russell, Inc. 1962)

Jones on Evidence (Lawyers Co-Op. Pub. Co. 6th ed. 1972)

A. Julien, *Opening Statements* (Callaghan & Co. 1980)

Y. Kamisar, W. LaFave & J. Israel, *Modern Criminal Procedure* (West 6th ed. 1986)

G.W. Keeton, *Harris's Hints on Advocacy* (Stevens & Sons, Ltd. 18th ed. 1943)

R. Keeton, *Trial Tactics and Methods* (Little, Brown & Co. 2d ed. 1973)

G. Kennedy, *The Art of Persuasion in Greece* (Princeton Univ. Press 1963)

G. Kennedy, *The Art of Rhetoric in the Roman World* (Princeton Univ. Press 1972)

J. Kestler, *Questioning Techniques and Tactics* (Shepard's/McGraw Hill, Inc. 1982)

A. Kruger, *Modern Debate: Its Logic and Strategy* (McGraw-Hill 1960)

W. LaFave & J. Israel, *Criminal Procedure* (West 1985)

L.W. Lake, *How to Cross-Examine Witnesses Successfully* (Prentice-Hall 10th ed. 1970)

S. Landsman, *The Adversary System: A Description and Defense* (American Enterprise Institute 1984)

R. Lempert & S. Saltzburg, *A Modern Approach to Evidence* (West 2d ed. 1982)

A. Lincoln, *The Collected Works of Abraham Lincoln* (R. Basler ed. 1953)

D. Louisell & C. Mueller, *Federal Evidence* (Lawyer's Co-op. Pub. Co. 1979)

T. Mauet, *Fundamentals of Trial Techniques* (Little, Brown 2d ed. 1988)

D. McCarty, *Psychology and the Law* (Prentice-Hall 1960)

McCormick on Evidence (West 3d ed. 1984)

Moore's Federal Practice (Matthew Bender 2d ed. 1989)

E. Morgan, *Some Problems of Proof Under the Anglo-American System of Litigation* (Columbia Univ. Press 1956)

A.E. Morrill, *Anatomy of a Trial* (C.P.I. 1968)

A.E. Morrill, *Trial Diplomacy* (C.P.I. 1971)

J. Nolan, *Trial Practice: Cases and Materials* (West 1981)

B. Palmer, *Courtroom Strategies* (Prentice-Hall, Inc. 4th ed. 1966)

J. Reed, *Conduct of Lawsuits* (Little, Brown 2d ed. 1912)

S. Schweitzer, *Cyclopedia of Trial Practice* (Lawyers Co-op. Pub. Co. 2d ed. 1970)

L. Smith & L. Malandro, *Courtroom Communication Strategies* (Kluwer Law Book Publishers, Inc. 1985)

J. Sonsteng, R. Haydock & J. Boyd, *The Trial Book — A Total System for the Preparation and Presentation of a Case* (West 1984)

H. Spellman, *Direct Examination of Witnesses* (Prentice Hall 1968)

J. Stein, *Closing Argument* (Callaghan & Co. 1989)

L. Stryker, *The Art of Advocacy* (Zenger Pub. Co., Inc. 1979)

J. Tanford, *The Trial Process: Law, Tactics and Ethics* (The Michie Co. 1983)

R. Traver, *Anatomy of a Murder* (Dell 1958)

S. Turow, *Presumed Innocent* (Farrar Straus Giroux 1987)

T. Twiss, *Life of Lord Eldon* (1844), *reprinted in* D. Shrager and E. Frost, *The Quotable Lawyer* (Facts on File Pub. 1986)

Webster's New World Dictionary (Simon & Schuster Second College Ed. 1980)

Weinstein's Evidence (Matthew Bender 1989)

F. Wellman, *Day In Court* (MacMillan Co. 1926)

J. Wigmore, *Evidence* (Little, Brown & Co. Chadbourn rev. 1979)

H. Wouk, *The Caine Mutiny* (Doubleday 1952)

C. Wright & A. Miller, *Federal Practice and Procedure* (West 1973)

W. Wyse, *The Speeches of Isaeus* (Cambridge Univ. Press 1904)

I. Younger, *The Art of Cross-Examination* (A.B.A. Monograph Series 1976)

I. Younger, *Trial Techniques with Irving Younger* (R. Oliphant ed. 1978)

G.K. Zipf, *Human Behavior and the Principle of Minimum Effort* (Addison-Wesley Press, Inc. 1949)

Newspapers and Periodicals

Alschuler, *Courtroom Misconduct by Prosecutors and Trial Judges,* 50 Tex. L. Rev. 629, 636 (1972)

Annotation, 5 A.L.R. 2d 893 (1949)

Brown, *A Juryman's View,* 2 Ga. B.J. 225 (1965)

Buchanan, "Keep up the Pressure, George," *reprinted in* The San Diego Union, Aug. 30, 1988

Evans and Novak, "The Tower Scorecard," *reprinted in* Wash. Post, Mar. 15, 1989, at A23

Frederick, *Jury Behavior: A Psychologist Examines Jury Selection,* 5 Ohio No. U. L. Rev. 571 (1978)

Jefferson, *Declarations Against Interest: An Exception to the Hearsay Rule,* 58 Harv. L. Rev. 1 (1944)

Ladd, *Impeachment of One's Own Witness — New Developments,* 4 U. Chi. L. Rev. 69 (1936)

Markus, *A Theory of Trial Advocacy,* 56 Tul. L. Rev. 95 (1981)

N.Y. Times, June 12, 1989

N.Y. Times, May 30, 1989

N.Y. Times, Oct. 6, 1988

Nelson, *Her Life is Her Job,* Wash. Post, June 12, 1988 (Magazine)

Note, *Drawing an Inference From the Failure to Produce a Knowledgeable Witness: Evidentiary and Constitutional Considerations,* 61 Cal. L. Rev. 1422 (1973)

Seymour, *Why Prosecutors Act Like Prosecutors,* 11 Record of NYCBA 302 (1956)

Suggs & Sales, *Using Communication Cues to Evaluate Prospective Jurors During the Voir Dire,* 20 Ariz. L. Rev. 629 (1978)

Sward, *Values, Ideology, and the Evolution of the Adversary System,* 64 Ind. L.J. 301 (1989)

Thomas, *The Rule Against Impeaching One's Own Witness: A Reconsideration,* 31 Mo. L. Rev. 364 (1966)

Trial Preparation: An Interview with Louis Nizer, 2 Trial Dip. L.J. 6 (1979)

Wash. Post, Feb. 23, 1989

Wash. Post, June 9, 1989

Cases

Arnold v. United States, 511 A.2d 399, 416 (D.C. 1986)

Austin v. United States, 382 F.2d 129, 138 (D.C. Cir. 1967)

Boyles v. State, 46 Wis.2d 473, 175 N.W.2d 277 (1970)

Brady v. Maryland, 373 U.S. 83 (1963)

Brooks v. Tennessee, 406 U.S. 605 (1972)

Bruton v. United States, 391 U.S. 123 (1968)

Carter v. Kentucky, 450 U.S. 288 (1981)

Cooper v. State, 201 Tenn. 149, 297 S.W.2d 75 (1956)

Cooper v. United States, 415 A.2d 528 (D.C. 1980)

Curley v. United States, 160 F.2d 229 (D.C. Cir. 1947)

Dent v. United States, 404 A.2d 165 (D.C. 1979)

Doman v. Baltimore & O.R. Co., 22 S.E.2d 703 (W.Va. 1942)

Edward J. Sweeney & Sons, Inc. v. Texaco, Inc., 478 F. Supp. 243 (E.D. Pa. 1979)

Estrella-Ortega v. United States, 423 F.2d 509 (9th Cir. 1970)

Evans v. Multicon Const. Corp., 6 Mass. App. 291, 375 N.E.2d 338 (1978)

Freeman v. Commercial Union Assurance Co., 317 S.W.2d 563 (Tex. Civ. App. 1958)

Griffin v. California, 380 U.S. 609 (1965)

Illinois Central Railroad Co. v. Staples, 272 F.2d 829 (8th Cir. 1959)

Inglett & Co. v. Everglades Fertilizer Co., 255 F.2d 342 (5th Cir. 1958)

Kean v. Comm'r of Internal Revenue, 469 F.2d 1183 (9th Cir. 1972)

Lakeside v. Oregon, 435 U.S. 333 (1978)

Lockett v. Ohio, 438 U.S. 586 (1978)

Lokos v. State, 434 So.2d 831 (Ala. 1983)

Luttrell v. United States, 320 F.2d 462 (5th Cir. 1963)

Manson v. Brathwaite, 432 U.S. 98 (1977)

McLhinney v. Lansdell Corp. of Maryland, 254 A.2d 177 (Md. App. 1969)

Miranda v. Arizona, 384 U.S. 436 (1966)

Onufer v. Seven Springs Farm, Inc., 636 F.2d 46 (3d Cir. 1980)

Oscanyan v. Arms Co., 103 U.S. 261 (1880)

Patton v. Rambo, 20 Ala. 485 (1852)

People v. McClellan, 80 Cal. Rptr. 31, 457 P.2d 871 (Cal. 1969)

People v. McKee, 235 N.E.2d 625 (Ill. 1968)

People v. Schofield, 124 Mich. App. 134, 333 N.W.2d 607 (1983)

Pointer v. Pointer, 251 S.W.2d 334 (Mo. App. 1952)

Resurrection Gold Mining Co. v. Fortune Gold Mining Co., 129 F. 668, 675 (8th Cir. 1904)

Sherrod v. United States, 478 A.2d 644 (D.C. 1984)

Shurman v. United States, 233 F.2d 272 (5th Cir. 1956)

Silkwood v. Kerr-McGee Corp., Civ. No. 76-0888 (W.D. Okla. May 14, 1979)

State v. Vincent, 24 Iowa 570 (1868)

Thomas v. United States, 447 A.2d 52 (D.C. 1982)

United States v. Bernard, 625 F.2d 854 (9th Cir. 1980)

United States v. Blood, 806 F.2d 1218 (4th Cir. 1986)

United States v. Burke, 781 F.2d 1234 (7th Cir. 1985)

United States v. Currier, 454 F.2d 835 (1st Cir. 1972)

United States v. Dreitzler, 577 F.2d 539 (9th Cir. 1978)

United States v. Insco, 365 F. Supp. 1308 (D.Fla. 1973)

United States v. Karnes, 531 F.2d 214 (4th Cir. 1976)

United States v. Leslie, 542 F.2d 285 (5th Cir. 1976)

United States v. Lopez, 575 F.2d 681 (9th Cir. 1978)

United States v. Lumpkin, 448 F.2d 1085 (D.C. Cir. 1971)

United States v. Mallis, 467 F.2d 567 (3d Cir. 1972)

United States v. Robinson, 108 S. Ct. 864 (1988)

United States v. Sblendorio, 830 F.2d 1382 (7th Cir. 1987)

United States v. Taylor, 599 F.2d 832 (8th Cir. 1979)
United States v. Young, 463 F.2d 934 (D.C. Cir. 1972)
Weiss v. Chrysler Motors Corp., 515 F.2d 449 (2d Cir. 1975)
Williams v. State, 251 Ga. 749, 312 S.E.2d 40 (1983)

Statutes and Rules

18 U.S.C. § 1951(a)
2 U.S.C. § 441d(a)
2 U.S.C. § 441d(a)
33 F.R.D. 53 (1963)
Federal Rules of Appellate Procedure
Federal Rules of Civil Procedure
Federal Rules of Criminal Procedure
Federal Rules of Evidence
Model Code of Professional Responsibility, DR 7-103(B)
American Bar Association, Standards for Criminal Justice (2d ed. 1980)
Criminal Jury Instructions, District of Columbia (3d ed. 1978)
A.B.A. Standards Relating to the Prosecution Function and the Defense Function (1971)

Index

B

D

E

J

N

O

P

S

T

V

W